"This book surveys the case law on property from an economic perspective, with the goal of offering new insights into the resolution of actual legal disputes drawn from several countries. It will be of interest to law professors and students, practicing lawyers with an interest in economics, and economists with an interest in law."

— **Thomas J. Miceli**, *Professor of Economics, University of Connecticut, USA.*

"This book will be a welcome addition to those who teach law and economics and those of an interdisciplinary disposition. With its primary focus on cases and how Coasian/Post-Coasian economics might give new light to the issues that encapsulate these cases it makes classic economic concepts such as externalities come alive again as ideas to be taken out of the textbooks and experimented with as a practical tool to understand the human condition."

— **Daniel Blackshields**, *School of Economics and Teaching Fellow Reflective Practice, University College, Cork, Ireland; Chair for Academic Standards, Cork University Business School.*

# Economic Analysis of Property Law Cases

The discipline of law and economics has earned a reputation for developing plausible and empirically testable theories on the social functions and the impact of legal institutions. Property rights are a field in which this has been very successful. In this book, economic property rights theories are applied to case law in order to examine the practice and solution of real life conflicts. The author examines the economic problems which are dealt with in these cases and evaluate the courts' decisions from an economic angle.

Cases are examined from across the UK, the US, Germany, Belgium and Canada to allow international comparisons to be made. These comparisons reveal that, regardless of the legal system, many legal issues have similar economic roots and therefore similar models of economic analysis can be applied. The analysis of these cases also shows that the discipline of law and economics is not only successful in developing explanatory models but also useful to generate better considerations and solutions for legal conflicts in individual cases.

This book aims to bridge the gap between the academic and professional literature and demonstrate the benefits of the economic analysis of property rights cases to all those who are interested in law and economics.

**Boudewijn R.A. Bouckaert** is an emeritus professor at the Law School of Ghent University. He is a guest professor at the Erasmus University in Rotterdam, at the CEVRO-Institute in Prague and at the University of Torino.

**The Economics of Legal Relationships**
Sponsored by Michigan State University College of Law
Series Editors:
Nicholas Mercuro
*Michigan State University College of Law*
Michael D. Kaplowitz
*Michigan State University*

**Predatory Pricing in Antitrust Law and Economics**
*Nicola Giocoli*

**The Role of Law and Regulation in Sustaining Financial Markets**
*Edited by Niels Philipsen and Guangdong Xu*

**Law and Economics**
Philosophical issues and fundamental questions
*Edited by Aristides N. Hatzis and Nicholas Mercuro*

**Public Procurement Policy**
*Edited by Gustavo Piga and Tünde Tatrai*

**Legal Origins and the Efficiency Dilemma**
*Nuno Garoupa, Carlos Gómez Ligüerre and Lela Mélon*

**Law and Economics of Public Procurement Reforms**
*Edited by Gustavo Piga and Tünde Tátrai*

**Law and Economics as Interdisciplinary Practice**
Philosophical, Methodological and Historical Perspectives
*Péter Cserne and Magdalena Malecka*

**Extraterritoriality and International Bribery**
A Collective Action Perspective
*Branislav Hock*

**Economic Analysis of Property Law Cases**
*Boudewijn R.A. Bouckaert*

For a full list of titles in this series please visit www.routledge.com/The-Economics-of-Legal-Relationships/book-series/ELR

# Economic Analysis of Property Law Cases

Boudewijn R.A. Bouckaert

Routledge
Taylor & Francis Group
LONDON AND NEW YORK

First published 2020
by Routledge
2 Park Square, Milton Park, Abingdon, Oxon OX14 4RN

and by Routledge
52 Vanderbilt Avenue, New York, NY 10017

*Routledge is an imprint of the Taylor & Francis Group, an informa business*



*British Library Cataloguing-in-Publication Data*
A catalogue record for this book is available from the British Library

*Library of Congress Cataloging-in-Publication Data*
A catalog record for this book has been requested

ISBN: 978-1-138-02167-9 (hbk)
ISBN: 978-1-315-77758-0 (ebk)

Typeset in Times New Roman
by Apex CoVantage, LLC

# Contents

# Figures

# Tables

# Preface

Some university classes are the stuff of legends.

Aaron Director's class on *Antitrust* at the University of Chicago Law School, for instance, marked the beginning of the integration of economic analysis into the core curriculum of US law schools.

Likewise, Boudewijn R.A. Bouckaert's *Property Law and Economics* fits the bill of a legendary, field reforming class.

While law and economics was still very much in its infancy in Europe in 1989, several European universities founded a very ambitious Master program in Law and Economics that today, thirty years later, still thrives. With this major academic enterprise came the task of devising the first ever curriculum for a master's program in law and economics. As co-founder of the program, Professor Bouckaert took it upon himself to develop the first full course on the law and economics of property law.

In the lectures, Professor Bouckaert combined his passion for economic analysis with the broader philosophical and historical perspectives that inhibit the mind of a true intellectual. Additionally, moving from theory to practice, the course was innovative in applying the concepts of law and economics to case law. Each year, every student was tasked with an assignment to read and present to other students a legal case from an economic perspective. The case law method, totally alien to civil law training, was used in a clever way to expose the trade-off inherent in property law disputes and identify the policy goals at stake in the creation of legal precedent.

The sad thing about legendary classes, especially prior to the age of podcasts and digital recordings, is that they come to their natural end and only alumni end up being privy to the unique experience that such classes and their professors offered. Certainly, some of the thoughts and deliberations of classic classes find their way into articles that the professor and former student disciples write during their careers. But such writings never get close to capturing the immersive experience of a legendary course.

This book mercilessly mercifully saves us from the fate that befell Aaron Director's antitrust class. With this book, Professor Bouckaert generously shares his classic course on the law and economics of property law with future generations of students and scholars of law and economics. But the book is much more than a transcript of that course, of course. *Economic Analysis of Property Law Cases* provides the most comprehensive economic and comparative analysis of the economics of property law to date.

As much as the course was pioneering and ground-breaking at its inception, it has been updated through the years. The book provides a broad overview of property law ranging across a diverse array of disputes: the definition of property rights, the concept of possession and the instruments of registration of private property rights, the relationship between owners of a common property, private and public nuisance disputes, the fragmentation of property in the context of servitude law, and the law of eminent domain.

Although the basis of the book is theoretical, it truly shines in its combination of concept and application. The case law section is a veritable treasure trove. The various property disputes truly bring to life the trade-offs and the value added by economic analysis to law. The thirty cases present the full gamut of property law disputes, traversing between, on the one hand, the edible nuisance disputes among petty neighbours (such as the noise of roosters case) and, on the other hand, cases that present major economic disputes. Some cases, such the German gnomes of frustration case (*Frustzwerge in Nachbars Garten*) cannot be unread – you will never forget them. This book brings you on a memorable trip through law, economics, philosophy and history. The book is a little masterpiece that was already influential long before it was published – through the legendary classes of Professor Bouckaert.

Ben Depoorter
Max Radin Distinguished Professor of Law
UC Hastings College of the Law
EMLE Coordinator
Ghent University
Gerrit De Geest
Charles F. Nagel Professor of International and Comparative Law
Washington University, St. Louis

# Introduction

This book is a long term result of my teaching in the European Master of Law and Economics course. I started up this master course, together with Gerrit De Geest, in 1989. This master course involves now ten universities in Europe and India and awards annually between eighty and one hundred degrees to students with a legal or economic training. For nearly thirty years (1990–2018), I taught the course Property Law and Economics in Ghent. In order to make my teaching more varied I organized, in addition to the formal teaching of the theory, sessions in which each student was assigned a case and was expected to briefly explain the case to the class audience and make an economic analysis of it. The presentation was followed by a brief discussion among the students. As years passed by, an impressive and rich stock of case analyses piled up. As I thought that this stock of intellectual experience was too valuable to get sent to the shredder or to be deleted from my computer files, the idea came to my mind to integrate these case analyses in a book in which theory on the economics of property rights would be combined with a discussion of cases. Although many case analyses made by the students were quite inspiring for me, I redrafted the analyses entirely. All factual errors, imperfections, omissions, logical mishaps, wrong legal constructions, flawed economic reasoning and empirical mistakes that one may discover in this book are all on my account. On a website especially set up for this book, all names of the students of the last twelve classes (2006–2018) are mentioned. In this way, I thank them for their contribution, and I hope that when this message reaches them it may resuscitate good memories of their stay at the Ghent University.

The interdisciplinary character of this book is three-pronged: comparative legal theory on six subjects of property law, economic theory on these subjects and economic analysis of cases dealing with property issues. It is my conviction that such a three-pronged approach can contribute to the usefulness of law and economics for society. Law and economics' potential for improving the efficiency of social institutions runs along two paths.

The best-known path follows policy advice on legal and regulatory reform. A key example is the introduction of procedures of regulation management in many countries. Such management requires the drafting of Regulatory Impact Assessment (RIA) before a new regulation is submitted to political decision-making. The rise of regulation management would have been unthinkable without law and economics, for this approach was able to develop a systematic assessment of the possible cost and benefits of proposed regulations (Renda 2011).

The second path of influence of law and economics in society concerns the judiciary. Depending on structures and traditions in legal systems, judges can have narrow or wide margins within which to make the law. Familiarizing judges with legal and economic arguments can enhance the efficiency of court decisions, which may have the authority of a precedent. In the US, exposure of the judiciary to law and economics has been successfully realized through initiatives of judicial training. Famous in this respect is the Law and Economics Center (LEC), associated with the George Mason University and founded by Henry Manne. In the 1970s, this law and economics scholar initiated weeklong seminars for federal judges. By 1990, 40 percent of federal judges had completed such seminars (Butler 1999).[1] Law and economics education for judges continues to be provided by the Mason Judicial Education Program. As of now more than five thousand federal and state judges from all fifty US states, including three current Supreme Court Justices, have attended such a program. It is likely that other countries offer courses in law and economics in judicial education programs, but the US experience is by far the most elaborate and has been the most enduring.

Besides enhancing judicial training programs, law and economics can influence case law through publications with a focus on case analysis. Of course, most law and economics textbooks refer amply to cases for a variety of reasons. Sometimes court decisions are referred to in order to strengthen the theoretical argument. Authors tend to invoke the authority of the court in order to show that even judges, not familiar with law and economics, share intuitively his/her viewpoint. Sometimes cases are analyzed to provide a flesh and blood illustration of the economic problem that the discussed legal rule is attempting to solve. In rare cases, court decisions are pioneering in the development of law and economics. The *United States v. Carroll Towing Co.* case, 159 F.2d 169 (2d. Cir. 1947), in which Justice Learned Hand articulated his famous formula, is one of the most striking examples in this respect. Common to all these textbooks however is that the references to cases have a mainly sustaining function, that is, the author picks out cases that sustain her/his point of view. This is useful because it relates the theoretical

1 Ash, Chen, and Naidu (2019) studied the impact of the 'Manne' seminars on the decisions and the language use of judges. They found out that the judges who followed the seminars made decisions that are more conservative while non-Manne judges, exposed to Manne-judges in previous cases, started to use more economically influenced language. Depending on the viewpoint about the merits and ideological background of law and economics, this study proves that these courses are either a blessing or a curse. It is a blessing if one believes that the greater the impact of law and economics on case law, the more efficient law will be and, consequently, the better off society will be. It is a curse when one believes that such influence makes the judiciary subservient to a conservative, pro-capitalistic agenda. I believe, rather, that the first is the case, but this is of course a matter of further discussion. Finally, suggesting, as the authors do, that more than half of federal judges in the US can be lured into a conservative agenda by attending a week-long course at a nice resort is not particularly flattering for the intellectual integrity of the American judges.

viewpoint with real life situations, but the case analysis does not function as an independent intellectual enterprise. It remains subservient to the theory.

However, some law and economics textbooks have been published in which case analysis is the central aim. Such textbooks do not pick cases to illustrate the theory but select cases as research subjects on their own merits and analyze them with the intellectual tools developed by law and economics. Here, cases are the starting points and theory follows, and not the inverse. A pioneering book in this respect is *Tort Law: Cases and Economic Analysis*, published by Richard Posner in 1982. More recently and closer to our subject is *Land Use Controls: Cases and Materials*, published in 2005 by Robert Ellickson and Vicki Been. Finally, we should mention *Cases and Materials on Law and Economics,* published by David Barnes and Lynn Stout in 2006. None of these casebooks, however, deals exclusively with property. Moreover, they focus exclusively on American case law. In that respect, this book is original. The focus is entirely on property law, and the case analyses are mostly of a European blend. The distribution of countries is as follows:

UK: 18
Germany: 6
Belgium: 4
US: 3
Canada: 1
Total: 32

The cases originate from common law as well as from civil law countries. By applying legal economic analysis to cases from these two seemingly different legal families, deep similarities concerning the type of problems and the basic legal reasoning may be revealed. Common law and civil law tradition are probably more distinct from each other with regard to style, terminology and the structuring of the legal materials, but much less on the level of the type of litigated problems and the underpinning logic of the decisions.

I did not select the cases in the process of the writing of this book. As has been mentioned already before, cases were selected since the 1990's for the student' sessions in class. From this wider stock the most relevant cases for this book were selected. I selected the cases for the student sessions on the base of two criteria: subject and language.

First, each case's relevance to a typical problem in property law was established. As shown by the order of the chapters the main subjects are related to

1 the definition and extent of property rights,
2 the relationship between owners of a common property,
3 problems of nuisance either between neighbours or within the public space,
4 the relationship between holders of fragmented property,
5 the extent of taking law and the meaning of the public use requirement, and
6 problems about possession, prescription and registration of property.

It is important to emphasize that I did not select the cases based on their ability to illustrate the particular viewpoints, adopted by law and economics-scholars. The selection was totally blind in this respect. Our enterprise would become vulnerable to the criticism of circular logic if we tried to show the adequacy of law and economics for analyzing cases by selecting only such cases that are adequate in this respect.

Another criterion concerns language. The author of this book believes he has the linguistic ability to read cases in four languages: English, Dutch, German and French. Cases in other languages were consequently excluded. Students from other linguistic areas than these four were assigned an English case, for English is the teaching language of EMLE. This explains the overwhelming majority of English cases. German cases were assigned to German students, Dutch to Dutch students and French or Dutch cases to Belgian and French students.

In order to further clarify our methodology of the case analyses, three preliminary remarks are in order.

First, often some elements of the case were totally irrelevant for an analysis from a property law and economics point of view. Such elements mostly concerned procedural questions. They may be interesting for the economic analysis of procedural law and administration of justice, but they are outside the scope of this book. Consequently, we filtered them out of our analyses.

Second, most selected cases concern legal questions in which judges have a wide margin of discretion. Consequently, the efficiency or inefficiency of the decision and the considerations of these cases can be fully ascribed to the court itself. Sometimes judicial discretion is narrowly restricted to the application of a detailed rule of legislation. In these cases, the efficiency/inefficiency of the decision and consideration has to be ascribed to the legislator because even the judge is bound by inefficient legislation. When this was the case, we also discussed the efficiency or inefficiency of the legislative rule by which the judge was bound.

Third, my main concern is that this book finds its way not only to legal and economic academics but also to all people involved in the functioning of the legal system. This includes practicing lawyers as well as judges. In order to facilitate this acceptance by the legal community I composed theory and case analyses in a way that is legible to the layperson. The use of graphs is very limited and the included graphs are very easy to understand. Mathematical equations and derivations, which usually figure in economic papers, either in the full text or in appendices, are nearly completely absent in this book.

The overall result of the efficiency check on the analyzed cases is quite positive. Of the thirty-two cases, twenty-three cases were deemed to have resulted in an economically sustainable decision. In five cases, this was only partly true, and in four cases a decision was reached that was deemed inefficient. In most cases, however, the considerations leading to the decision were deemed intellectually flawed because obvious economic reasons were not advanced. This seems to confirm the general thesis of Richard Posner (1972) about the efficiency of the common (and civil) laws. Judges are intuitively aware about what makes sense economically in their decision-making but do not have the background and training necessary to articulate the economic rationality of their own decisions in a more systematic way. This seems to suggest that case law within the common and civil law tradition does not need a revolution. Most decisions go in the economically right direction. Case law in private law, rather, needs gradual intellectual improvements in order to become more precise in terms of the economically sustainable reasons underpinning the decisions taken. I hope this book will contribute to this intellectual upgrade, for citizens deserve a system of justice in which the available stock of rational arguments, as developed by social sciences such as economics, are exhausted to the maximum extent to legitimize enforceable decisions. The only alternative for this is authoritarianism, dogmatism, vagueness and traditionalist inertia. Our citizens, our taxpayers, our companies, our associations and our future generations in general deserve better!

## Bibliography

Ash, Elliott, Daniel L. Chen and Suresh Naidu (March 20, 2019) 'Ideas Have Consequences: The Impact of Law and Economics on American Justice', unpublished paper

Barnes, David and Lynn Stout (2006) *Cases and Materials on Law and Economics*, West Academic Publishing, St.-Paul, MN

Butler, Henry N. (1999) 'The Manne Programs in Economics for Federal Judges', *Case Western Reserve Law Review*, Vol. 50, no. 2, 351–371

Ellickson, Robert C., Vicki L. Been, Roderick M. Hills and Christopher Serkin (2005) *Land Use Controls: Cases and Materials*, Alphen aan den Rijn, Wolters Kluwer Law & Business, The Netherlands

Posner, Richard A. (1973) *Economic Analysis of Law*, Little Brown and Company, Boston and Toronto

Posner, Richard A. (1982) *Tort Law: Cases and Economic Analysis*, Little Brown and Company, Boston

Renda, Andrea (2011) *Law and Economics in the RIA-world*, European Studies in Law and Economics (EDLE), Intersentia, Mortsel

# 1 Definition and extent of property rights

## 1.1 Definition and extent of property rights in the economic theory of law

1 **Divergence between traditional legal definition of property rights and definitions within the economic theory of law.** Within law and economics literature the term 'property' is used in a much wider and less precise way than in the classical legal tradition, especially the Roman and civil law tradition. This divergence about such a crucial legal notion spawns confusion and irritation in the relationship between classical lawyers and legal economists and certainly did not contribute to a better mutual understanding between the two approaches to law. In this section (1) the differences between the classical and economic notion of property will be analyzed and (2) explanations will be provided for why legal economists prefer to work with another and much wider notion of property.

2 **Property within the civil law tradition.** The civil law tradition stretches back in history to the tradition of Roman law, which encompasses the law in the Roman Republic, the law in the Roman Empire – especially the law as it was codified under Emperor Justinian I – and the Roman law as it was reintroduced and adapted in Medieval Europe and evolved until the great civil law codifications in continental Europe.

The Latin term for property is *dominium*. As Roman lawyers were sceptical about definitions ('*Omnis definitio in iure civili periculosa est*') they never attempted or agreed on a definition of *dominium*. It is, however, possible to derive some characteristics of this right of *dominium* from the Roman classification of actions (*actiones*). Probably one of the oldest categories, developed in law, concerns the distinction between '*actiones in personam*' and '*actiones in rem*'. The distinction was developed by the legal scholar Publius Mucius Scaevola (second century BC) but came to us via the works of Gaius and the Institutes of Justinian. In case of '*actiones in personam*' it is possible to identify ex ante the persons or the group of persons against which the action can be directed. 'Ex ante' means before facts that may lead to a claim have occurred. An example of such an action is the '*legis actio per condictionem*', the action to enforce a contractual obligation (a '*stipulatio*' to '*dare, facere, praestari*') (Van Oven 1948: 204). One knows ex ante, that is, before eventual facts consisting of a breach of contractual obligations have occurred that the action can only be directed against the promisor in the contract.

The '*actiones in rem*' on the other hand concern actions which can be introduced against anybody who might interfere with the dominium. In difference with the '*actiones in personam*' it is impossible to identify ex ante, that is, before facts occur which may lead to a claim, against which person or persons the action can be introduced. In theory everybody is a potential intervenient into your dominium. As a consequence the '*actiones in rem*' are considered as potentially directed 'against the whole world'. 'The whole world' has as such an obligation to abstain from any interference into the dominium. It is only when an act of interference actually occurs that the party, against whom an '*actio in rem*' can be introduced, can be identified. An example of such an action is the '*actio negatoria*', originally an action against a person who claims to have a legal interest on your *dominium*. Later on this action acquired a larger scope: it could be introduced against the author of any nuisance, disturbing the enjoyment of *dominium* (see Van Oven 1948: 105, see also Chapter 3). Only when a nuisance occurs in fact, one knows against whom the '*actio negatoria*' can be introduced.

The distinction of '*actiones in rem*' and '*actiones in personam*' underwent a substantial theoretical change in the medieval Roman law. As law was more and more conceptualized, not as a collection of actions, but rather as a system of rights ('*iura*'), a new distinction, '*iura in personam*' versus '*iura in rem*' became prominent. The fourteenth-century legal scholar Bartolus defined *dominium* as the right to use a corporeal good, to withdraw from it all the proceeds and to alienate/ destroy the good ('*ius utenti, fruendi et abutendi*'). Within the logic of Bartolus *dominium*, defined in this way, had to be considered as the 'mother real right' from which other real rights (e.g. usufruct, easements, emphyteosis) could be split off ('*demembratio*').

Later civil law theory built further on this original Roman law distinction in order to come to the following elaborated distinction:

| *Aspect* | *Real Right* | *Personal Right* |
|---|---|---|
| **Corresponding obligation** | Obligation of non-interference | Obligation to give, to perform, to abstain |
| **Opposability** | Ex ante against the whole world | Against promisor or injurer |
| **'Droit de suite'**[1] | Yes. A real right sticks with the good in whomever hands it is. | No. The holder has no direct claim on the good, only on an obligation from the promisor /injurer. |
| | For instance, A rents a car from B; B sells the car to C; A can claim it from C because he/she has a real right (abstraction is made here from prescription/ limitation statutes) | For instance, A promises to rent a car to B but A sells this car to C. B cannot claim the car from C but can claim damages for contractual breach from A |

(*Continued*)

(Continued)

| *Aspect* | *Real Right* | *Personal Right* |
|---|---|---|
| **Numerus Clausus** | The law determines which types of real rights are available in the legal system. As a consequence there are a limited number of real right-types. | Types of personal rights can be freely created by contractual parties. As a consequence the number of personal right-types is unlimited. |

1 Although using a different terminology, Yun-chien Yang and Henry E. Smith consider a '*droit de suite*' as a basic feature of a property right. Instead of '*droit de suite*' they use the term 'running with the assets' indicating that property rights (they mean 'real rights' in the continental sense) continue to stick with the asset even when the physical possession of it has changed hands, either through a fact (e.g. theft) or through a contractual transfer (Yun-chien Chang and Henry E. Smith, 2012: 35, 55).

By way of conclusion on this point, property (*dominium, propriété, Eigentum, eigendom, proprieta*) in the civil law tradition concerns a real right on a corporeal good allowing the owner to use the good, to withdraw the proceeds of the good, to alienate (partially of totally) his rights on the good, to destroy the good.

3 **Property in the common law tradition.** Until the end of the eighteenth century, theoretical concepts and categories such as *dominium* and real rights versus personal rights were not very influential in the common law tradition. There are two major explanations for this:

First, one of the general characteristics of the common law tradition is its reluctance from strong conceptualization and its preference for practical solutions for the problems as they appear. This is reflected in the way the common law evolved, during the twelfth to the fourteenth century from writ to writ, and later, from precedent to precedent. The reluctance to theorization is illustrated by the absence of academic teaching of the common law. A professorship in common law was only established in 1758 with the appointment of William Blackstone at Oxford.

Second, the absence of elaborated concepts on property in the common law tradition is also related to the feudal character of the rights concerning the use of land. The rights on land were conceived as tenures, that is, rights a person held from another person, who thus ranked higher within the feudal hierarchy. The highest instance in this feudal pyramid was the Crown itself, the ultimate holder of the whole realm. Within this feudal system a wide variety of tenures were developed: free tenures such as tenure in chivalry, socage, frankalmoign and unfree tenure. The plurality of tenures (legal estates) and their link with the feudal pyramid prevented the development of a single notion of property such as *dominium* in the Roman/civil law tradition. A person never held his/her right directly from the legal system but always from someone else.[1]

1 On the impact of feudalism on the common law property doctrines see Yun-chien Chang and Henry R. E. Smith. They contend that the feudal framework of estates survived feudalism itself because

Even after the power relationships behind the feudal system were gradually vanishing,[2] the concepts about the rights on land, as tainted by feudalism, remained. Also in strong difference with the Roman/civil law tradition is the distinction real/personal. While these notions relate in the Roman/civil law tradition to categories of rights, they relate in the common law tradition to categories of goods. Real property, real rights, real actions relate to immovable goods (real estate) such as land and buildings. Personal property, personal rights and personal actions relate to movable goods (chattel).

The common law tradition, however, evolved into the direction of the Roman/civil law tradition. First, on the theoretical level, the first academic common law commentator, William Blackstone defined property as '*that sole and despotic dominion which one man claims and exercises over the external things of the world, in total exclusion of the right of any other individual in the universe*' (Blackstone, *2; Merrill and Smith 2001b: 361). In this definition Blackstone captures two important elements also present in the Roman/civil law-definition, that is, the mother rights aspect and the *in rem* aspect of universal opposability. A more systematic elaboration of the concept of property as a real right was developed by the American legal theorist Wesley Hohfeld, distinguishing in rem property rights from personal rights in that they avail against '*persons constituting a very large and indefinite class of people*' (Hohfeld 1917: 710; Merrill and Smith 2001b: 364).

Also on the level of the law itself the common law tradition moved closer to the Roman/civil one. The English Property Act of 1925 reduced dramatically the number of legal estates. Only the fee simple and the term of years survived, while all other tenures were abolished. Other rights on real estate can only follow from contract (e.g. rent of houses, of land). The scope of the right of fee simple is that wide that it is very similar to the Bartolian definition of property as a mother real right.

Finally it has to be remarked that also within the common law tradition the *'numerus clausus'*- principle of real estates was developed. Although the legal estates, distinguished in common law systems are different from the real rights, distinguished in Roman/civil law systems, the system of legal estates is also conceived as a 'formalistic, box-like structure' (Merrill and Smith 2001a: 12–24).

By way of conclusion, it can be stated that, although the theoretical and practical paths were quite different, both Roman/civil law and common law

the fixed costs to overhaul it were too burdensome. Moreover, the complementary equity system and the institution of trust allowed enough flexibility to cope with eventual outdated features of the estate system (Yun-chien Chang and Henry. E. Smith 2012: 36–39).

2 The feudal power of the lords vis-à-vis tenants were gradually weakened by legal reforms such as the Statute Quia Emptores in 1291, the Statute of Wills in 1540 and the Tenures Abolition Act of 1660. Also, political and economic events weakened the position of the lords such as for instance the Black Death of 1348, causing huge scarcity of labour and strengthening the bargaining position of tenants, and the peasants' revolts of the fifteenth century.

tradition converge on the notion of property, that is, as a right on a corporeal good bestowing on its holder the widest array of competences, a right which is opposable to the 'whole world' and a right which is a standard right belonging to a limited category of legally defined real rights or legal estates.

4 **Property in law and economics: the School of Property Rights.** Since the nineteenth-century, economists like Fréderic Bastiat, John R. Commons, Jeremy Bentham, Karl Marx and Carl Menger[3] have been very interested in the impact of property institutions on economic growth and development. Their reflections were however rather of a general kind. A more systematic and applied economic analysis of property institutions, based on neo-classical micro-economics, emerged only in the 1960s. For some economists, labelled the 'School of Property Rights', such as Harold Demsetz, Svetozar Pejovich and Armen Alchian, property was the core institution of an economic system. Economic systems differ because they operate under different property institutions. Property institutions are decisive for the success or the failure of a social and economic system. The economists of the school of property rights and other neo-classical economists however did not use the notion 'property right' in the sense which is prominent in the Roman/civil law or common law tradition. As economists are primarily concerned with the problem of efficient use of scarce resources they were inclined to label any use right on a scarce resource as a property right. So for instance Armen Alchian: *'By a system of property rights I mean a method of assigning to particular individuals the 'authority' to select for specific goods any use from a non-prohibited class of* uses' (Alchian 1977: 130). Similar definitions are proposed by other legal economists such as Yoram Barzel, Thrainn Eggertson, Steven Cheung, Richard Posner and Harold Demsetz (see Merrill and Smith 2001b: 358). When one adopts the definition of Alchian every political-economic system can be described in terms of property rights. Even a Stalinist economy of central planning is a property rights' system for scarce resources have always to be allocated and used by somebody. Consequently the 'property rights' in this system are awarded to planning bureaucrats who select the uses of resources, which are not prohibited for them according to the rules of the bureaucratic hierarchy. It may be clear, with such a wide definition one is far away from Bartolus and Blackstone!

5 **Property in law and economics: the 'bundle of sticks' metaphor.** Often legal economists use a metaphor to clarify their property notion. Property is a 'bundle of sticks'. The 'sticks' are specific rights, which can be allocated by the holder of the bundle and which can be extended or restricted by the state. Merrill and Smith point to the intellectual ancestry of this 'bundle of sticks' metaphor. The American Realists preferred this vague and flexible definition to the strict Blackstonian notion because it fitted within their political program. By undermining the *'in rem'* and the absolute character

3 So, for instance, Menger: 'Property, therefore, like human economy, is not an arbitrary invention but rather the only practically possible solution of the problem that is, in the nature of things, imposed upon us by the disparity between requirements for, and available quantities of, all economic goods' (Menger 1871: 97).

of property government restrictions on property became intellectually more acceptable (Merrill and Smith 2001b: 365). As such however the 'bundle of sticks' metaphor is politically neutral. Also the Blackstonian-Bartolian notion of property can be depicted as such a bundle. The owner is then the one who has initially – i.e. before any alienation of a composing right – the sticks of *usus, fructus* and *abusus* in his bundle.

The economic notion of property as a 'bundle of sticks' however differs from the legal traditional notion of property in several aspects. As mentioned earlier, property is considered in the civil/common law tradition as a 'mother right', involving initially the widest possible span of competences for the owner. The owner has the right to alienate these competences but she/he will retain always a residual right ('a title'), that is, all competences which are not alienated in a legally valid way, remain retained by her/him. To put this in a concise way: $P^{ccl}$ = (UFA – IRA) where UFA is '*usus, fructus, abusus*' and IRA are the '*iura in re aliena*', the rights eventually alienated by the owner to thirds.

In the 'bundle of sticks'-notion of the economists this initially complete or residual character of property has evaporated. Property is depicted as a collection of specific rights but there is neither unanimity nor clarity which specific rights are necessary in order to have property and which types of specific rights can be or should be distinguished

Ostrom, for instance, defines a property right as 'an enforceable authority to undertake particular actions in a specific domain' (Ostrom 2000: 339). She distinguishes between the following:

- **Access**: The right to enter a defined physical area and enjoy nonsubtractive benefits (for example, hike, canoe, sit in the sun)
- **Withdrawal**: The right to obtain resource units or products of a resource system (for example, catch fish, divert water)
- **Management**: The right to regulate internal use patterns and transform the resource by making improvements
- **Exclusion**: The right to determine who will have access rights and withdrawal rights and how those rights may be transferred
- **Alienation**: the right to sell or lease management and exclusion rights[4]

On the base of this rights distinction she distinguishes five classes of property-rights holders according to Table 1.1.

However elegant, this scheme reveals strong terminological and conceptual differences with the traditional property notion. First, the notion of 'proprietor' and 'claimant' are used in a meaning quite different from their

4 How many 'sticks' can be/should distinguished within a 'bundle' seems to be an endless discussion. Honoré (1961) largely beats Ostrom by distinguishing eleven sticks in a property bundle: the right to exclusively possess, the right to use, the right to manage, the right to the income, the right to the capital, the right to security, transmissibility, absence of term, the prohibition of harmful use, liability to execution, the right to residuary character. According to Honoré, none of these rights is strictly necessary to be considered an owner of property.

*Table 1.1* Ostrom's matrix of property rights holders

| | *Owner* | *Proprietor* | *Claimant* | *Authorized User* | *Authorized Entrant* |
|---|---|---|---|---|---|
| Access | X | X | X | X | X |
| Withdrawal | X | X | X | X | |
| Management | X | X | X | | |
| Exclusion | X | X | | | |
| Alienation | X | | | | |

classical legal meaning. Second, the meaning of the notion of property rights in general is widened in an extreme sense. For instance someone who buys a ticket for Disney Land has acquired a 'property right' as an authorized entrant. Third, it is unclear whether the notion 'owner' in this scheme has a residual character. Suppose the owner in this scheme alienates her/his property rights of access and withdrawal. Is she/he still considered the owner, as is the case with the traditional notion?

A second difference of the economic 'bundle of sticks' notion of property with the legal traditional one concerns the distinction between real and personal rights and the 'in rem' character of the former. The 'in rem' character of the 'real right sticks' of the bundle implies that all third parties are submitted to an identical obligation, i.e. abstention from interference in the legal domain of the right-holder. Legal economists seem not to bother about this distinction among the 'sticks' of the bundle. At the contrary, the bilateral and reciprocal character of the Coasean bargaining process, which should be, when transaction costs are not prohibitive, at the origin of property rights, seems to suggest that obligations of third parties vis-à-vis the right-holder can vary from party to party (Merrill and Smith 2001b: 371).

Finally also the '*numerus clausus*' rule for real rights is mostly overlooked in the economic 'bundle of sticks' notion.[5] This rule implies that the holders of the bundle have only a limited number of 'sticks'-types at their disposal, at least as far as 'real rights' are concerned. From a classical legal viewpoint the holder of the bundle has two kinds of sticks, namely, the 'real right' sticks which are given in a limited number determined by law and 'personal right' sticks the content of which can vary according to the contract by which they are established.

6 **Why a different property notion in law and economics?** Accidental reasons such as superficial knowledge of the law and the impatience of economists to frame the law into theoretical and mathematical models are only a partial explanation of the conceptual divergence on property between classical lawyers and legal economists. There is also a deeper reason. Legal economists are

5 On the economic rationale of the 'numerus clausus' see Chapter 4.

in the first place economists aiming at economic explanations for the emergence of institutions and the impact of institutions. Their research is, unlike classical lawyers, not limited to the explanation, interpretation and eventually improvement (‘*de lege ferenda*’) of one particular legal system. For classical lawyers the choice for using an analytical concept is mainly determined by the particular content of the legal system they are concerned with. Classical lawyers in France, Italy, Spain, Belgium, and other countries work with a Bartolian concept of property because this concept is entrenched in their civil code. Economists are not submitted to this vocational limitation. Institutions of all humankind in all historical epochs constitute in principle their research field. Of course, common and civil law traditions have spread throughout the whole world through colonization and voluntary legal transplants. Consequently by using the classical conceptual tools of these traditions a very wide set of legal institutions in the world can be analytically caught. For two important fields of research however the use of these tools will generate analytical difficulties. First, the Bartolian-Blackstonian notion of property will be useless as an analytical tool for the study of pre-modern legal systems. How to analyze for instance a feudal system of tenures in terms of full property and derived rights when there are no such owners recognized and operational in such a system? Second, the Bartolian-Blackstonian notion of property will be of no help to analyze the persisting traditional/tribal legal systems in the present world. The territory of such systems may seem to shrink steadily on the official legal world maps. In many cases they persist even on an informal level and remain influential for the way scarce resources are used and distributed among large parts of the world population (Fitzpatrick 2006). As economists are more interested in the explanation of human behavior than in the meaning of statutory texts, the analysis of these persisting informal legal systems remains an interesting field of research and in this the classical notion of Bartolian-Blackstonian property will be of little help. As a consequence it is methodologically legitimate to develop a ‘property’ notion which is neutral vis-à-vis any legal culture and which can be used as a conceptual tool to analyze in principle all possible ‘property’ systems in the world.

The methodological legitimacy of a transcultural economic notion of property, different from the classical one, does not justify however the present handling of ‘property’ in the law and economics literature.

In the first place, one can question whether the unilateral capture of the term ‘property’ by the legal economists is productive for future interdisciplinary cooperation between lawyers and economists. The dreams of legal economists to see their viewpoints translated in legal statutory texts or opinions in case law can only become true through such cooperation, based on mutual respect. As a result it would be wise that legal economists adopt another term for their transcultural economic notion of ‘property’ and use the term ‘property’ exclusively in its traditional meaning.

Second, by using the same term for on one side a very encompassing and well protected right such as Bartolian-Blackstonian property and on the other side for very ephemeral and minimal rights such as one day access to Disney Land, legal economists tend to undermine, most often unintendedly, the political impact of property. Since the liberal revolutions of the eighteenth and nineteenth centuries property has been considered as pivotal, not only for the functioning of a genuine free market system but also for personal liberty and the pursuit of happiness. Property rights are conceived to be a part of the 'material constitution' of a free society, as a part of the 'nomocratic' order (Hayek 1973; Oakeshott 1975). By reducing property rights to a mere use right conceivable in endless variety property seems to be reduced to a mere policy tool, as an instrument of a 'teleocracy' (Hayek 1973; Oakeshott 1975). Avoiding this unintended political impact of the terminological downsizing of property is a second good reason to adopt another term for the economic notion of property.

The economic notion of property could be called for instance 'an acting with scarce resources right' (ASRR), in line with the German term for property rights in the economic sense: *Handlungsrechte*[6] (Schäfer and Ott 1995: 453). Building further on the distinction made by Ostrom (see earlier pp. 10–11) such an ASRR could be defined as an institutionally backed actual or future authority of an individual, family, group or organization to (1) get access to a resource, (2) to withdraw the flow from a resource, (3) to manage the use of a resource, (4) to exclude others from the right to (1), (2) and (3), (5) to destroy the resource and (6) to alienate the rights to (1), (2), (3), (4) and (5).[7]

Property in its traditional meaning should then be conceived as a particular case of an ASRR. Property can consist of an actual or future authority of acting with scarce resources. When the owner for instance has conveyed a usufruct on his estate the owner is regarded as a 'nude owner' with only a latent ownership, to be revived when the usufructor deceases. Property is initially a complete right, so it involves the authorities of (1, 2, 3, 4, 5 and 6). Other characteristics such as the '*droit de suite*', the '*in rem*' character, and the '*numerus clausus*' rule (see earlier pp. 7–8) are typical for property but not for many other forms of ASRR. The fact that these characteristics do not pertain to the 'naked' notion of an ASRR does not imply that they are economically not viable. In more recent economic literature ample reasons have been provided

6 Schäfer and Ott make the following distinction: '*Der Begriff von Property Rights oder Handlungsrechten ist nicht mit Privateigentum gleichzusetzen. Er umfasst neben dem Privateigentum auch Gemeinschaftseigentum (Allmende), das Eigentum aller* (free access), *Staatseigentum, Sicherungseigentum, Patente oder Urheberrechte, Wohnungseigentum, Wegerecht, Jagdrecht und im allgemeinen alle Rechtsformen, die die Kompetenzverteilung bei der Ressourcennutzung regelen*' (Schäfer and Ott 1995: 453).

7 The notion of ASRR, as defined here, is however much wider than the notion of property rights, developed by Yun-chun Chang and Henry E. Smith (2012: 54). They consider as property rights all rights involving three basic features: the '*in rem-erga omnes*' status, the right to exclude, the running with the asset. In the continental conceptual system this category would conflate with the category of 'real rights'. Many ASSR do not even match these basic features, such as for instance a right of access.

to justify these characteristics.[8] So it makes sense to argue that more ASRRs in the legal systems of the world should evolve towards genuine property rights. This is however an economic normative point of view. For analytical purposes it is preferable to work with a more neutral tool such as the one we propose.

7 **The extent of property rights in civil and common law traditions.** In both traditions the extent of property rights (as defined in these traditions, see earlier pp. 7–8) is substantially restricted. Some categories of goods escape in principle to any privatization. According to the Justinian Code the '*res communes*' are by law of nature common to mankind. '*Res communes*' encompass the air, running water, the sea and the seashores. The French Civil Code does not repeat this enumeration but refers to 'things belonging to nobody' and as such to be 'regulated through the police power of public authorities' (art. 714 French Civil Code). References to this category are less frequent in common law[9] but some scholars adhere to the public trust doctrine, claiming that goods such as the mentioned '*res communes*' are held by the government under a public trust which involves environmental obligations, eventually enforceable before court (Sax 1970; Velozo de Melo Bento 2009). In civil law countries also the so called '*res publicae*', or the goods of the public domain, are not open for appropriation. This category encompasses roads, streets, navigable rivers, beaches, ports, fortifications and all goods not adequate for appropriation (art. 538–541 French Civil Code). Also these goods are submitted to the police power of public authorities. During the nineteenth century civil law scholars introduced a distinction into the patrimony of public authorities: on one side the proper public domain involving the mentioned goods, on the other side the private domain of public authorities. In the latter case public authorities own goods in the way private parties do and are consequently submitted to the same rules. Goods of the private domain of public authorities can be sold, rented, seized by creditors[10] and are submitted to adverse possession rules. The goods of the public domain cannot be sold as such; they have to be first 'disaffected' from the public domain to the private domain by a legislative decision. In common law countries this distinction seems to be less popular. Goods held by public bodies, such as for instance the goods of the Crown Estate in the UK, are alienable upon decision of these bodies. This is however not the case for the land, belonging to the 'commons' as regulated in several legislation such as the Commons Act of 1876, the Property Act of 1925, the Commons Registration Act of 1995 and the Countryside and Rights of Way Act of 2000 (CRoW Act), the Commons

8 See pp. 19–21 and Chapter 2.

9 See however *Geer v. State of Connecticut* 161 U.S. 519 (16 S.Ct.600, 40 L. Ed. 793). In majority opinion Justice White refers to this category in order to justify the power of states to regulate hunting, even the interstate transfers of game.

10 Concerning the immunity of public authorities against seizure by creditors, the distinction between public and private became gradually less relevant. Rather another criterion, the continuity of the public service, has become decisive (see art. 1412bis Ger. W. – Belgian Code of Civil Procedure)

Act of 2006. Owners of lands, registered as 'commons', are submitted to several restrictions: they have to allow the right to roam for the general public, they cannot fence without permission. Finally there is the category of '*res nullius*' and '*res derelictae*'. These goods are open for appropriation but are actually not submitted to a private property regime either because they were never appropriated or were abandoned by the owner. Their appropriation is submitted to the rules of '*occupatio*' (first come, first served) in Roman law, treasure trove in Roman law ('*thesaurus*') to art. 716 of the French Civil Code and the rules on lost and found goods.[11] Concerning animals, the Roman legal scholar Gaius[12] distinguished between domesticated and wild animals. Domesticated animals have to be returned to the owner of the nest (e.g. pigsty, dovecot). For wild animals moving from place to place the rule of capture applies. This distinction is still valid in many civil law countries

8 **Extent of property rights and international law.** Effective property rights are only possible within organized human communities (tribes, religious communities, dynastic states, city-states, nation-states, etc.). Within modern nation-states the development of a legal framework of property devolves from the privilege of sovereignty. National sovereignty is as such the primary source of property rights. In dynastic states (before the English, French and American revolutions), this sovereignty resides with the monarch, also considered as the ultimate owner of the whole realm. In liberal nation states sovereignty resides with 'the people', represented by the parliament, which is supposed to develop a general framework of rules on property. Citizens then do not hold their property rights from a person ('tenure') but directly from the legal system, as developed by the representants of the people. However not all modern property institutions devolve directly from national sovereignty. Important property arrangements owe their development from treaties, i.e. agreements between several nation states, and from international organizations, devolving from treaties by their founding member states. These treaties concern most often areas of the world which are vital for all nations. An exclusive control on these areas by one nation state could result in highly conflictual situations. As a consequence the extent of property rights is not only determined by national arrangements but also by evolutions within international law. An important example of this concerns the Open Sea ('*Mare Liberum*'). Coastal states can only exercise their jurisdiction within territorial waters (12 nautical miles). Art. 87 of the UN-Convention on the Law of the Sea (10 December 1982) specifies:

1. the high seas are open to all states, whether coastal or land-locked. Freedom of the high seas is exercised under the conditions laid down under this

11 In civil law countries, goods found on the public domain have to be declared to the police, keeping the found goods at the disposal of the owner. After a certain period (e.g. six months) the non-reclaimed goods can be auctioned by the public authority. According to the German Civil code however the finder can claim a reward for the lost good ('*Finderslohn*'; below 500 € value: 5 percent, above: 3 percent; see § 971 BGB)

12 Gaius, D 41.1.1–5

Convention and by other rules of international law. It comprises, inter alia, both for coastal and land-locked States:

a) Freedom of navigation
b) Freedom of overflight
c) Freedom to lay submarine cables and pipelines, subject to Part VI
d) Freedom to construct artificial islands and other installations permitted under international laws, subject to Part VI
e) Freedom of fishing, subject to the conditions laid down in section 2
f) Freedom of scientific research subject to Parts VI and XIII

The '*Mare Liberum*' clause in the UN Convention prevents national states and eventual other political structures to develop schemes of property rights on resources, located within the open sea. This includes not only fish but also other economically profitable resources such as salt, potassium, magnesium, sand, gravel, limestone, gypsum, manganese nodules, phosphorite, silver, gold, cobalt, zinc, etc.

Another important example of international regulation of the extent of property rights concerns the air space. In the Convention of Paris of 13 October 1919, the first important treaty on the air space, an option, totally different from the one on the open sea, was taken. According to this Convention each country has full sovereignty on the air space, spanning over its territory and waters. This principle was reiterated by the Chicago Convention of 7 December 1944 (revised eight times during 1944–2006). Art. 1 states: 'Every state has complete and exclusive sovereignty over air space above its territory.' National states are allowed to regulate the use of 'their' air space and eventually develop property rights (in the broad economic sense, see earlier pp. 37–41) within it. An interesting question in this respect is how far the property rights of landowners stretch into the air. In civil law countries it was generally accepted that the owner of the land had a right to the air space above his land in so far as it was necessary to allow activities on his land. Owners were for instance allowed to let their trees grow into the air. The medieval Roman law scholar Accursius introduced the principle '*Cuius est solum, eius est usque ad coelum et ad inferos'*. The property of the land owner stretches from the middle of the earth to the infinite heights of the air space. The principle had been adopted in fourteenth-century common law but was expressly mentioned by Edward Coke in *Bury v. Pope* (1587)[13] and promulgated by Blackstone in his Commentaries (Blackstone 1776, Book 2, Chapter 2). The application of the principle was adapted in later cases of the common law (see further *Lord Bernstein v. Skyview Leigh*).

Another important question, dealt with by International Law, concerns the consequences of acquisition of territories by conquest and occupation. Does

13 In this case the owner of a house was allowed to erect the building thereby blocking the window of his neighbour, who had enjoyed during more than thirty years the sunlight in this window.

the conquering state have the right to overrun the established property system in the conquered territory and impose the system of the conqueror? In international law a distinction is made between the conquest of a country inhabited by institutionally organized communities and the occupation of non-inhabited territories ('*terra nullius*'). In the former case the established institutions of the conquered population remain valid until eventually changed by the new masters. In the latter case the laws of the conquering nation are immediately applicable after occupation. The distinction is however not always easy to draw and has often been interpreted according to the conqueror's interest. The acquisition of Australia by Great Britain has been qualified as an occupation because the aboriginals were not considered as institutionally organized communities. As a consequence, they could not claim any title to Australian land, while all the land devolved initially to the English Crown. This was changed by the famous Mabo case,[14] reversing this qualification and recognizing aboriginals' titles to land (Peter Butt 1996: 495–516).

9 **The tragedy of open-access goods.** Do we need property rights for a sustainable management of scarce resources? The discussion on this question is as old as Western philosophy. Plato advocated communism on goods and women for the praetorian guard of his model state. Aristotle replied 'that which is common to the greatest number has the least care bestowed on it' (Aristotle 1941: sec. 1262b34–35). Aristotle's viewpoint was adopted by the most famous medieval theologian Saint Thomas Aquinas,[15] by which acceptance of private property became part of mainstream Catholicism. In modern literature the argument was more systematically reframed by the ecologist Garret Hardin (Hardin 1968). The latter pointed to the fact that in a commons the users do not care about the impact of their individual behaviour on the total value of the resource for they don't own it. All commoners are induced to externalize negatively on all the other commoners, ultimately leading to a tragedy: the tragedy of the commons. Hardin however was not the first in modern literature to address the problem of non-owned resources. More than ten years before, Scott Gordon analysed the problem of resource depletion in the fisheries. The lack of private property in ocean resources induced fishermen to fish beyond the point where marginal costs intersect with marginal productivity. Fishermen cannot take into account the Net Present Value of the resource because they do not own it and only consider the actual value of it (Scott Gordon 1954). As it will be argued further, Hardin and Scott Gordon have it right in their theoretical analysis but the title 'tragedy of the commons' was misleading and thus ill chosen. Many authors (Ostrom 2000; Ciriacy-Wantrup and Bishop 1975) correctly referred to the numerous historical and current examples of 'commons' which were and are all but a tragedy but often examples of rational management of resources. In fact, all these cases

14 *Mabo v. Queensland*, (1992) 66 ALJR 408

15 Thomas Aquinas, Summa Theologiae, II-II, 9.66,9.2

concern resources managed by well-defined and organized groups able to exclude outsiders from the use of the resource. The tragedy arises not merely because resources are owned and managed by a group, but arise when (1) there is complete absence of an owner-manager, or (2) when the owning group is so vague and ill-defined that there is a lack of effective exclusion or (3) when the law provides an excluding agent (e.g. public authorities), who is however ineffective in practice. These cases should be rather qualified, not as 'commons' but rather as 'open-access' situations, in which resources are either legally or de facto open to a rule of capture.

Theoretically the tragedy of open-access resources has a three pronged character. Open access (1) leads to inefficient overuse, (2) leads to inefficient timing of harvesting; (3) leads to suboptimal investment in the resource.

1. Inefficient overuse

   Consider an open access lake which is a fishing ground for fishermen, living around the lake. For the fishermen, operating in teams, there is no restriction to fish on the lake.

   The optimal number of teams, fishing in the lake, is 4 (see Table 1.2). At this number the net total return is the highest (i.e. $800). When there is however no restriction for the fishermen, the number of teams will rise to 10, for the number of teams will rise up to the point where the average return equals the marginal private cost (i.e. $150). As a consequence the open access character of the lake causes a rent dissipation of $800, i.e. the difference between the net total return at 4 fishing teams and the one at 10 fishing teams.

*Table 1.2* Inefficient overuse of open-access goods

| *Teams* | *Marginal return* | *Total return* | *Average Return* | *Marginal private Cost* | *Total Private Cost* | *Total Wealth* |
|---|---|---|---|---|---|---|
| 1 | $500 | $500 | $500 | $150 | $150 | $350 |
| 2 | $400 | $900 | $450 | $150 | $300 | $600 |
| 3 | $300 | $1200 | $400 | $150 | $450 | $750 |
| 4 | $200 | $1400 | $350 | $150 | $600 | $800 |
| 5 | $100 | $1500 | $300 | $150 | $750 | $750 |
| 6 | 0 | $1500 | $250 | $150 | $900 | $600 |
| 7 | 0 | $1500 | $230 | $150 | $1050 | $450 |
| 8 | 0 | $1500 | $175 | $150 | $1200 | $300 |
| 9 | 0 | $1500 | $160 | $150 | $1350 | $150 |
| 10 | 0 | $1500 | $150 | $150 | $1500 | 0 |
| 11 | 0 | $1500 | $136 | $150 | $1650 | – $150 |

2. Inefficient timing of harvesting

   Consider a forest with trees planted more or less at the same time. The trees get bigger which makes them more difficult to cut, by which cutting costs are rising (see table 1.3). After some time trees are aging, get sick and fall down, which makes returns of cutting decrease. Costs of waiting are due to the fact that by leaving the trees in the wood rents on returns are foregone. In the example, the rents are set at 5 percent. The variable of waiting costs causes a divergence between technical optimality of cutting (at T9 = 30,000) and the economic optimality of it (at T6 = 24,000).

*Table 1.3* Inefficient timing of harvesting of open-access goods

| *Time period* | *Total Return of Cutting* | *Total Cost of Waiting* | *Total Cost of Cutting* | *Total Net Return* |
|---|---|---|---|---|
| T1 | 1,000 | 0 | 5,000 | −4,000 |
| T2 | 5,000 | 50 | 7,000 | −2,050 |
| T3 | 10,000 | 300 | 9,000 | +700 |
| T4 | 15,000 | 800 | 11,000 | +3,250 |
| T5 | 20,000 | 1,550 | 13,000 | +5,450 |
| T6 | 24,000 | 2,550 | 15,000 | +6,450 |
| T7 | 27,000 | 3,750 | 17,000 | +6,250 |
| T8 | 29,000 | 5,100 | 19,000 | +4,900 |
| T9 | 30,000 | 6,550 | 21,000 | +2,450 |
| T10 | 29,000 | 8,050 | 19,000 | +1,950 |
| T11 | 27,000 | 9,500 | 17,000 | +500 |
| T12 | 24,000 | 10,850 | 15,000 | −1,850 |

An owner of the forest (a lumber company, a village community, a landlord etc.) able to exclude outsider-lumbermen would harvest at T6, that is, when total net return is the highest. When the wood is under open access, lumbermen will harvest at T3, that is, when the return of cutting becomes higher than the cost of cutting, thereby dissipating (6,450–700 = 5,750) in wealth.

3. Inefficient underinvestment in the resource

Often the productivity of a resource is not static but can be enhanced by additional investment. A prime example of such an investment regards the use of fertilizers to improve agricultural productivity. Suppose Steve and Laura are open-access users of agricultural land and are able to improve productivity with fertilizers. The cost is $6 for each, the total result of fertilization is $10 for each, $20 in total. The following diagram indicates the payoffs: in the case none of both fertilizes (0; 0), in case both do {(10–6) + (10–6)} = 8, in case one does while the other not (5–6) + (5+0) = −1. Because both can profit from fertilization of the other while not doing it by him/her both will bet on no fertilization, which brings them in a suboptimal situation and rent dissipation. The optimum is both fertilize with total result of 8. No fertilize, the expected outcome (Nash equilibrium) leads to 0, a rent dissipation of 8. In fact, investment in an open-access good has a public good character, leading to prisoners' dilemmas with suboptimal equilibria as a result.

*Table 1.4* Underinvestment in open-access goods

| | | Steve | |
|---|---|---|---|
| | | Fertilize | No Fertilize |
| **Laura** | Fertilize | (10–6)(10–6) | (5–6) (5–0) |
| | No Fertilize | (5–0)(5–6) | 0; 0 |

Concerning the depletion of resources, and especially the cases of rapid and dramatic depletion, two remarks should however be made: (1) depletion is not per se a consequence of a tragedy of open-access goods, and (2) not all tragedies of open-access resources can be solved by the introduction of property rights.

Regarding the first remark, in some cases a rapid and thorough depletion of a resource can be the result of rational resource substitution. Hill (2014) analyses the case of the extinction of the bison in North America, commonly regarded as a case in point of an open-access goods-tragedy. Hill argues that the extinction consisted of a rational substitution of the bison by cattle, leading to a more efficient use of the basic resource, namely, the vast plains in the Mid-West. Several variables, such as meat productivity and the comparative monitoring costs of bison versus cattle point to this conclusion. Whether rapid and dramatic depletion of resources has its origins either in inefficient institutions or, at the contrary, in efficient management of resources depends of course on empirical data, to be sorted out in case-by-case analyses.

About the second remark: the institutional switch from an open-access situation towards an ordered and effective property system involves costs: exclusion costs. Such costs encompass the elaboration of property rules and institutions to litigate property conflicts, negotiation costs to build a social consensus around a property system, costs of delineation of property rights (e.g. fencing), costs of identification of property rights ('verification rules' such as registration of property rights) and costs of protection of property rights. Such costs can be very high, even infinite, and can outweigh the benefits of internalization, realized by the establishment of possible property rights.

This latter remark fits entirely with the general Demsetz-theory about the emergence of property rights. According to Demsetz (Demsetz 1966, 1967) property rights emerge in society when the benefits of them outweigh significantly the costs. Benefits vary foremost with the evolution of the value of the concerned items. An increase of value will elicit social pressure to envelop these assets with property rights. Increased demographic pressure for instance will necessarily lead to an increase of arable land value which may be a decisive push factor for the development of property rights (Ault and Rutman 1979). A decrease in value may lead to a neglect of protection of property rights and a return to open access. Anderson and Hill (Anderson and Hill 1998) analyse the impact of the dramatic price drop of horses in post–World War I America due to the massive introduction of cars and trucks. Property claims and protection of the lands of horse ranches in the northern Mid-West plains were neglected or even abandoned and the lands returned to a de facto open-access situation as was the case before the Homestead Law of 1862 and the introduction of barbed wire some years later. A decrease in exclusion costs will predictably lead to the establishment of more property rights within an already established legal system or of the introduction of such a system. Again, Anderson and Hill point to the dramatic increase of land claims under the American Homestead Law due to the use of barbed wire instead of wooden fences, the former being far less costly than the latter (Anderson and Hill 1998). Finally, an increase in exclusion cost will predictably lead to a drop in protection of property rights. Due to the high demand of powder of the rhino-horn, believed by Far Easterners to be an adequate cure for several diseases, the protection costs of rhinos against poachers increased steeply. As a result the protection of the rhino with the horn was given up and limited to protection without a horn, by cutting it (Allen 2000).

This negative relationship between the viability of property rights and exclusion costs indicates that the establishment of property rights in many open-access areas is currently not possible and will may be never be. Other solutions, such as regulations, will consequently be necessary. It is for instance clear that the air space cannot be submitted to property rights, at least in their classic legal sense (see earlier pp. 7–8). This does not prevent that other types of rights (property rights in the economic sense, 'acting with scarce resources rights', ASRR) may be possible (see earlier pp. 8–9). The same applies for the open sea. It is clear that the introduction of a property rights scheme, modelled after territorial property right systems, is not a solution for the exploitation of the open sea fugitive resources. New technologies may however pave the way for the development of new types of property rights on open sea resources. De Alessi refers to the development of the 'robo-tuna', a digitalized artificial tuna fish which could act as a 'fish-herder' goading schools of tuna fishes from feeding ground to feeding ground. This technology could allow fishermen to own schools of tuna fish, while still swimming in the sea and to exploit them more rationally, as owners of cattle on land are able to do (De Alessi 1998: 52). As long as such technologies are not adequately developed and made operational, reliance on regulation seems to be to only remedy for open-access tragedies.

10 **New forms of property rights.** The wider and more flexible economic notion of property rights (see earlier pp. 12–14) is also applicable to a specific type

of environmental regulatory policy, the so called trading schemes. Basically environmental policy has to address two categories of fundamental problems:

1) The control of activities which produce **external effects** harming environmental goods, which are under an open-access regime, either for economic reasons (too high exclusion cost, see Chapter 2, 7. The Optimal Commons) or for political reasons (preference for collective government). Examples here include pollution of the air space, pollution of rivers, lakes, seas and oceans, and pollution of aquifers.
2) **The control of consumption- and/or use-levels** of natural resources which are under an open-access regime, again either for economic or political reasons. Examples here are the fisheries, virgin forests.

In order to cope with these problems governments have developed a wide battery of regulatory instruments which can be categorized in different ways (Cole 2010: 235). The most basic categorization is twofold:

1) **Command and control regulation**: the government imposes on externalizers and users of environmental goods detailed behavioural standards and technically specified prevention devices (e.g. scrubbers) in order to curb down externalization and depletion.
2) **Market-based regulation:** the government relies partially on market forces in order to enhance the efficiency of its environmental policy. This can be done by

   a **Taxation/subsidy**: the government either increases the costs of externalizers/users/consumers by imposing taxes or diminishes the costs of agents abating their externalities, consumption or use levels.
   b **Trading systems:** the government relies on a combination of general regulation and the allocation of tradeable rights ('cap and trade').

The basic structure of such trading schemes is two-tiered. First the government determines a general level of allowed externalization or of allowed use /consumption. Second, the general levels of externalization or of use/consumption are 'unitized', that is, split up in identical quantities ('quota'). These quotas are then submitted to a market allocation process. The quota are initially either given away, for instance to incumbent users, or auctioned. The initial quota-holders are then allowed to transfer their quota to other market participants.

The economic advantage of such trading schemes resides in the fact that the production costs structures of firms can differ substantially. One firm can produce more than another at the same equivalent of pollution. Under a command and control system both firms will be treated in the same way. Under a trading system the more productive firm will acquire more pollution quotas and the less productive one less. As a result, at ceteris paribus concerning allowed pollution, productivity in society is comparatively higher under a trading system than under a command and control system.

Are these quotas, awarded under the different trading systems property rights? The American Congress for instance stated clearly in §403(f) of the 1990 Clean Air Act Amendments (42 U.S. C §765(f)) that an 'allowance' to emit is not a property right and it expressly authorized the EPA to terminate or limit allowances when necessary to achieve environmental goals without having to pay just compensation for taking property under the Fifth Amendment of the US Constitution (Cole 2010: 245). When comparing with a property right in the classical legal sense (see earlier pp. 27–33) the differences are substantial. Although the right of a quota-holder under a trading system is related to corporeal goods (air, water, fish) the 'bundle of sticks' of the quota-holder is far more restricted than the one of a Bartolian-Blackstonian owner. Of the six components encompassed by a classical legal property right (see earlier pp. 34–37), the quota holder can only claim a limited right of access, a limited right of use/consumption, and depending on the specific rules of the concerned trading system, some right of alienation of these two rights. The rights of a quota holder can certainly be qualified as a property right in the legal economic sense (or better: an acting with scarce resources right-ASRR, see earlier pp. 34–37) but not I the classical legal sense.

The intellectual father of environmental trading systems is Dales (1968). His seminal writings inspired the US legislation in its air-pollution policy to develop alternatives to command-and-control approaches. After experimenting with softer systems such as netting, bubbles and banking, a market of SO2-emission allowances was established in 1979 in which an allowance was the equivalent of one ton of SO2 emissions (Cole 2010: 243).

Another important example of trading systems concerns the EU-Emission Trading System. This system is designed to cope with the emission of greenhouse gases and the famous global warming problem. The system covers thirty-one countries and applies to 11,000 power stations, industrial plants and aircraft-operators. As such it is the most ample in the world. The general aim is to reduce emission of greenhouse gases over time by which emission allowances will become scarcer and more expensive. With 2005 at a 100 percent reference base the ambition is to reduce in 2020 to 79 percent and in 2030 to 57 percent. The emitting companies can buy and trade allowances and credits from emission-saving projects around the world (e.g. creating greenhouse gas sinks by foresting).

Trading systems concerning the use and consumption of open-access resources are most common in the fisheries.

Throughout the world national governments have developed ITQ (Individual Transferable Quota) or IFQ (Individual Fish Quota) in order to cope with the treat of fishing ground depletion. The basic scheme is everywhere the same: the government, hereby advised by specialized institutes on marine resources, determine each year the Total Allowable Catch (TAC) of the concerned fish species, 'unitizes' this TAC and awards IFQ's to the fishing companies. There are however differences mostly related to the initial awarding process (only auction, free gifting to incumbent) and to the degree of free alienability.

New Zealand introduced in 1975 an IFQ-system for thirty-two fish species in ten management areas, covering about 90 percent of total fish value (Major 1999).

The USA introduced in 1990 an IFQ for surf clam and ocean quahog fishing in the Mid-Atlantic and New England waters, in 1992 for wreck fish in the Southern East coast waters, in 1995 for halibut and sablefish in Alaska. Italy introduced IFQ for clams (Garcia and Newton 1997), Australia introduced IFQ for fifteen species (Pascoe 1993), South Africa for abalone fishing. Canada developed IFQ for the Atlantic, the Pacific and the Great Lakes. The Netherlands developed ITQ for sole and plaice (Davides 1997). The country which has the most encompassing IFQ-system however is Iceland, a country quite dependent on fishery (Gissurarson 1999). Between 1965 and 2000 ITQ systems were gradually introduced. Because Iceland was able during the notorious cod wars to extend its Economic Exploitation Zone (EEZ) to 200 miles, migratory movements of fish remained mainly within the jurisdiction of this country by which the tragedy of the open sea could by coped with by a national scheme. Each year the TAC of different fishes such as cod, are determined by the Ministry of Fishery on the advice of the Marine Research Institute. Most often this advice is more or less followed. IFQ are awarded to fishing companies. Only agents disposing of an operational fishing vessel can bid for ITQ's and only 50 percent of the annual catch quota can be transferred.

## 1.2 Case analyses

### *1. Lord Bernstein of* Leigh v. Skyviews & General Ltd*; Queen's Bench Division [1977] 2 All ER 902*

**A Facts and legal sources.** The plaintiff is the owner and a resident at premises comprising a country house and surrounding land in Kent. On 3 August 1974, an aeroplane of the defendant overflew the area on the height of several hundred feet and took aerial photographs of the house of the plaintiff. The defendant offered the photographs for sale to the plaintiff, but the latter was offended by this behaviour. He wrote a letter to the defendant complaining about the invasion of his privacy and asked the defendant to hand over or destroy all the negatives of the photographs. The secretary of the defendant did however not see the letter but the letter was responded by a young lady who had recently joined the defendant. In her answer she offered the plaintiff to buy the negatives for £15. Offended by this reaction the defendant went to his solicitors who wrote again a letter asking to deliver prints and negatives and to apologize, but again the secretary of the defendant did not see this letter either. Receiving no answer the solicitors introduced an action against the defendant.

This case concerns in the first place the question whether the flights above the premises of the defendant and the taking of the photographs can be qualified as common law trespass or nuisance. Behind this qualification there is the larger question whether the property rights of the land owner stretch into the air space above his land according to the maxim '*cujus est solum ejus est usque ad coelum et ad inferos*' (see earlier pp. 45–46). If so, the activity of the defendant has to be qualified as trespass, to be remedied by damages and injunction. In the second place, however, air traffic is regulated by statute law, namely, the Air Navigation Act of 1920, replaced by the Civil Aviation Act of 1949, s40 (1) of which specifies that:

> No action shall lie in respect of trespass or in respect of nuisance, by reason only of the flight of an aircraft over any property at a height above the ground, which, having regard to wind, weather, and all the circumstances of the case is reasonable, or the ordinary incidents of such flight so long as the provisions of Part II and this Part of this Act and any Order in Council or order made under Part II of this Part of this Act are duly complied with.

B **Claims and defences.** The defendant claims to be a victim of trespass and consequently claims (1) damages for trespass and/or invasion of the plaintiff's right to privacy; (2) an injunction to restrain the defendants from entering the premises of the plaintiff and the air space above them; (3) an injunction to restrain the defendants from invading the privacy of the plaintiff by taking unauthorized photographs of his home and (4) an order for immediate delivery up, alternatively the destruction of all negatives and prints of the photographs. According to the plaintiff the Civil Aviation Act does not preclude his claim for this act has to be read in a restrictive way and applies exclusively to the right of passage of aircraft and not to accompanying activities such as taking photographs.

C **Sentence and considerations.** In his opinion, Judge Griffiths discusses first the claim of the plaintiff that the defendant committed trespass by entering wrongfully the air space above his land. To assess this claim the exact reading of the maxim '*cujus est solum ejus est usque ad coelum et ad inferos*' within the case law of the common law has to be analysed. According to the judge this maxim was never understood in common law case law as if a full property right on the air space up to the heaven was granted to the land owner. The cases in which the maxim was used concern structures attached to the adjoining land such as overhanging buildings, signs, telegraph wires, branches of trees. For the solution of these cases it has not been necessary to cast the eyes towards the heavens. They concern only the rights of the owner in the air space immediately adjacent to the surface of the land. In some cases the overhanging of these structures has been qualified as nuisance (*Lemmon v. Webb*), in other cases as trespass (*Wandsworth Board of Works v. United Telephone Co, Gifford v. Dent*). As far as the passage through the air space above land is concerned the judge remarks that the overflight with a balloon is not considered a trespass (*Pickering v. Rudd, Saunders v. Smith*) and that an overflight by an aircraft will only constitute a trespass if they fly so low as to come within the area of the ordinary user (*Kelsen v. Imperial Tobacco Co. Ltd*) (Wilburforce 1954: 379). The judge concludes with the words of Lord Wilberforce in the case *Commissioner for Railways v. Valuer-General*:

> In none of these cases [where the maxim was invoked] is there an authoritative pronouncement that 'land' means the whole of the space from the centre

of the earth to the heavens: so sweeping, unscientific and unpractical a doctrine is unlikely to appeal to the common law mind.

The judge concludes that the plaintiff cannot find support in the common law for his claim that his rights on air space were infringed and that the overflight constituted a trespass.

Finally the judge also analyses the claim of the plaintiff that the mentioned provision (see earlier p. 25–26) in the Civil Aviation Act concerns only the passage through the air space and does not cover other activities such as taking photographs. According to the judge there is no indication that this provision has to be read in such a restrictive way. Taking photographs is not a crime as such, so there is no reason to exclude it from the application of the mentioned provision. The judge admits however that considering the taking of aerial photographs as a nuisance is not excluded, for instance when it is done systematically in a harassing way with the intention to harm the other party.

D **Economic analysis.** The case concerns in the first place the use of air space which is from a legal viewpoint (see earlier p. 17–18) an open-access area. According to the judge property rights on land should not be extended upwards into heaven. The land owner's property right only extends into the air as far it is necessary for his/her activities on land.

From a legal economic viewpoint this position can be fully sustained for two reasons. In the first place, exclusion costs necessary for the establishment of an effective system of aerial property rights as an extension of landed property rights will prove to be very high, if not completely prohibitive. In theory, radar control, registering the crossing by airplanes and allowing the charge of tolls by landed owners is thinkable but in practice utterly costly. Moreover, any change in land ownership would necessitate a reshuffling of the corresponding aerial property rights. The quasi utopian character of an aerial property scheme as an extension of land ownership does not entail that no aerial property rights can ever be developed. Limited schemes such as tradeable property rights on air routes may be practically feasible and economically recommendable in order to make air traffic more efficient (Bouckaert 1993).

There is however an even more compelling reason than the high bill of exclusion costs. Even in the case that exclusion costs were more or less manageable, perhaps due to technological innovation, aerial property rights as an extension of such rights on land would not be recommendable. The main economic impact of such a scheme would be a huge wealth transfer from air travellers (business, tourists, freight, etc.) to land owners. Wealth would be transferred but not created. In this respect the open-access area of the air space is different from open-access area such as the open sea, where the problem of rational exploitation of natural resources (see earlier pp. 17–18) is involved. A property rights scheme, provided it is technically possible, could improve dramatically the exploitation efficiency of these resources. This is not the case with the air space, where mainly the problem of traffic is concerned. The wealth transfer, provoked by the introduction of this property rights scheme would however involve enormous transaction costs. The air traffic sector has to negotiate prices with a gigantic number of land owners, which could elicit strategic behaviour, hold-up strategies and anti-commons problems. In total, the introduction of such a scheme would result in huge social costs and virtually no gains.

The second problem the judge deals with in this case concerns the non-restrictive or restrictive reading of provision 40 of the Civil Aviation Act. Also here the decision of the judge in favour of a non-restrictive reading can be sustained from a legal economic view. A restrictive reading, by which the provision is limited to mere passage through the air, would necessitate steady interventions by the legislator to broaden the exemption from nuisance- or trespass-claims for other activities in the air. By a non-restrictive reading these legislative interventions can be avoided through evolutionary adjustment by case law. Both possibilities involve their own problems. In the former the slowness of the legislative procedures often contaminated by inefficient influences by lobbyists, have to be mentioned. In the latter courts have to draw the line, which may elicit many and costly litigation in order to arrive at authoritative precedents. According to Kaplow (2000: 502–528) legal systems can rely either on standards or on rules. By the first is meant general clauses or principles (e.g. good faith) which allow courts a large margin of deliberation and decision. By the second is meant detailed rules limiting or even eliminating any margin for the court. Standards are the best solution for legal systems which can rely on a judiciary with high professional standards of intellect and integrity. If this is not the case, it is better to rely on detailed rules, made up in the legislative centre of the system. It is beyond doubt that the English judiciary, at least comparted with many other legal systems in the world, has a reputation of integrity and intellectual capacity. As a consequence it is better to leave to the courts a wide margin of interpretation of the mentioned provision in order to adapt the categories of allowed activities into the air spaces to the evolving social and economic needs.

E **Economic evaluation of the decision.** The final decision of the judge in this case reflects without doubt a lot of common sense based on sound economic intuition. This is well expressed by the quoted Lord Wilberforce when he considers an extreme reading of the maxim *'usque ad coelum'* as unscientific and unpractical and not appealing to the common law mind. However, in so far the judge had to rely on the common law case law, he was only able to explain why a land owner should have aerial rights just above his land in order to allow her/him to pursue his/her activities, but not why these rights should not stretch any further. To draw the limit of landed property rights the judge had to invoke the statute law of the Civil Aviation Act. Legal economics would have provided the judge here a firmer base for his decision by providing also a convincing general reason not to extend the landed property rights further into the air space.

### 2. Eigentum an Entflogenem Falken *(Ownership of Escaped Falcons), LG Bonn,* Urt. V. 15.10.1992,- *8 T 114/92; NJW 1993, Heft 14, 940*

A **Facts and legal sources.** The claimant (in appeal) was the owner of a saker falcon ('falco cherrug') since 1973. The falcon carried a ring with the number NRWR 433. At a training flight on 8 February 1992 the falcon flew away and did not return to the owner. Two weeks later the falcon was captured by a third person and brought it, at latest 22 February 1992, to the birds' asylum, managed by the defendant. The presence of the falcon was signalled to the claimant and consequently the claimant requested the restitution of the falcon. The defendant refused this by arguing that the claimant had lost his ownership of the falcon.

The question of ownership of escaped or lost animals (wild or domesticated) is dealt with in §960 I, II and III of the German Civil Code (BGB). The first section provides that wild animals are unowned as long they are in freedom. Wild animals kept in zoos and fish kept in pounds and other private waters are owned. The second section provides that a wild animal regaining its freedom becomes unowned again when the owner does not pursue it persistently or when he/she quits the pursuit. The third section provides that a domesticated animal becomes unowned when it stops returning to its nest. Finally §985 BGB provides that the possessor has to restitute the good to the owner.

B **Claims and defences.** The claimant asks for the restitution of the falcon because he pursued the animal after its escape. According to §960, II BGB the animal has never been unowned, so he can ask for restitution from the possessor. The defendant however argued that the claimant had lost his ownership on the falcon by the escape.

C **Sentence and considerations.** By a mandatory injunction the *Ambtsgericht* had ordered on 27 May 1992 the restitution of the falcon. The defendant first filed his opposition against this injunction but restituted later on the falcon to the claimant. The parties made also an agreement to stop further proceedings and to arrange for their mutual costs. The *Ambtsgericht* had assigned the litigation costs to the claimant because he did not prove fully the legitimacy of his claim. The claimant made an appeal to the *Landesgericht* against this decision, which was allowed. In order to decide about the allocation of the litigation costs the court has to decide whether the claimant had lost his ownership on the falcon or not. In the first case the litigation costs have to be bore by the defendant, in the second case by the claimant. According to the *Landesgericht* the claimant did never lose his ownership on the falcon because he immediately started the pursuit and notified this pursuit to the competent instance. Moreover the court stated that this condition also applied to domesticated animals although this condition was not explicitly mentioned in §960, III BGB, the provision which applies to the loss of domesticated animals. In case of the contrary, the owner of a domesticated animal would be treated worse than an owner of a wild animal, which would conflict with the underlying intention and aim of the law. As the condition applies on wild animals and domesticated animals as well, the court does not have to decide in this case to which category the animal in question belongs. As the claimant never lost his ownership on the falcon, §985 BGB applies and the defendant, who is a mere possessor, has to restitute the falcon to the claimant who has always been the owner. As a further consequence the defendant has to bear the litigation costs of the case.

D **Economic analysis.** This case concerns the extent of property rights to a kind of fugitive resource, namely (wild and tamed) animals. The central legal question in this case is whether ownership of animals continues even when the owner lost his physical control on the animal or whether ownership is discontinued by the escape and consequently the rule of capture applies to the animal. In the latter case the property regime of animals would be remarkably different from that of corporeal goods, as the ownership of goods is not necessarily discontinued by the loss of possession of the good. In case of adverse possession the owner remains owner and can recover his good through actions like restitution and replevin unless of course prescription periods have elapsed.

Contrary to the opinion of the *Landsgericht* the distinction between wild and tamed animals is relevant from a legal-economic viewpoint.

As far as wild animals, such as large predators (lions, tigers, wolves), large reptiles (crocodiles, snakes, varans, leguans) and large and predator birds (eagles or, as in this case, falcons) are concerned, their escape does not only impose a loss to the owner, but also an increased risk to third parties. This implies that the optimal level of monitoring and prevention should be eventually higher than the monitoring costs the owner is willing to make for maintaining the pleasure of his ownership. When $EEC^O$ are the expected escape costs for the owner (i.e. the real costs of escape or loss of the animal multiplied with the ex ante assessed risk of escape) and when $EEC^T$ are the expected costs of escape for third parties (the risk to be killed or wounded by the escaped animals, or the killing of other animals, the theft of food, etc.) then the optimal level of monitoring is where the marginal monitoring cost ($\Delta MC$) is equal to the marginal expected cost of escape for owner and thirds ($\Delta EEC^O + \Delta EEC^T$). This is illustrated by Figure 1.1:

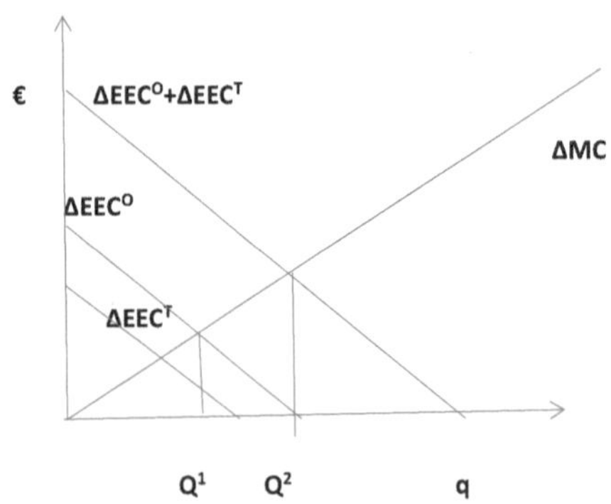


*Figure 1.1* Optimal level of monitoring by animal owner

The optimal level of monitoring by the owner is at $Q^2$. Without additional incentives, provided by the law or other social pressures, owners of wild animals will monitor only at level $Q^1$. Classical incentives through the law are primarily in tort law and in criminal law. If damage is inflicted by a wild animal and the owner of it has been negligent in monitoring, he has to compensate the victim. The law can strengthen this incentive by adding criminal punishment such as fines and even imprisonment or by awarding punitive damages. The question here arises whether property law can be used as an incentive to optimize prevention through monitoring. By applying the rule of capture in case of escape, the owner is 'punished' through the loss of his animal. The treat of such a loss is beyond doubt an incentive to be more careful in guarding the animal. Using property law in this way has the advantage of a low-cost remedy. If a third person captures the escaped animal the case is closed in most cases (see further, however, on immediate pursuit). The capture by a third is the punishment of the negligent owner. It provides also an incentive to thirds to capture the animal and end possible danger as soon as possible. Further intervention through litigation is not necessary. The question however is whether such a property rule is sufficient as an incentive for optimal monitoring and when and how it should be supplemented.

Whether this remedy is sufficient depends on the relationship between the expected escape costs for the owner ($EEC^O$) and such costs for third parties ($EEC^T$). When $EEC^0$ is large in relationship to $EEC^T$, then the possible loss of the animal will provide an effective incentive to reach an optimal monitoring level. Suppose a very expensive yet untamed falcon, precious for successful hunt. Such a bird will be expensive for the owner but rather a low risk for third parties. The treat by the rule of capture will be sufficient here. When $EEC^0$ is rather small in relationship to $EEC^T$, then an exclusive treat with a capture rule will be ineffective for optimal monitoring. Wolves for instance are rather inexpensive but can be quite dangerous. The loss of the wolf may be a too low incentive for the owner to monitor efficiently.

The possible variation in the value of the lost animal and the possible danger inflicted to thirds implies that the rule of capture, despite its cost advantages, cannot be the exclusive remedy for escape of wild animals. Criminal sanctions, supplementing the rule of capture have to remain possible. In using these sanctions, courts should look to the relationship between the variables of the value of the escaped animal and the potential danger of the escaped animal.

A further question concerns the exception of hot pursuit. §960 II BGB provides that ownership on the wild animal stops when the owner does not pursue it persistently or has stopped altogether the pursuit. This provision takes account of the grey zone lying between the physical escape (e.g. leaving the cage) and the full disappearance of the animal. Often the animal remains a while in the immediate neighbourhood of its nest or cage during which the owner (e.g. staff-members of the zoo) remains 'on the heels' of the animal. When the rule of capture would also apply to this 'grey zone' it would lower the incentives of the owner to start an effective immediate pursuit. This would be inefficient as the owner is often the 'best capturer' because he knows his animal and its habits the best. The flip side of this hot pursuit – rule is its cost of complexity. When does hot pursuit stops to be hot or stops altogether? This may be unclear in many cases and lead to more litigation.[16] As the escape can lead to severe wounding and even killing, i.e. damages which are not fully compensable, swift capture of the animal should be the first priority and outweigh the eventual higher litigation cost. For this reason the hot pursuit rule of §980 II BGB is efficient.

Domesticated animals differ from wild ones in that respect that human beings were able to change to a certain extent their instinct. Domesticated animals are for instance trained to leave and return to their nest or cage. They adopted, as the Roman legal scholar Gaius stated, a '*consuetudo revertendi*'. Due to this, characteristic ownership is continued during this moving from and to home.

From an economic point of view this position has to be nuanced somewhat for one should make a distinction whether the domesticated animal is captured by a third party during its regular move or during a real escape, during which it deviates from its regular pattern.

If a simple rule of capture would apply in cases where a third party captures a domesticated animal during its regular move, it would constitute a strong disincentive for animal keepers to invest in domestication efforts. It would become very risky to let your animal move away as any third person can catch and keep it at any moment. The real enjoyment of domestication, namely, giving your animal full liberty to leave and yet having good expectations that it will return, would largely disappear. Such a brutal rule of capture would lead to disinvestment in domestication and inflict a welfare loss on society.

If the capture happens however during a real escape, which can only be caused by an obvious loss of the '*consuetudo revertendi*', then a rule of capture should apply. In these cases the rule of capture provides to the capturer an incentive to re-educate the animal again. If the ownership remains uncertain because the former owner can always reclaim it, this incentive is seriously impaired. There are further reasons to apply a rule of capture here. As in the case of wild animals, former domesticated animals may mean a danger for other human beings and animals. Moreover, because the animal may have lost some instincts of hunting or food gathering, it may not survive if it is not captured soon.

16 See for instance Dean Lueck (1995) in his comment on the case *Post v. Pierson*. In this case the fox was awarded to Pierson who shot the animal and not to Post who pursued it during a long time. From an efficiency viewpoint one can criticize this outcome as pursuing efforts are discouraged and free riding is encouraged. Nevertheless Lueck prefers this solution as it opts for a clear sign of possession by which future litigation costs can be minimized.

The question arises however how the court should make the difference between capture during a regular move and capture during a real escape. There is of course not a watertight solution for this. The court will have to rely on proxies such as duration and distance of the escape. Zoological expertise can indicate when a particular duration or distance still fits with a '*consuetudo revertendi'* of a domesticated animal.

E **Economic evaluation of the decision** The *Landesgericht* Bonn decided that it is not necessary to make the distinction between wild and domesticated animals in this case as the legal rule concerning ownership is identical. An identity, constructed through an 'a fortiori'-reasoning applied to the rule on domesticated animals (see earlier pp. 29–30). Following the legal economic viewpoint the court is however wrong as efficiency considerations indicate that the ownership question of escaped wild and domesticated animals should be different and that according to the category to which the animal belongs, the court would have had to investigate something different. If the saker falcon would have been qualified as a wild animal, then the court should have investigated whether the owner was still in hot pursuit. When the animal would have been qualified as a domesticated animal, then the court had to investigate whether the falcon was captured during its regular moves or whether it was captured when having lost its '*consuetudo revertendi'*. The saker falcon was treated as if it was a wild animal. If it had be treated as a domesticated animal the court had to made another research and this could have led to the result that the falcon had lost its '*consuetudo revertendi'* and that the defendant, the manager of the birds' sanctuary, could consequently keep the falcon.[17]

### *3.* Lyme Valley Squash Club Ltd v. Newcastle under Lyme Borough Council and another*; Chancery Division Manchester, [1985] 2 All ER, 405–414*

A **Facts and legal sources.** In 1978, the city council of Newcastle under Lyme made the decision to open the area of the Lyme valley for development. The main idea of the plan was to keep the valley merely for open space and recreational use. Against this background the city council decided that squash courts would be a desirable amenity and advertised the possibilities of such an investment. Mr. Hall, the owner of the club, put forward a proposal to invest in the valley. Early 1980 the city council made a decision on the

17 The neglect by the court to make the distinction between wild and domesticated animals is also criticised by Dr. Martin Avenarius in a comment on the case (Avenarius 1993). His argument is however merely based on the Roman tradition which should constitute the historical background through which §960 I, II and III BGB should be interpreted. The argument based on tradition leads in this case to the same conclusion as the argument based on economic reasoning.

precise location of the club. On 11 April it sent a letter to Mr. Hall with an offer to sell the land for £15,000. In a plan, joint with the letter, the location of the site was made more precise: the site of the club would be surrounded by an existing car park, except from the North side. During the summer of 1980 no progress was made and Mr. Hall became impatient and urged for a contract. The city council allowed him on 5 January 1981 to take possession of the land, upon which Mr. Hall started to build the buildings of the club. On 13 March 1981 a draft contract was sent to Mr. Hall and on 16 April the sale contract was signed by both parties. On 28 April a draft conveyance, drafted by the solicitor of the club was sent to the city council and approved on 30 April. On 17 June 1981 the solicitor of the club explained in a letter that the conveyance was not yet signed nor sealed because he wanted the deed to be registered on the same day as the mortgage deeds to save on registration costs. On 19 June 1981 the conveyance was sent to the council and signed and sealed. On 11 September 1981 the squash club was opened. End 1981 Mr. Hall was, to his appalment, informed on proposals by the city council to build a retail store in front of the windows of the lounge of the club.

The contract of sale was drafted by a legal trainee of the club. He included, as usual, into the contract the general conditions of sale from The West Midland Association of Law Societies. Clause 4(2) (c) of these conditions provides that '*purchaser shall not acquire any rights or easements restricting free use of vendor's adjoining land.*' The legal trainee did not know the sold land was part of a larger tract of land. Mr. Hall did not remark the clause either. The clause was however not included into the later conveyance.

The central legal question in this case concerns the right of light of house dwellers in relationship with their neighbours. The crucial precedent in this question is *Colls v. Home & Colonial Stores Ltd* (1904). According to this precedent the right to light concerns 'the light required for the beneficial use of the building for any ordinary purpose for which it is adapted.'

Another legal source relevant for this question is the *derogation from grant-doctrine*, endorsed by Judge Parker in the case *Brown v. Flower* (1911). This doctrine implies that a grant confers to the grantee all rights and advantages, connected with the granted real estate.

A last relevant legal element concerns section 62 of the Law of Property Act 1925. This section formulates the general wording of a conveyance, supposed to be part of the conveyance if not explicitly excluded. Paragraph (1) of the *'General words implied in conveyance'* provides that:

> A conveyance of land shall be deemed to include and shall by virtue of this Act operate to convey, with the land, all buildings, erections, fixtures, commons, hedges, ditches, fences, ways, waters, water-courses, liberties, privileges, easements, rights, and advantages whatsoever, appertaining or reputed to appertain to the land, or any part thereof, or, at the time of

conveyance, demised, occupied, or enjoyed with, or reputed or known as part or parcel of or appurtenant to the land or any part thereof.

B **Claims and defences.** The plaintiff stated four claims: (1) a declaration that neither of the defendants is entitled to construct a building upon land lying to the south west of the plaintiff's premises, (2) that the plaintiffs are entitled to a right of uninterrupted light through the said windows, (3) an injunction to restrain the defendants from building so as to interfere with the light and (4) a rectification of the contract, more precisely of clause 4(2) (c).

The first defendant (the city) refers to clause 4(2) (c) in the sale contract and claims the right to erect the building. The second defendant, the constructor of the retail store, offered a proposal to the plaintiff, that is, a gift to the club of a twenty-foot space between the buildings and laying out a sort of patio. This would necessitate a redesigning of the entrance of the club. The cost of this proposal for the second defendant is estimated at about £10,000.

C **Sentence and considerations.** Judge Blackett-Ord V-C awards to the plaintiff a right to light, based on precedents from case law, on the derogation from grant doctrine and section 62 Law of Property Act 1925. Clause 4(2) (c) from the original sale contract can be sidestepped as the parties had the mutual intention to grant a right to light. The fact it was not included into the later conveyance proves that no one gave it a thought. Awarded the right to light, the second question is whether this right will be infringed by the building. According to experts the amount of light will be at 30–35 percent while a minimum of 50 percent is required. The lounge will be used mostly at lunchtime and from 4:30 pm on and during the weekends. There will be also additional light coming through the windows on the north side. Finally, the bar of the lounge is lit by strip lighting. The judge decides that an injunction is not justified here and awards a compensation of £10,000.

D **Economic analysis**

D1 **The right to light.** Because the court did not accept the binding force of clause 4(2) (c) in the sale contract as it was probably based on a mistake and not included into the final conveyance, the question whether the squash club had an initial right to light vis-à-vis the owner of the adjacent land, became the central one in this case. The question on the legal validity of the clause in the sale contract will be discussed later. The focus is first on the question whether owners should be awarded an initial right to light. This question can be analysed from a Coasian perspective on rights and transaction costs.

Concerning the right to light, two opposed rules can be chosen by the rulemaking authority.

The lawmaker can opt for an initial right to light rule for owners. In this case the owner of land acquires automatically, that is, without any contractual deal with neighbours being necessary, a right to light, or in other words the right to require from his/her neighbours to respect distance and altitude rules so that daylight in his building is guaranteed. The purchase of land is in this case a kind of package deal. The purchaser acquires not only his/her land but at the same time a negative easement towards his neighbours.

The lawmaker can opt for a no initial right to light rule for owners. In this case the owner cannot claim any right to the owners of adjacent land. In order to acquire rights to light the owner has to negotiate such rights with the adjacent owners. The owner can eventually buy more land or negotiate a negative easement involving the respect of distance and altitude rules.

From a legal economic, more particularly Coasean, viewpoint the choice of the rules will, under certain conditions, not affect the allocation of the rights to light and the application of both rules will lead to an efficient outcome.

The first condition for this Coasean efficiency concerns only the initial right to light rule (Figure 1.2). This rule should be mutual and apply to first- and latecomers alike.

Suppose there are no buildings on the two parcels in the figure and A arrives and builds on the border with his neighbour B. Later on B wants to build but A claims a right to light against B and forces B to keep the necessary distance and altitude-rules. In this case the right to light applies only to later-comers and not to first-comers. In this case the initial right to light rule would lead to very inefficient results. It would stimulate inefficient racing among builders, for the first-comer acquires a legal advantage on the later comers. This would lead to inefficient premature building. The effect would be similar as with the inefficiencies caused by the homestead-rules on land and the coming to the nuisance-rule (see Chapter 3). The initial right to light rule is consequently only efficient when its application is mutual. In the mentioned example: also first comer A has to respect distance and altitude rules even when there is no building yet on the adjacent parcel.

A second and more general condition concerns the transaction costs, either to acquire contractually rights to light or to negotiate away already

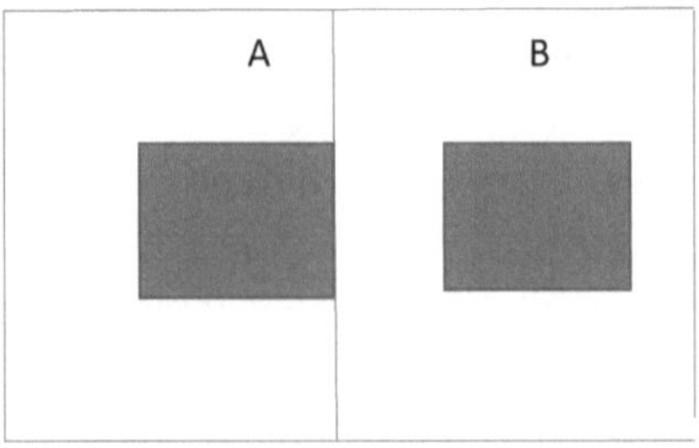


*Figure 1.2* Right to light

initial rights to light. Coasian efficiency will only be reached under the two rules when transaction costs are zero or at least infra-marginal.

Suppose this latter is the case and suppose that A values the right to light at 10 while B values the costs of complying with distance and altitude rules at 8.

Under the initial right to light rule A will stick with his initial right to light and B will suffer the costs of it because there are no gains from trade to be realized. The willingness to sell of A is at least 10 while the willingness to pay of B is at maximum 8.

Under the no initial right to light rule A will buy the right to light from B because gains from trade can be realized. The willingness to pay of A is 10 while the willing to sell of B is 8.

Whatever the rule, the allocation result will be the same: A will get the right to light and B will respect distance and altitude rules and in both cases the result is efficient.

When transaction costs are however higher than infra-marginal (i.e. higher than gains from trade), the choice of the rule can matter. The most efficient rule is then the one the implementation of which entails the lowest transaction costs. This latter cost category involves information costs (costs to find parties to trade with), negotiation costs and the risk of costs of enforcement of the contract when no voluntary compliance.

Concerning right to light deals information costs are trivial as the parties are the owners of adjacent land.

Negotiation costs may be considerable however as the party who has to sell the right to light in order to arrive at an efficient allocation can behave strategically and adopt a hold up strategy. As both parties are caught into a bilateral monopoly situation this hold up strategy may lead to a breakup of the negotiation by which possible gains of trade are not realized. This possibility is however the same for both rules. Under the initial right to light rule the owner of the initial right can apply an extortion strategy towards his neighbour who wants to buy away the negative easement of distance and altitude. Under the no initial right to light rule the owner, from whom a right to light has to be bought, can evenly apply such an extortion strategy. As a consequence, negotiation costs are not an indicator for the efficiency of one of the two rules. The probability of hold up-strategy could however be, under both rules, a reason to give the court the power to impose parties a deal under a rule of abuse of right (civil law) or duress (common law).

Finally it has to be remarked that the so-called endowment-effect will impose certain inertia on the reallocation of rights to light. According to this effect an incumbent owner of a right to light will value this right more than he/she would be willing to pay for this right in the case he/she has not the right. But also this endowment effect would be present under the two rules and is as such not a reason to opt for one or another rule.

From a legal economic and Coasian viewpoint it does not matter which right to light rule should be adopted, prohibitive transaction costs or not. As a consequence, the decision of the judge in this case to apply the right to light rule as articulated in case law (*Colls v. Home & Colonial Stores Ltd*) can be sustained. This rule, in fact an initial right to light rule, in which the amount of light should be awarded according to the type of the building, is efficient as long as parties have the right to trade this initial right and as long this rule is applied consistently over time towards the real estate market. If the latter should not be the case this would frustrate legitimate expectations of many parties in this market. Suppose the lawmaker (legislator or courts through case law) would switch suddenly from an initial right to light rule to a no initial right to light rule. Many parties relied implicitly on the first rule and did not anticipate through negotiation the possibility of neighbouring buildings blocking their daylight. This rule induced the parties in fact to a moral hazard attitude regarding the preservation of daylight. By switching the rules these parties are in fact submitted to a kind of regulatory taking and should be compensated as such. A switch of the rules would impose transaction costs on society while the switch as such involves no apparent benefits, as the rules are both efficient.

In case of infringement of a right to light the court can choose between two remedies: injunctive relief or damages. In legal economics this choice is framed as a choice between a property rule and a liability rule (see more on this in Chapter 3 in the section on "Calabresi and Melamed"). In the first case the protection of an entitlement is absolute and the entitlement can only be 'infringed' by consent of the entitled party. In the second case the protection is only relative and the entitlement can be infringed at the condition the 'infringing' party compensates ex post for the damage. According to Calabresi, a property rule has to be preferred when transaction costs are low and the costs of administration of justice (especially the assessment of the damages) are high. In the opposite case a liability rule has to be preferred. One can also frame this choice as a choice between an exclusion regime of a governance regime (see further Chapter 3 on exclusion and governance regimes).

According to this theory the preferred remedy in case of right to light should be damages. As stated before, transaction costs can be considerable due to bilateral monopoly and strategic behavior. The assessment costs of damage on the contrary are not considerable as only goods (real estate) are involved and courts can rely on proxies such as a comparison of house prices with daylight provision and without. Courts should however compensate beyond market prices when subjective value is involved (e.g. a family farm enjoying since years sunlight).

**D2 Mistake in contracting.** The former legal economic analysis is of course only correct when there were good economic reasons to disregard clause 4(2)(c) from the original sale contract. If not, the squash club had in fact alienated his right to light in a legal valid way. As we stated before, rules on the right to light are only efficient when the owners of land are allowed to negotiate freely over allocation and reallocation of the right to light. Consequently, when the mentioned clause is legally valid, the allocation of the right to light to the defendants was efficient.

The court overruled this clause although it was included in the sale contract, which had become binding for the parties because they had signed it and exchanged copies of it. The fact that the clause was omitted in the final conveyance does not undermine this binding force for the conveyance does not contradict this clause either. As a consequence the court disregarded an expressed and not contradicted will of the contractual parties.

The court however suggests, however not very explicit, that the clause is based on a mistake on behalf of one party, namely, the seller. The court relies here on two facts: (1) the inclusion was done by a legal trainee who was not familiar with the local situation, more precisely the expectation from Mr. Hall, the owner of the squash club, that the adjacent land would remain a car park, and (2) the lack of attention from Mr. Hall to the clause because he was convinced that the adjacent land would anyhow remain a car park.

From a legal economic point of view an exchange is only efficient when the involved parties are well informed about the exchanged goods and the committed obligations. Wrong information may lead to wrong evaluation by which a mutual benefit operation is not guaranteed. As a consequence the law should provide incentives to minimize mistakes in contracts. This is done by making the party, which is the best information gatherer (BIG) (e.g. the professional in the contract), responsible for the consequences of the mistake. By this the party, which can produce the relevant information in the cheapest way, will get the incentive to provide effectively this information during the process of contract formation.

The question however is, which party should be considered in this case as the best information gatherer.

At first sight, the BIG seems to be the plaintiff, as he consulted a legal professional, solicitor Mr. Dennis Hall. The latter is supposed to know what could be the legal consequences of such a clause and he should have advised to take out this clause from 'The West Midlands Association of Law Societies Contract of Sale' model. By respecting this clause, mistakenly included, professional lawyers will be stimulated in the future to be more diligent.

On the other side, the mentioned clause is no problem for the plaintiff as long as the defendant, the City, maintains its plan to keep the adjacent land as a car park. Daylight to the squash club is then guaranteed by the factual use of the land by the defendant. The BIG about the plans of the city with the adjacent land is of course the city itself. By leaving the impression that the car park would remain and by not revealing clearly that the use of the land might change by light blocking investments, the plaintiff did not pay attention to the mentioned clause. As a consequence, the defendant should be considered as the main responsible for the mistake in the contract and should bear the costs of the mistake. By making the city responsible and by disregarding the clause, public bodies such as the cities will be stimulated to be clearer towards potential buyers about their plans on the lands, adjacent to the sold land. As a result, the decision of the court to disregard the clause can be sustained from a legal economic point of view.

E **Economic evaluation of the decision** Although the final decisions of the court, i.e. stepping over the clause in the sale contract, awarding a right to light to the plaintiff, awarding only damages to the plaintiff can be sustained from a legal-economic viewpoint, the considerations in which these decisions are grounded are open to some criticism.

The decision to step over clause 4(2) (2) of the sale contract is barely motivated by the court. The court refers vaguely to a probable mistake by the legal trainee in the law office of the defendant but does not motivate why this should be a reason to deny the legal validity of the clause. By this the court may give a signal to future parties in contracts that contractual clauses can be set aside at random by courts, by which uncertainty in contracting and transaction costs will increase. This can be avoided by explaining in a more precise way why the clause can be denied any effect in this case (and thus not in other cases).

The decision concerning the right to light is based in former case law which grants an initial right to light to the owner of land. This initial entitlement is nearly framed as a natural right. In his opinion in the case *Colls v. Home & Colonial Stores ltd*, the guiding precedent in this case, Lord Davey states 'generally speaking an owner of ancient lights is entitled to sufficient light according to the ordinary notions of mankind for the comfortable use and enjoyment of his house'. According to legal economics, however, there is no compelling argument to give or to refuse initially the right to light to the owner of land as long the right to light can be shifted through exchange from one party to another. Inefficiencies occur through institutional instability by changing the basic rule during the game. As a result, not a substantive initial right to light is decisive in this case, but the argument of institutional stability. Case law seems to have assigned since long an initial right to light to landowners. It is efficient to keep it like that.

## 4. Government of the State of Penang and another v. Beng Hong Oon and others; *Privy Council, 5 October 1971, [1971] 3 All ER PC, 1163–1175*

A **Facts and legal sources.** The case concerns the property right on sea alluvium, which accreted to a strip of land, adjacent to the sea (Strait of Malaysia) in the state of Penang in Malaysia (under colonial rule the province of Wellesley). By an indenture the East Indian India Company had conveyed in 1853 this strip to a private person. In the indenture the borders of the strip on the north, east and south side were well indicated. On the west side (the sea side) however a straight line, called *'Beach'* was marked as border. In 1895 a survey was made of the area and a plan published. This showed that the strip was subdivided into lots, including lot 275 (1 and 3) and that marking stones were placed along the western boundary. These stones formed a straight line and west of it was marked as 'Sea' (see Figure 1.3). The plan did not indicate that any alluvium had been formed. In 1924 a government plan was published indicating an alluvium between 75 and 100 feet in breadth. A similar plan published in 1935 showed that the alluvium had increased to a width of 116 feet. The defendant (Mrs. Beng Hong Oon) came to live in a house on the strip in 1938. During the Japanese occupation she was forced to leave and on her return she found that the alluvium had increased again. She became owner of the strip between 1942 and 1947. In 1949 she was granted temporary occupation licenses of the alluvium, renewed until 1958. In 1959 the first plaintiff (the Government of Penang) leased the alluvium to the second plaintiff (the Central Electricity Board of the Federation of Malaya) who went into occupation of the alluvium. The defendant went to court to claim the property of the alluvium. The trial judge dismissed this claim. The defendants appeal was allowed by the Federal Court and the plaintiffs appealed against that decision at the Privy Council.

In the common law the property of alluviums is dealt with by the doctrine of accretion. This doctrine is clearly stated in the judgment of Lord Wilberforce in *Southern Centre of Theosophy v. South Australia* [1982] AC 706–716:

> This is a doctrine which gives recognition to the fact that where land is bounded by water, the forces of nature are likely to cause changes in the

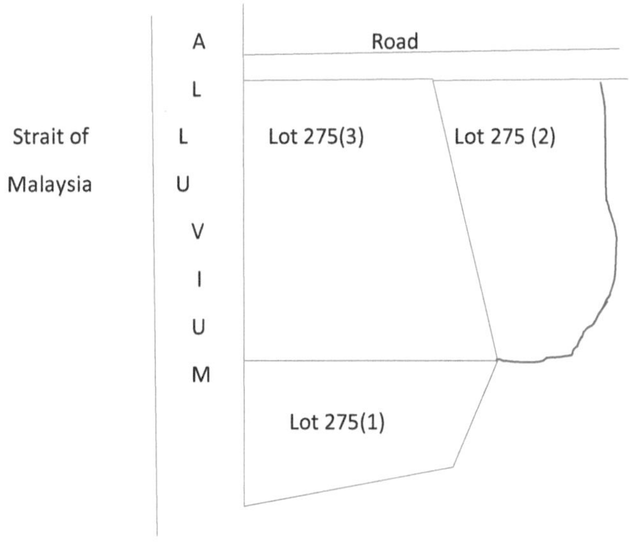


*Figure 1.3* Map of lots and alluvium

> boundary between the land and the water. Where these changes are gradual and imperceptible the law considers the title to the land as applicable to the land as it may be so changed from time to time. This may be said to be based on grounds of convenience and fairness. Except in cases where a substantial and recognizable change in boundary has suddenly taken place (to which the doctrine does not apply), it is manifestly convenient to continue to regard the boundary between land and water as being it is from day to day or year to year. To do so is also fair. If part of an owner's land is taken from him by erosion, or diluvion (i.e. advance of the water) it would be most inconvenient to regard this boundary as extending into the water: the treated as losing a portion of his land. So, if an addition is made to the land from what was previously water, it is only fair that the landowner's title should extend to it.

Another rule, relevant for this case is Section 116 of the Evidence Ordinance of 1950 stating that a licensee is estopped from denying the title of his licensor.

B **Claims and defences.** The state of Penang and the Central Electricity Board claim the property on the alluvium. Their claim is based on three arguments. First, they argue that the defendants did not provide the proof that the alluvium results from a gradual and imperceptible recession while the onus of proof is on their side. Second, by accepting a license on the alluvium from the plaintiffs all claims denying that the plaintiffs had no title on the licensed land are estopped according to Section 116 of the Evidence Ordinance of 1950. Third, from the construction of the indenture it follows that the straight line on it should be considered as the fixed boundary on the west side. If the parties of the indenture would have had the intention to include in the grant also the possible alluvium, they would have used the term 'sea shore' and not 'sea beach'.

C **Sentence and considerations.** The Privy Council dismisses the appeal by which the sentence of the Federal Court, which was in favour of the defendants, is confirmed. The Privy Council based its decision on the following considerations.

First, concerning the alluvium point. The Council agreed that even under the assumption that the onus of proof concerning the gradual and imperceptible formation of the alluvium was on the defendants, she had discharged that onus. According to the Council the different and sequential plans show indeed a gradual and imperceptible accretion of alluvium.

Second, on the point of estoppel. According to the Council Section 116 of the Evidence Ordinance of 1950 does not imply that a licensee is forever estopped from denying the title of his licensor. He is entitled to do so after he has given up his possession.

Third, on the point of the construction of the Indenture (dissenting Viscount Dilhorne). By the term 'seashore' it is usually meant 'foreshore', that is, the land lying between the lines of medium high and low tide. The Council sees no reason why the term 'sea beach', used in the Indenture, should not have the same meaning as 'sea shore'. The western boundary line, drawn on the plan of the Indenture, was very probably not meant as a line, delineating the property as it is unlikely that the Crown was intending to retain land between the land conveyed and the foreshore.

**D** **Economic Analysis** The main question in this case concerns the property on land, accreted by alluvium. According to an ancient doctrine in the common law, the doctrine of accretion, the land, formed through a gradual, imperceptible and permanent regression of the sea or a river (the *alluvium*), belongs to the riparian owner of the adjacent land. When the shoreline of the sea or the river moves inwards the land (the *diluvium*) the riparian owner incurs the loss of land without any compensation. A similar doctrine is followed in the civil law. Art. 556 and 557 of the Civil Code (France, Belgium) provide that riparian owners gain the land formed by *alluvium* and lose the land taken by *diluvium*. Art. 556–557 Civil Code only apply to shores of rivers.

Is this doctrine of accretion optimal from a legal economic point of view?

The optimality of this doctrine is quite obvious in case of mobile goods (chattel). When an item gets connected with another item owned by another person (e.g. a jewel with a ring) and the costs of separation are large, then it is efficient to assign the property of the whole to one owner who has then to compensate the other owner for his/her loss. According to the civil law the owner of the most valuable component of the whole will be assigned the property right (art. 566 Civil Code).

As land gained by alluvium or lost by diluvium is concerned, the optimality of this doctrine is less evident prima facie. However, the analysis of possible alternatives of the accretion doctrine shows that this doctrine is rather efficient.

One could apply *the first come, first serve*-rule to *alluvium* land. The outcome of this rule would be in most cases the same as by applying the accretion doctrine. As the riparian owner is most often the cheapest cost observer of the movements of the sea, he will very probably also be the first one to take possession of the *alluvium* land. This is however not necessarily the case. The riparian owner can be an absentee owner, living far from the concerned area so that others, living more close by, will take possession first. The *first come first serve* rule will then lead to a situation in which the former riparian owner is cut off from the sea (or river). As the sea regresses however only slowly the alluvium-strip, taken into possession will be only narrow and without any utility for the first possessor (except may be for fishing purposes). The first possessor can however use his possessory position to start a hold-up game against the (former) riparian owner. This could at maximum lead to a mere redistribution of rents between the new strip possessor and the (former) riparian owner. This redistribution involves transaction costs by which the whole process would result in a negative sum game. By time elapsing, the alluvium strip will become wider and eventually economically valuable, for instance for building purposes, for beach exploitation, for fishing, etc. During that time the (former) riparian owner could become alerted and also claim first possession of the alluvium strip which could result in a costly conflict between the two involved owners.

Under most assumptions about the factual development under a first come first serve rule the result will be economically negative and not efficient.

As a second possibility one could apply a government rule. When alluvium is formed it becomes public property (public domain, see before Chapter 1, I. Theory, 7. The extent of property rights in civil and common law traditions) and governed by public authority. It is however very doubtful that public authorities would be the initial best users of the alluvium. Riparian owners, living close by the shore, the sea or the river are very probably the best informed users of the alluvium and will perceive the highest valued use of it. If the alluvium strip is initially assigned to the public authorities the strip has to be reallocated to the riparian owner which could involve transaction costs which can be a lot higher than in case of a private parties. Public authorities may be under pressure of interest groups, urging for less valuable uses of the alluvium strip. Also corruption can be involved. For efficiency reasons it is, as a result, better to assign the *alluvium* initially to the riparian owner. If the government perceives better economic opportunities for its use, it can eventually purchase or take the alluvium strip.

E **Economic evaluation of the decision.** From a legal economic point of view the Privy Council took the right decision by assigning the alluvium strip to the riparian owners. The only criticism concerns the fact that the court did not put the doctrine of accretion and its efficiency within the centre of its arguments. The largest part of the opinions concern secondary aspects such as the construction of the Indenture, the meaning of the line on the plan and the point of estoppel. A more explicit reconfirmation of the accretion doctrine would have given a stronger precedent value to this case.

### 5. Finderlohn für Gestohlenen PKW *(Finder's Fee for stolen car); AG Hamburg, 16 March 1993, NJW 1993, Heft 40, 2627*

A **Facts and legal sources.** The defendant, the owner of a car rental company, was the victim of the theft of one of his cars during the night of 4 to 5 June 1992. The plaintiff made a call to the defendant to tell him that his car was parked on the P+R Parking Place close to the railway station. The defendant told him that this car was stolen and that the plaintiff had to declare this to the police, what he subsequently did. The police brought the car to Autohaus R. The value of the car as new is 32,0000 DM. The car was one year old. At the moment of the theft there were 33,561 km on the counter, at the moment of the rediscovery 33,625 km. The car was not damaged.

Two provisions of the *Burgerliches Gesetzbuch* (German Civil Code) are relevant for this case. Section 965 BGG provides that the finder has to notify the owner immediately and when the owner is not known to notify the competent authorities (most often the police). Section 971 BGB provides that the finder can charge a finder's fee to the owner. The finder's fee is 5 percent of the first 500 Euro of the value, above this value the fee is 3 percent.

**B Claims and defences.** The plaintiff claims a finder's fee of 770 DM according to the mentioned BGB provisions. The plaintiff argued that he had watched the car for twelve to fourteen days and that during this time nobody had used the car. Consequently the thief had given up his possession of the car so that the car qualifies as a lost good. The defendant however argues that the thief has not given up his possession. The car was locked at the moment of the discovery, so probably the renter of the car was still using the car or has made a copy of the key and given it to a third person. Consequently the car was not lost and a finder's fee cannot be charged.

**C Sentence and considerations.** According to the court the car should be considered as a lost item. It is not relevant whether the car has been given by the letter of the car to a third or that it has been stolen, for also stolen cars can be lost. It is relevant to find out whether the thief, or another adverse possessor, has given up his/her possession and whether no new possession had been established at the moment of the discovery. The court observes that the car was parked at the P+R Parking Place for twelve days and that only 64 km had been driven with it since the theft or loss. It is, consequently, very plausible to assume that the thief or other adverse possessor has driven with the car only during a short period and has then abandoned the car for the rest of the period. The fact that the car was closed cannot be considered as an act of permanent possession, as closing a car is a normal act after each ride. The court consequently awards a finder's fee to the plaintiff, to be calculated on 98 percent of the value of the car as new.

**D Economic analysis.** A first question concerns the most efficient acquisition rule of lost items: a finders' keepers rule or the continuation of the property right of the original owner. In contrast to abandoned goods ('*res derelictae*') one may assume that on average the original owner attaches a higher value to the lost good than the occasional finder. If a return of the lost good from the finder to the original owner could be operated in a costless way, the continuation rule is superior to a finders' keeper-rule. Moreover a finders' keepers-rule for lost goods, which means also a zero prescription rule for the finder, would increase the monitoring costs for owners as a physical loss of the good would equal automatically its legal loss. A second question concerns the provision of incentives for finders to return the good to the original owner. Important variables concerning the probability of such a return are(1) the value of the found for the finder ($V^f$),(2) the probability of being legally divested and/or punished as an adverse possessor ($p^{DP}$),(3) the moral guilt feeling for keeping a someone else's good (G).

When ($V^f < p^{DP} + G$) then the finder will return the good either to the original owner or to the competent authority.

When ($V^f > p^{DP} + G$) then the finder will keep the good for him/herself.

In order to stimulate the returning of lost items either apprehension rates of adverse possessors or moral guilt feelings have to be increased. The increase of both variables imply most often high cost: either higher monitoring by police authorities, or higher education efforts by parents and schools.

Within this perspective the introduction of a finder's fee can be a low cost instrument to stimulate returns of lost items.

With a finder's fee (F) lost items will be returned when ($V^f < p^{DP} + G + F$) and will be kept by the finder when ($V^f > p^{DP} + G + F$).

By increasing the finder's fee also the probability of returning lost items will be increased. This has however also its limits. When the finder's fee would be fixed at a very high levels (e.g. 40 percent, 50 percent, 60 percent) the cost of a loss to owners would be high also by which monitoring costs will be driven up. The smaller the difference between the value of the good for the owner and the finder's fee, the less owners will invest in search to find their good by which returns will be diminished. A very high finder's fee might also stimulate fee chasing behaviour: thieves might be more tempted to cover up their theft as a found and collect the high finder's fees. In fact very high finder's fees bring the situation closer to the effect of a finder's keepers-rule and its mentioned inefficiencies.

Legislators or courts, 'finding' the law, should keep these cost considerations in mind when introducing finder's fees and the levels of them. Empirical studies, assessing the difference between the value of goods for owners and occasional finders, the impact of moral feelings, the costs of increasing the apprehension rates of adverse possessors, could result in a more scientific base of fixing the levels of finder's fees. By way of conclusion, it is very plausible to state that the introduction as such of a finder's fee by the German civil legislator is efficient. Whether the fee is too high or too low is difficult to say by lack of empirical studies on this field.

The discussion in this case did not concern the efficiency of the finder's fee, for this is provided by the law. The discussion concerned the question whether the car was still possessed by someone at the moment of the discovery and the declaration to the police, or not. In the first case it was not a found and finder's fee did not apply, in the second case, it did.

From an economic point of view it is important that the law determines clear signs of possession and does not leave a veil of uncertainty around this. Clarity on the signs of possession or non-possession might save on litigation costs, provides a clear starting point for prescription periods, determines when a possessor is protected against violent or surreptitious dispossession and determines when a good can be considered as a found.[18]

By stating that the immobility of a car during 12 days constitutes a clear sign of giving up possession, the court has given a clear signal for later similar

18 Clarity on possession is, according to Dean Lueck (1995), the deeper reason of the decision in the famous case *Post v. Pierson* in which the court awarded the shot fox to the free riding hunter and not to the hunter who had chased and exhausted the fox. The court preferred the consideration on clarity of possession (the final shooting) to the eventual consideration of discouraging free riders.

cases. If the court had ruled for instance that locked doors constituted a sign of possession it would have lengthened the period of possessory uncertainty and have impeded the smooth return of lost items in future cases.

E **Economic evaluation of the decision.** Although it is difficult to state whether the legal level of the finder's fee is fixed efficiently the decision of the court to award the fee by qualifying the car as a lost good is certainly sustainable from an economic point of view. By such a decision the court diminishes uncertainty about possessory situations and stimulates the return of lost items to original owners.

### *6.* Beteiligung der Künstler am Verkaufserlös der Berliner Mauer-Bilder *(Share of artists in proceeds of auction of parts of Berlin Wall); BGH, 23 February 1995, NJW 1995, Heft 2, 1556–1558;*

A **Facts and legal sources.** During 1985–1988, some painters (the plaintiffs) painted artistic images on parts of the Berlin wall, more precisely in the section of the Waldemarstreet. During this period the painters also repaired continuously the damages on their paintings. In the end of 1989 the wall was destroyed by GDR border troops. The painted concrete parts were split and moved away. The defendant bought the painted parts from the VEB L, the foreign trade state company of the GDR. On 21–23 June 1990 the concerned painted parts were offered for sale on an auction organized by the defendant in Monte Carlo-Monaco. In the catalogue of the auction pictures of the painted parts, together with the names of the artists, were included. The auction yielded a profit of 1.9 million DM (about 920,000 Euros).

The law on intellectual property and copyrights (*Gesetz über Urheberrecht und verwandte Schutzrechte*) guarantees the author of art works, such as paintings (§2.4) the right of multiplication and distribution to the public ('*Verbreitungsrecht*', §15, §17).

Civil property law on the other hand states that when a new item is created out of one of more materials, the creator acquires a property right on the whole (§950 BGB). If somebody incurs a loss due to this acquisition, he is entitled to a compensation (§951 BGB).

Further the civil code and the constitution protect the property rights on corporeal goods (Artikel 14 GG, §823 BGB). Violation of a property right entails compensation to the owner.

The civil code also states that when somebody acquires something through the performance of somebody else without any legal foundation (unjust enrichment), he is obliged to some compensation (§812 BGB).

The civil code of the GDR stated that property of the people ('Volkseigentum') cannot be alienated (art. 17, 18 DDR ZGB).

B **Claims and defences.** The plaintiffs (the painters) claim a reasonable share of the sales revenue of the auction. They claim to have an intellectual property right on the paintings on the segments of the wall and that part of the revenue of the auction is related to their artistic fame and reputation. In order to be able to assess that part of the revenue which is related to the sale of their paintings, they also claim a right to information on the structure of the total revenue.

The defendants claim that they acquired legally the segments from the state authorities of the GDR (VEB L). This authority made the selection of the segments which could be sold. The artistic component of the segments was fully included in the price of the segments.

Further they contend that the expenses made for the sale of the concerned segments, exceed the revenue of the sale of these segments.

Finally they argue that the paintings were applied to the wall without the consent of the owners of the wall. As a consequence they cannot pretend to have any right on the segments.

C **Sentence and considerations.** The *Landesgericht* (Court of First Instance) sentenced in favour of the plaintiffs and awarded a compensation to them. The *Berufungsgericht* (Court of Appeal), however, reversed this decision and denied compensation. The *Revision* (appeal to the Supreme Court) was admitted by which the *Bundesgerichtshof* (Supreme Court) has to decide on the case.

According to the *Berufungsgericht* the plaintiffs cannot invoke their intellectual property right of distribution (UrhG §15, §17) because they exposed their art work freely to the public by their own choice. Moreover, as the wall was placed some meters on GDR-territory, they knew that border troops could always overpaint their paintings. Their real 'salary' was not an expected income from distribution of an artwork protected by an intellectual property right, but rather the satisfaction from the recognition and appreciation by the general public. Finally also an appeal to provisions §950 and §951 BGB (Civil Code) are not appropriate as these provisions apply to mobile corporeal goods and have nothing to do with intellectual property rights.

The *Bundesgerichtshof* reversed this decision with the following arguments.

First, the fact that the paintings were painted before the unification of Germany and placed some meters on GDR-territory does not preclude the application of §15 §17 UrhG, because German citizens (and by extension all citizens of an EU country) can enjoy their intellectual rights on their artistic creations, wherever they are located.

Second, the fact that the paintings were illegally painted on a wall, not belonging to plaintiffs, is not relevant with regard to the question whether they can enjoy the mentioned intellectual property rights. The property right on a thing, which serves as a canvas, and the intellectual property right on an art work applied to that canvas, are two different rights existing independently from each other. This entails that the owner of the canvas is not allowed to alter the canvas in a way that this violates the intellectual property right of the author. This principle does not apply however when the artist has expressed his art work on a canvas, belonging to somebody else, in a way that violates the property right of the owner of the canvas (e.g. graffiti painted on the wall of a private house). This can be sanctioned according to civil and criminal law. Artistic freedom, protected by the Constitution (Artikel 5.3), is limited by the protection of property rights also provided by the Constitution (Artikel 14) and the civil code (§903 BGB). This entails that the owner of the canvas can make full use of his property right even when this would entail the alteration or even destruction of the art work. This, however, does not imply that the owner of the canvas can make use of the rights, especially provided for the protection of art works. The owner of the canvas is by this not allowed to multiply, to distribute and to commercialize the art work. These rights are especially provided for the artist, and not for the owner of the object, on which eventually the art work was illegally applied. The intellectual property rights of the artists, which are independent from the property rights on the wall segments, were neither extinguished by the segmentation of the wall. The artists were well known by the public and their names were mentioned in the catalogue of the auction. In this way one cannot argue that there was a 'dereliction' of the intellectual property rights by the artist. Moreover and differently from a property right on a corporeal good, an 'ownerless' (*Herrenlos*) intellectual property right is unthinkable.

Third, the fact that the painters painted their art work on a publicly visible wall does not mean that they have given up their intellectual property rights. It is true, when an artist makes his art work public, he/she has given up his/her claim to intellectual property rights. This principle is however only valid when the artist is able to charge royalties for his work. When an artist makes his work public under this condition, he/she implicitly abandons his/her right to charge royalties. Taking into regard the circumstances of this case, it is impossible to suppose that the artists have consented in some way to abandon their intellectual property rights and consequently their right to charge royalties. During the period of painting (1985–1988) the Berlin wall was, according to the GDR-Constitution (art. 17–18 DDR-ZGB) 'socialist property'. This type of property was legally inalienable. By this, the artists were during that period not able to trade and to distribute their art works. From these special circumstances one cannot derive any neither explicit nor implicit abandoning of intellectual property rights. From the moment of the fragmentation of the wall, the art works became physically and legally tradeable. This latter implies that from that moment on also the intellectual rights of the artists, including the right to distribute (§15, §17 UrhG) and to charge royalties, became operational.

Fourth, because the defendant, the organizer of the auction, has unjustly violated the right of distribution of the plaintiffs, the artists, the latter are entitled to a claim of 'unjust enrichment', as provided by the civil code (§812 BGB). The defendant has intervened in the right of distribution of the plaintiffs and has obtained revenue on the expense of the plaintiffs. Such an 'unjust enrichment' consequently justifies a compensation for the plaintiffs.

Fifth, the circumstance that the buyers in the auction also valued the segments as a historical item and not only as an art work, does not invalidate the claim of the plaintiffs as such, but should be taken into consideration when the damages have to be assessed.

D **Economic analysis.** This case concerns a conflict on scarce resources. The segments of the Berlin wall and the paintings are both scarce resources. The first because of their historical peculiarity. The second because of their artistic peculiarity. The two scarce resources cannot be physically separated. When two different parties claim one of the two resources the inseparability creates a conflict and this conflict can only be solved by an assignment of property rights.

The first question about this assignment concerns the right of the physical use of the joint resource. Two possibilities can be distinguished here: a) the owner of the corporeal thing on which the art work has been put up (the property right-holder: PRH) has all the rights of any owner of a corporeal thing and is not restricted by any rights of the author of the artwork. PRH is allowed to use, to rent, to sell and to destroy the good without needing any consent from the author (the intellectual property holder IPRH)); b) PRH is restricted in his rights on the canvas by rights of IPRH; for any act which may affect the integrity of the artwork, the consent of IPRH is needed.

According to Coase, the initial assignment of these rights (whether a) or b)) does not matter for efficiency when transaction costs are zero. An efficient outcome will always be reached.

Suppose the law opts for a) and PRH values his right to eventually destroy the canvas, including the artwork, at 800, while IPRH values the integrity of his artwork at 1,000. IPRH will offer to PRH not to destroy and a deal will be reached at a price between 800 and 1000. The outcome is efficient because the more valuable outcome has persisted. Suppose, still in the shadow of a) that PRH values his right to destroy at 1,000 and IPRH the integrity of his artwork at 800. Canvas and artwork may be destroyed but again, this is the most efficient outcome.

Suppose the law opts for b) and PRH values his right to destroy the canvas at 800, while IPRH values the integrity of his artwork at 1,000. The canvas will not be destroyed and the artwork will remain the efficient outcome. Suppose, still under the shadow of b), that PRH values his right to destroy at 1,000 and IPRH the integrity of his artwork at 800. In this case PRH will offer to IPRH to destroy and a deal will be reached between a price of 800 and 1,000. Again the efficient outcome.

When the assumption of zero-transaction costs is dropped, these efficient outcomes are far from guaranteed. Transaction costs in this setting will be nearly exclusively related to the existence of a bilateral monopoly and the ensuing hold up-strategies the concerned parties may follow. Neither for PRH nor for IPRH is there a market. For efficiency enhancing trade they are condemned to each other. This may seduce parties to apply a hold-up strategy, i.e. trying to extort the other party by willing to sell or to buy only at the respectively highest or lowest possible price. The party, towards which the extortion strategy is directed, may not accept this and a breakdown of the negotiations may follow by which the parties remain in an inefficient situation. The probability of prohibitive transaction costs due to possible hold-up-strategies indicates that often efficient outcomes will not be reached. It does not indicate however which original assignment of property rights would be the most adequate to cope with this problem of transaction costs because the problem of transaction costs is symmetrically given for both parties. Whether PRH of IPRH is given the initial right, both parties can abuse the bilateral monopoly position and play hold up.

If the case is considered in isolation from impact on future similar situations, efficiency concerns do not indicate any preference for one or another property assignment. Without transaction costs efficiency will always be reached and with transaction costs the barrier to efficient outcomes will be as big in both possible initial assignments. If we place such cases back within the context of institutional reality however, the decision in one case does influence, through the precedent rule (stare decisis) future decisions of judges and by this the behaviour of actors in similar situations, who will anticipate the decisions of the courts. When this institutional reality is taken into consideration, the choice of the initial assignment of property rights will indeed matter for efficiency in society. Rule b) implies that an artist acquires a property right through a non-consensual invasion of a property right on the canvas. A classic example here is the graffiti-painter, painting on the wall of a private house, without bothering about the consent of the owner of the house. Under rule b) acquisition can consequently occur through externalization: the artist takes for himself a free canvas and acquires by this some further veto-rights on the use of the canvas. Such a rule will have an impact on incentives. The rule of free canvas will ceteris paribus stimulate artists to use property of third parties for their art works and eventually charge a fee to the owner when he wants to change the canvas (e.g. destruction of the wall with graffiti). This might also change the incentives of canvas-owners. In order to avoid similar situations they may start to build in another, more costly way (e.g. building walls at some distance from the border and putting barbed wire on the border). Due to this possible impact on incentives rule a) has to be preferred from an economic point of view. It is more efficient to allow PRH use fully their property rights and in case of an involuntary putting up of artworks on the property leaving it to the author of the art work to negotiate with the PRH in order to preserve eventually his art work. This position follows from the constitutional and legal protection of property rights and is consequently also the opinion of the *Bundesgerichtshof* in this case.

Another question concerns the ownership of intellectual property rights in case of a split between ownership of the canvas and authorship of the art work, put up the canvas without consent of the owner of it. This question is, as the BGH stated clearly, different from the question whether the PRH is limited in the use of his property right by the need to preserve the integrity of the art work on his canvas. Since more than two centuries the law on intellectual property, more precisely on copy rights, awards to the authors of art works a monopoly on the multiplication ('*Verbreitung*') of their creation. This monopoly relieves the authors to use physical concealment or virtual concealment ('coding' such as for software) in order to prevent multiplication without their consent. Consequently it allows them to charge a price (a royalty) for the multiplication and to recoup eventually the fixed costs of their creative investment.

Should, in case of a split canvas-ownership and authorship of the artwork put up on it, the intellectual property rights go to the canvas-owner or to the author? Again, one can apply here a Coasean analysis, which would point out, as in the former question, that at zero transaction costs an efficient solution will always be reached and that in a real world such an efficient outcome will be unlikely, because of possible strategic behaviour from both sides. Again, also this conclusion is only valid for the case, taken in an isolated way, but not when the precedent-impact on similar future situations is taken into consideration.

To analyse this, the difference in purposes of property rights and intellectual property rights are of importance.

The primary function of property rights regards the orderly use of scarce resources and the avoidance of costly conflicts in case of incompatible uses. In the case of art works and the eventual multiplication of it, such incompatibility is not a problem. Art works and software can be reproduced without intruding in the use opportunities of the author. Copying a painting on a calendar does not prevent the painter to admire his own work and eventually sell the painting on the canvas; copying a software programme does not prevent the author of it to use his programme on the computer. In difference with property rights on corporeal goods intellectual property rights find their ratio exclusively in providing creativity and innovation incentives for future authors. As stated already, awarding authors a monopoly on the multiplication allows them to recoup eventually their fixed creation costs by charging royalties. The incentive character of intellectual property explains also the temporary character of it. The longer the period, the longer the author enjoys the monopoly and the higher his/her revenue, but also the higher the monopoly and transaction costs for the rest of society (Posner 2005). The optimal time period stretches to the point where marginal monopoly and transaction costs intersect with the marginal revenue of the author.

Consequently, awarding intellectual property rights to the owner of a canvas, on which occasionally an art work was put up, does not award and stimulate creativity in society. It just provides the owner of the canvas an occasional rent. On the contrary, the fact that the owner of the canvas is able to free ride on the creativity of the artists will impose disincentives on artists to put their artworks in public places and visible for the general public. This will inflict a loss in artistic enjoyment among the public.

On the other side, by providing this disincentive less situations of split between canvas-ownership and authorship might occur which saves costs of administration of justice. These latter costs are easy to quantify by checking the number of cases involving such a split. The 'artistic loss' is more difficult to assess. In cities such as Berlin, with a tradition and culture of public graffiti art, such loss is probably significantly higher than the costs of administration of justice. Intuitively a cost-minimization balance seems to tilt towards respecting the intellectual property rights of the artists and not to shift them to the canvas-owner.

Finally, it is not possible to keep silent, also in an economic analysis, about the very specific circumstances of this case. Specific circumstances may justify a deviation of the decisions, usually reached in normal circumstances. As long as the court can establish clearly the link between the '*ratio decidendi*' of the deviation with the specificity of the circumstances, there is no danger that this deviation will undermine the principles of 'normal' case law in the future.

The historically specific circumstances here, seem to even strengthen the case in favour of the artists and their claim on (a part of) the returns of the auction.

The canvas-owner in this case is for two reasons of a very special kind. In the first place the 'canvas', that is, the Berlin Wall, was the property of the German Democratic Republic, a state which was not recognized by the Federal German Republic and most countries in the Western democratic world. Although this non-recognition does not relieve foreigners to respect the laws of the non-recognized state, it undermines the legitimacy of the owner of the wall and certainly does not stimulate citizens to respect this type of property. Secondly, the special purpose of the wall, namely, to keep GDR citizens as prisoners within their own state and deny them the basic human right of travel, bestowed a quasi-criminal character on this 'monument'. The criminal character of the wall and the often lethal practices of the GDR border troops were later on confirmed by the trials against border guards who killed refugees.

These two special circumstances about the Berlin wall may let suppose that this item was not perceived by the public as an object of a legitimate property right, such as for instance the private houses of fellow citizens, residing under the same legal order. Painting on the wall was not perceived as an invasion of a property right, although it was from a positive law viewpoint, but rather as an act of protest against an oppressive regime. This lack of legitimacy reflected very probably also on the buyers of the segments of the wall. They were probably perceived, not as usual art traders but as persons, shrewd enough to make easy profits in these exceptional circumstances.

Finally it was not clear whether the defendants really paid to the GDR state agency for the surplus-value due to the paintings or whether they just paid for the special '*souvenir*'-value of the Berlin wall segments. Very probably the second is the case, as the GDR state agency had no reputation to be familiar with modern graffiti art.

E **Economic evaluation of the decision.** The decision of the German Supreme Court (BGH), that is, to award damages to the artists, can be sustained from an economic point of view. The Supreme Court makes the right distinction between the rights of the owner of the corporeal thing used as a canvas in this case, and the intellectual rights of the artists. The Court recognizes the intellectual property rights of the artists without infringing on the legitimate rights of the owner of the canvas. The decision, however right in its outcome, might have gained strength in its motivation, if the court had made the distinction between the different economic purposes of the law concerning property on corporeal things and intellectual property.

## Cases

*Beteiligung der Künstler am Verkaufserlös der Berliner Mauer-Bilder (Share of Artists in Proceeds of Auction of Parts of Berlin Wall); BGH, 23 February 1995, NJW 1995, Heft 2, 1556–1558;*

*Eigentum an Entflogenem Falken (Ownership of Escaped Falcons), LG*

*Bonn, Urt. V. 15.10.1992,- 8 T 114/92; NJW 1993, Heft 14, 940*

*Finderlohn für Gestohlenen PKW (Finder's Fee for Stolen Car); AG Hamburg, 16 March 1993, NJW 1993, Heft 40, 2627*

*Government of the State of Penang and Another v. Beng Hong Oon and Others; Privy Council,*

*5 October 1971, [1971] 3 All ER PC, 1163–1175*

*Lord Bernstein of Leigh v. Skyviews & General Ltd; Queen's Bench Division [1977] 2 All ER 902*

*Lyme Valley Squash Club Ltd v. Newcastle under Lyme Borough Council and another; Chancery Division Manchester, [1985] 2 All ER, 405–414*

## Bibliography

Alchian, Armen A. (1977) *Economic Forces at Work*, Liberty Fund, Indianapolis

Allen, Douglas W. (2000), 'The Rhino's Horn: Incomplete Property Rights and the Optimal Value of an Asset', *The Journal of Legal Studies*, Vol. 31, no. 52, 339–359

Anderson, T.L. and P.J. Hill (1998) 'From Free Grass to Fences in the American West: Transforming the Commons of the American West', in J.A. Baden and D.S. Noonan, eds. *Managing the Commons*, Bloomington, 119–134

Aristotle (1941) 'Political', Jowett, B. (trans.), in Richard McKeon, ed. *The Basic Works of Aristotle*, Modern Library, New York, 1113–1316

Ault, D.E. and G.L. Rutman (1979) 'Development of Individual Rights to Property in Tribal Africa', *Journal of Law and Economics*, Vol. 22, 163

Avenarius, Martin (1993) 'Der Freiflug des Falken – mobilia non habent sequelam', *NJW Heft*, Vol. 40, 2589–2590

Blackstone, William (1766) *Commentaries on the Laws of England*, Clarendon Press, Oxford

Bouckaert, Boudewijn (1993) 'Airport and En Route Slot Allocation: A Property Rights Approach', *European Transport Law*, Vol. XXVIII, no. 1, 77–99

Chang, Yun-Chien and Henry E. Smith (2012) 'An Economic Analysis of Civil Versus Common Law Property', *Notre Dame Law Review*, Vol. 88, no. 1, 1–56

Ciriacy-Wantrup, Siegfried V. and Richard C. Bishop (1975) 'Common Property as a Concept in Natural Resource Policy', *Natural Resources Journal*, Vol. 15, 713–727

Cole, Daniel H. (2010) 'New Forms of Private Property: Property Rights in Environmental Goods', in Boudewijn Bouckaert, ed. *Property Law and Economics Volume 5 Encyclopedia of Law and Economics*, Edward Elgar, Cheltenham, 223–269

Dales, J.H. (1968) *Pollution, Property and Prices: An Essay in Policy-Making and Economics*, Edward Elgar, Toronto

Davides, W. (1997) 'ITQ's in the Netherlands', in G. Pettursdottir, ed. *Property Rights in the Fishing Industry*, University of Iceland Press, Reykjavik

De Alessi, Michael (1998) *Fishing for Solutions*, Studies on the Environment no. 11, Institute of Economic Affairs, London

Demsetz, Harold (1966) 'Some Aspects of Property Rights', *Journal of Law and Economics*, Vol. 9, 61–70

Demsetz, Harold (1967) 'Towards a Theory of Property Rights', *American Economic Review*, Vol. 57, 347–373

Fitzpatrick, Daniel (2006) 'Evolution and Chaos in Property Rights Systems: The Third World Tragedy of Contested Access', *The Yale Law Journal*, Vol. 115, 996

Garcia, S.M. and C. Newton (1997) 'Current Situation, Trends and Prospects in World Capture Fisheries', in E.K. Pikitch, D.D. Huppert and M.P. Sissenwine, eds. *Global Trends: Fisheries Management*, American Fisheries Society, Bethesda

Gissurarson, H.H. (1999) 'The Fishery: A1greeing on the Rules', in R. Arnason and H.H. Gissurarson, eds. *Individual Quota in Theory and Practice*, University of Iceland Press, Reykjavik

Gordon, H. Scott (April 1954) 'The Economic Theory of a Common Property Resource: The Fishery', *Journal of Political Economy*, Vol. 62, no. 2, 124–142

Hansmann, Henry and Reinier Kraakman (June 2002) 'Property, Contract, and the Divisibility of Rights', *Journal of Legal Studies*, Vol. XXXI, 373–420

Hardin, Garret (December 13, 1968) 'The Tragedy of the Commons', *Science*, Vol. 162, no. 3859, 1243–1248

Hayek, Friedrich A. (1973–1978) *Law, Legislation and Liberty*, University of Chicago Press, London, Vol. 1–3

Hill, Peter J. (Spring 2014) 'Are All Commons Tragedies? The Case of Bison in the Nineteenth Century', *The Independent Review*, Vol. 18, no. 4, 485–502

Hohfeld, Wesley Newcomb (1917) 'Fundamental Legal Conceptions as Applied in Judicial Reasoning', *The Yale Law Journal*, Vol. 26

Honoré, Toni (1961) 'Ownership', in Anthony Gordon Guest, ed. *Oxford Essays in Jurisprudence*, University of Oxford Press, London, 107–147

Kaplow, Louis (2000) 'General Characteristics of Rules', in Boudewijn Bouckaert and Gerrit De Geest, ed. *Encyclopedia of Law and Economics*, Vol. V, Edward Elgar, Cheltenham, 502–528

Lueck, Dean (1995) 'The Rule of First Possession and the Design of the Law', *Journal of Law and Economics*, Vol. 38, 393–436

Major, P. (1999) 'The Evolution of ITQ's in New Zealand', in R. Arnason and H.H. Gissurarson, eds. *Individual Quota in Theory and Practice*, The University of Iceland Press, Reykjavik

Menger, Carl (1871) *Principles of Economics*, Online Version, Von Mises Institute, Auburn

Merrill, Thomas W. and Henry E. Smith (2001a) 'Optimal Standardization in the Law of Property: The *Numerus Clausus* Principle', *The Yale Law Journal*, Vol. 110, 1–70

Merrill, Thomas W. and Henry E. Smith (2001b) 'What Happened to Property in Law and Economics', *The Yale Law Journal*, Vol. 111, 356–398

Oakeshott, Michael (1975) *On Human Conduct*, Oxford University Press, Oxford

Ostrom, Elinor (2000) 'Private and Common Property Rights', in Boudewijn Bouckaert and Gerrit De Geest, eds. *Encyclopedia of Law and Economics*, Civil Law and Economics, Edward Elgar, Cheltenham, Vol. II

Pascoe, S. (1993) 'ITQ's in the Australian South East Fishery', *Marine Resources Economics*, The University of Chicago Press, Chicago, Vol. 8, 395–401

Peter, Butt (1996) 'The Mabo Case and its aftermath: Indigenous Land Title in Australia', in G.E. van Maanen and A.J. van der Walt, eds. *Property on the Threshold of the 21st Century*, MAKLU, Antwerp, 495–516

Posner, Richard A. (Spring 2005) 'Intellectual Property: The Law and Economics Approach', *Journal of Economic Perspectives*, Vol. 19, no. 2, 57–73

Sax, Joseph L. (1970) 'The Public Trust Doctrine in Natural Resource Law: Effective Judicial Intervention', *Michigan Law Review*, Vol. 68, no. 3, 471–566

Schäfer, Hans-Bernd and Claus Ott (1995) *Lehrbuch der ökonomischen Analyse des Zivilrechts,* Springer, Berlin

Van Oven, J.C. (1948) *Leerboek van Romeinsch Privaatrecht*, E.J. Brill, Leiden

Velozo de Melo Bento, Lucas (2009) 'Searching for Intergenerational Green Solutions: The Relevance of the Public Trust Doctrine to Environmental Preservation', *Common Law Review*, Vol. 11, 7–13

Winfield, Percy Henry (1954) *Tort*, London

# 2 Common property

## 2.1 Common property in the economic theory of the law

### *1. Common property: institutional variety*

1 **Definition.** In its most abstract sense common property relates to the legal situation in which more than one individual hold similar property rights (in the economic sense – ASRR – see Chapter 1) on the same asset. This definition implies a notion of equality. The commoners are legally equal in their relationship vis-à-vis the asset. As a consequence situations in which more than one individual has rights towards the same asset but where the rights are unequal, such as is the case with lord-tenant relationships either in feudal or modern common-civil law contexts, are not covered by the notion of common property.[1]

The legal world of common property is extremely varied and covers legal situations which are very different in a historical, socio-anthropological and economic sense.

2 **Number of commoners.** A first variable in common property concerns the number of commoners. Theoretically this number stretches from two people to seven billion. Many resources are held in common property by married couples, depending on the adopted matrimonial system. Even in so-called extremely individualist societies most of the family patrimonies are not held by an individual but by a couple. At the other side of the spectrum some resources are, according to international law, held by humanity as such, such as the open sea (see Chapter 1). As further stated, this variable is important for the efficient management of resources held in common. As 'humanity' for instance is not an effective excluding agent it is very likely that assets under a 'humanity-commons' regime will face problems characteristic for an open-access regime (Ostrom and Hess 2010: 55).

1 This means that cotenants (or joint tenants) have to be considered as commoners as they have the same property rights (in the economic sense: ASRR) on the asset. The owner-landlord of the cotenants however is not a commoner as he has other property rights than the cotenants. On cotenancy see Tracht 2000: 63.

3 **Type of rights.** A second variable in common property concerns the type of rights the commoners hold towards the asset. The wide variety of property rights in general (see Chapter 1) applies also to the rights of commoners. Commoners can hold full Blackstonian-Bartolian ownership rights towards the asset but also lesser rights such as tenants' rights, withdrawal rights, etc. The type of rights commoners hold can be exogenously or endogenously determined. Exogenously in case the rights of the commoners are determined by the legal system as such (modern or traditional). Ostrom and Hess, for instance, mention many cases in which the traditional law limits rights of commoners to resources to proprietorship, that is, it deprives them of the right of alienation (Ostrom and Hess 2010: 61). Endogenously in case the commoners themselves determine their rights towards the common asset and further regulations. Modern liberal legal systems allow commoners within certain margins freedom to determine which rights they have (e.g. full ownership rights, only usufructuary rights, only more limited rights), how the common property is divided (equal shares, unequal shares) and by which rules the use of the common resource will be regulated. Major examples here are apartment buildings and condominiums in civil and common law countries.

4 **Ideology versus empirical research.** The choice between common and private property regimes and the historical analysis of these regimes has often been the subject of mere ideological approaches, which run against the results of empirical, historical and anthropological research. In general, such research points out that during all historical periods and in all human civilisations economic production and forms of habitations were organized through often complicated combinations of private and common property arrangements. Some Marxist versions of history completely neglect this complexity.[2] According to these versions human history went first through the phase of primitive communism during which common property exclusively prevailed. This was succeeded by a long trend of privatization culminating in the extreme individualist regime of industrial capitalism. This will in its turn be succeeded by communism on a high technological level in which private property can be abolished because the scarcity of natural resources has disappeared. Liberal/conservative thinkers of the nineteenth century on the contrary perceived a long and unilinear trend throughout human history from common property towards the complete dominance of private property (Ostrom and Hess 2010: 53). Neither the claim of exclusive dominance nor that of unilinear evolution withstand the confrontation with the findings of empirical research. In Western capitalist societies, for example, the

2 Marx himself changed several times his ideas about this question. First he believed that pre-capitalist forms of common property were inevitably doomed by the rise of individual property and capitalism. Later, by studying the works of Maurer on the German *Mark* and the Russian village communities, he believed that persisting forms of common property could bypass individualism and capitalism and link up with modern socialism (Tairako 2016: 1–10)

modernization of agriculture has led indeed to a strong reduction of common property regimes. On the other hand, common property arrangements, such as condominiums, are steadily on the rise in urban residential areas (Tracht 2000: 73). Private and common property regimes often prevail within one and the same community. Swiss and Italian villagers in mountain areas combine private property on arable land in the valleys with common property on the meadows in the mountains (Netting 1981; Casari 2007). Sometimes the combination applies even on one and the same asset. In the open field system in medieval England private property prevailed on the strips of arable land from the sewing season until harvest. During the autumn, winter and early spring, the land became a commons for the pastoring of the cattle of the villagers (Smith 2000).

5 **Common property rights and politico-legal systems.** Common property regimes prevail in very different politico-legal systems. The nature of these systems have however a strong impact on the common property regimes. A very broad categorization generates the following fourfold distinction:

   a **Common property within traditional legal systems.** In these systems common property regimes are legally embedded in tribal or local customary law. The structure and the rules of common property are mostly exogenously determined by the customs of the tribe or the village. Although these customary rules are sometimes adapted to changing circumstances, there is no explicit procedure for changing the custom. As with customary law in general, the custom is enforced, neither by formalized state agencies, nor by feudal overlords, but by a general and horizontal peer pressure from the members of the tribe or village. Nearly all common property regimes in less developed countries (LDCs) pertain to this category.

   b **Common property and feudal manorial systems.** Often feudal manorial systems of land exploitation existed side by side with traditional common property. Sometimes this coexistence was only transitional; sometimes it was permanent. In many areas in which feudalism was introduced, not all land was integrated into the feudal chain. Besides land held in tenure from lords, some land remained under allodial household property while other land remained under a regime of common village property. Feudalism and common property not only existed merely side by side. Sometimes feudalism triggered and strengthened some forms of common property. The main example here is Russia. Agriculture in the largest part of Russia was organized around the *obshchina* or the *mir*, the agricultural commune. Farmer households had no property; all arable land belonged to the commune. The assembly of the commune, the *skhod*, determined what crops were to grow, regulated crop rotation, the organization of the common labour (sewing, reaping, tilling, fertilizing, ploughing, etc.) and the distribution of the harvest. The system was hailed by Slavophiles as the true expression of the Russian collectivistic soul. One cannot deny, however, the impact of feudal relationships on the persistence of this system, which hampered individual initiative and agricultural innovation. The peasants had to pay heavy taxes to their lords and to the czarist state. In order to ensure tax collection, peasants were placed under a regime of vicarious liability for their tax debts. In order to avoid moral hazard peasants preferred to keep their land pooled into the commune. This situation persisted even after the abolishing of serfdom in 1861 for peasants were obliged to pay to the lords for their liberation. Also for these payments the vicarious liability remained in place (Stahl-Role 2000). In 1912 minister Stolypine abolished the *obshchina-mir* system and introduced household-ownership. After the revolution of 1917 the Bolsheviks reintroduced the communal system again.

c **Common property in collectivistic systems.** In these systems common property is imposed through state policy. The state imposes common property either by making already existing traditional common property compulsory and formalizing the customary rules about it or by imposing a compulsory pooling of former private households. The first occurred rather as a result of decolonization. Postcolonial political leaders, often influenced by Marxism, attempted to build further on traditional communalist institutions in order to realize a modern socialist system. The main example here is the *ujamaa* in Tanzania under the impulse of Julius Nyerere's ideology of 'African socialism'.[3] The second occurred rather in communist countries such as Russia, China and the Central- and East-European countries. Most often the pattern was the following: the communist party won the hearts and the minds of the peasants by redistributing land from expropriated large landholders to small and middle peasants; then the communist party obliged the peasants to pool their land in large common farms (e.g. the *kolkhozes*); first the proceeds of the farms were distributed according to the land pooled in the commune; later according to the labour input or more egalitarian rules. Often this compulsory process of collectivization was met with violent resistance, eliciting brutal repression, starvation and even mass murders of genocidal proportions (Conquest 1986). Sometimes the state did not impose common property but stimulated it by propagating and subsidizing it. The main example here is Israel with its *kibbutzim* (Ellickson 1993: 1347). Surfing on socialist ideas brought from Europe and the enthusiasm of building a new state, many Jewish settlers opted voluntarily to live in communalist farms, without however being forced by the state.

d **Common property in liberal legal systems.** In modern common and civil law systems the principle of individual autonomy has a central place. As a consequence common property can only exist in accordance with this principle. This has two very important consequences. First,

3 In the beginning of Nyerere's rule *ujamaa* collectivization was rather voluntary. Later on it was more and more imposed from above and bureaucratized. Productivity in *ujamaa*-villages was only at 50 percent of the independent farms (Boesen, Madsen, and Moody 1977). The program was abandoned in 1985

common property arrangements should be the result of a voluntary pooling of property by individuals and by a mutual consent about the regulations on the exploitation of the commons.[4] Second, individuals cannot be compelled to remain in common property-arrangements or in indivisibility. Commoners have a right to exit.[5] This latter consequence implies of course further complications concerning the eventual breaking up of the common property arrangement and the division of the assets.

Although voluntary common property and right to exit are the rule in modern liberal legal systems, there are some important exceptions.

Sometimes common property has an involuntary origin. At the decease of a person his heirs are in common property of his inheritance. This is necessary as the abstract division of their parts, determined by law or by will, has to be converted into a concrete division of the assets in the inheritance. This involuntary common property lasts as long a concrete division has not been reached, either consensually or by decision of the court.

Sometimes common property is imposed by law, also in liberal legal systems. A first case concerns the so-called party wall. An owner whose land is bordered by a wall of his neighbour can require that this wall becomes common to the two neighbours at the condition of compensation of the neighbour. This allows this owner to use also this wall and avoids a duplication of wall-building.[6] A second, far more important case concerns apartment buildings. The law imposes common property among all owners of an apartment in one building of all common parts such as the roof, the outside walls, the staircase, the elevators, the lobby, the basement, the central heating and so forth. The law also imposes that all apartment owners administer this common property through an assembly of co-owners.[7]

## 2. *The economics of common property*

6 **Common property. Open-access goods. Common pool resources.** As explained in Chapter 1, I. Theory, 9. The tragedy of open-access goods, legal economics draws a distinguishing line between open-access goods and

4 Civil law distinguishes voluntary, involuntary and imposed common property. The partners in voluntary common property are free to determine their shares and the regulations on the use of the common asset. The civil code only provides some default rules on this (e.g. art. 577/2 Belgian Civil Code)

5 The right to exit common property has traditionally been based on art. 815 Civil Code, providing that 'nobody can be forced to remain in indivisibility'. This article allows however clauses that prevent parties to exit but no longer than a five years' period. Recent case law rejects however art. 815 Civil Code as the base of a general right to exit. It is argued that art. 815 Civil Code belongs to a section in the code dealing with involuntary common property of heirs and does not apply to voluntary common property. As a consequence it is up to the partners to deal with the exit problem within their common property-contract.

6 See art. 661 Belgian Civil Code.

7 See art. 577/3–577/14 Belgian Civil Code; for the UK see The Party Wall etc Law of 1996;

commons. The first notion refers to a lack of any effective excluding agent about the use of the asset by which the asset becomes vulnerable to overuse, untimely use and underinvestment. In a commons, as understood by legal economics, the problem of exclusion of outsiders can be solved, however often at a cost, the so called exclusion costs. For excluding outsiders commoners, operating within the context of a well-organized legal system, can rely on the protection this system offers to all owners, private as well as common ones. Inhabitants of an anti-capitalist-anarchist commune for instance, who are the victim of robbery of their common assets, can call upon the police of (what they consider as) the 'liberal capitalist legal system' to recover their stolen goods. When such an effective legal system is lacking commoners will have to rely for the exclusion on self-defence, as was often the case in human history. When it is assumed that the outsiders' problem is solvable for a commons, the specific kind of problems of the management of a commons concerns the insiders: how to coordinate the behaviour of the commoners in such a way that an efficient management of use of the common asset is guaranteed.

Before dealing with this question, another source of confusion has to be addressed, namely, the distinction between common property and a common pool resource. Common property refers to the legal situation of an asset, while a common pool resource refers to economic characteristics of the consumption of a good. Typical for common pool resource-consumption is its rival and non-excludable character. In the matrix of the classification of goods according to the characteristics of consumption a common pool resource has the following position:

| | **Rival Consumption** | **Non-rival Consumption** |
|---|---|---|
| **Excludable Consumption** | **Private Goods**<br>**Optimal regime: markets** | **Club goods**<br>**Optimal regime: clubs** |
| **Non-excludable Consumption** | **Common pool resource**<br>**Optimal regime: regulation** | **Public Goods**<br>**Optimal regime: state intervention** |

*Figure 2.1* Economic classification of goods

Concerning the relationship between the classification of legal regimes (private property, common property, state property, open access, etc.) and the economic classification of goods, illustrated by the matrix, it has to be remarked that there is no strict relationship between the two and that many combinations are possible.

A private good, as for instance a car, can be owned in common by several households. Technically it has the characteristics of a private good but because of the chosen legal regime problems, typical for common pool resource – use, may arise and the households will have to make some internal deals.

A club good, as for instance a bridge, can be owned either by a private owner, a group or a public authority, but whomever the owner of the bridge is, solutions typical for club goods, such as admission prices (tolls) and measures to prevent overcrowding will have to be taken.

A public good, such as for instance police patrolling can be provided by public authorities but also by private initiative. In any case however, there will be problems with free ridership. While public authorities will try to solve this by taxation and regulation, private operators will have to rely on other strategies such as moral education, tribal sentiments and repeated games.[8]

The relationship between the economic notion 'common pool resource' and legal regimes is somewhat more complicated. Private goods, club goods and public goods[9] derive their consumption characteristics (rival or not, excludable or not) from technical qualities. In case of common pool resources the non-excludable character can be the result of a legal regime. Inshore fisheries of salmon on the US north-west coast for instance became a common pool resource due to the legal ban on territorial and harvesting restrictions by local fishermen (Higgs 1996). In this case the legal regime is not a strategy for solution but the source of the problem.

Whatever the source of the rival and non-excludable character of consumption, be it technical or legal, the management of common pool resources will always be faced with problems of overuse, untimely use and underinvestment. When the resource is owned by the government, these problems will be coped with by public regulations, when the owner is a group internal group deals will be necessary, when the owner is a private individual or a company, restrictions will be necessary vis-à-vis the users-customers of the resource.

7 **The optimal commons.** Why do individuals pool their resources in a commons or why would they exit an existing commons, provided they have the freedom to decide this?[10] This question is dealt with in the theory of the

8 See, for instance, Anthony de Jasay (1989: 192) and his 'ethics turnpike', listing different social strategies to overcome free ridership in public good-provision.

9 Although some goods, labelled by mainstream economic literature as 'public', owe their public character also to legal and political interventions (see Foldvary 1994)

10 'Quod non' of course in compulsory collectivistic systems such as Soviet Russia and People's Republic of China.

optimal commons. Barry Field (1985) developed a cost-minimization model, attempting to identify the most important cost-variables for this choice. The Field model departs from a stable population in relationship with a fixed asset, for instance a certain amount of land. The population faces a continuum of choice from dividing the asset in as many property units (m) as there are members in the group(n) (m=n), to have the asset in common for the whole group (m=1). On the continuum there are intermediate positions between this extreme individualism and extreme communism. The population can for instance split up in subgroups to which property units are allotted ($m= n/x^1$, $m=n/x^2$, $m=n/x^3$, etc.). As the main cost-variable pushing groups to fragment the property rights on the asset Field considers the transaction costs. By this is meant all the costs groups have to spend to prevent or alleviate internal conflicts, free ridership, overuse of, untimely use of and underinvestment in the asset. To prevent this the group has to find out the appropriate rules which involves information costs, has to convince the members about the utility of these rules which involves negotiation costs, has to watch the members about the compliance with the rules which involves monitoring costs. The larger the group and the more common the property rights on the asset the higher these transaction costs.

As the main cost-variable pushing groups to pool their resources Field considers the exclusion costs. By this is meant all costs involving the setting up and the running of an effective property order. When property rights on the asset are fragmented the borders separating these property rights are lengthening. Borders involve costs, as the owners have to delineate their properties, fence in their cattle and provide devices to internalize externalities such as dust, smoke, smell and noise. Fragmentation increases also the possibility of border conflicts, triggering the need for conflict solving social institutions such as mediation and court adjudication. Beside the internal exclusion costs the concerned population also faces exclusion costs towards outsiders. Although an external threat imposes a risk to the whole group, the pooling/fragmentation degree is not neutral vis-à-vis these exclusion costs. In case of thorough fragmentation the members will be inclined to defend first their own property and may put the defence of the whole group in second order. Consequently fragmentation may have a positive impact on the costs of exclusion of outsiders. In case of thorough pooling members may feel more inclined to defend the whole community which has a negative impact on exclusion costs.

Both cost variables constitute the basis for a cost-minimization model about the optimal commons.

When fragmenting, thus moving from (m=1) towards (m=n), costs will rise. When pooling, thus moving from (m=n) towards (m=1), transaction costs will rise. The number of property units is optimal when the sum of both exclusion costs and transaction costs is the lowest. On the graph this point is (x). The optimal point is not necessarily at the intersection of both cost curves. This will depend on the concavity-non-concavity of both curves. In this model transaction costs and exclusion costs are both the independent

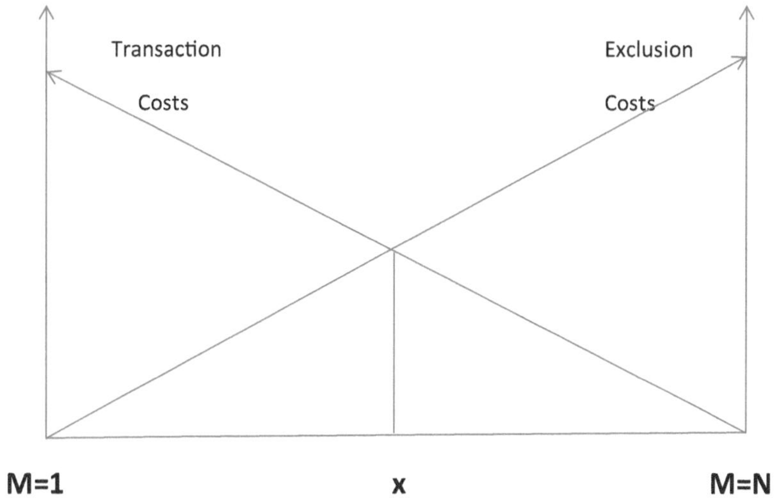


*Figure 2.2* Optimal commons

cost-variables where the degree of pooling/fragmentation is the dependent variable. When due to exogenous evolutions transaction costs rise and *ceteris paribus*, one can expect a push for more fragmentation. When exclusion costs rise at the other hand and *ceteris paribus*, a push for more pooling can be expected.

The model is helpful to explain several historical evolutions on property rights, as well on the micro as on the macro scale.

Acheson (1979), for instance, analyzes the evolution within the indigenous management system employed in Maine lobster fisheries. Although the fishing waters are officially 'common' and everybody who obtains a license has the right to fish lobster, the fishing is in effect controlled by the 'harbour gangs' of each port who divided the fishing waters among them. These gangs protect their 'informal common property' against 'poachers' through intimidation and if necessary by destroying the fishing gear of the interlopers. Acheson observed during the sixties an evolution towards pooling of the territorial units and consequently of the groups of fishermen controlling them. This evolution was explained by the higher intensity of 'poaching' as demand for lobster rose considerably during this period. In terms of the Field model the pooling is the result of higher exclusion costs resulting from the higher frequency of 'poaching'.

Jodha (1985), for instance, analyzes the evolution on the common property resources (community pastures, forests, waste lands) in the West of Rajasthan. Since the land reforms of the 1950s these common resources are in decline, as well as in quantity as in quality. Jodha indicates several factors as explanation of this evolution such as commercialization, population pressure and large scale introduction of tractors, but also institutional factors, included in the land reform program were effective in this evolution. The common pasture lands were, before the reforms, managed by a feudal landlord who rented the land to the peasants in exchange for different taxes. Although this system (the Jagirdari system) was certainly exploitative towards the peasants it also resulted as a by-product in a management that protected, maintained and regulated the use of the common resources. The reforms lead not only to the privatization of large parts of the common property land but also to a change of the management of the remaining common land. Instead of the feudal land lord the management was entrusted to a village council (*Panchayats*). These councils were not effective at all in levying the necessary taxes to invest into or even maintain the infrastructure of the common lands. The result was decay in quality of the exploitation of these lands. In terms of the Field model the evolution towards more privatization and decline in common property lands management is a result of the higher transaction costs within the village councils. Management under feudalism was cheap in terms of transaction costs as only one authority had to decide. By democratizing the management transaction costs increased considerably which led to either privatization or decay in the management of the commons.

8 **Elinor Ostrom: social-ecological systems.** The model of Field indicates that common property management may be sustainable at the condition that transaction costs are significantly lower than exclusion costs. Elinor Ostrom (Ostrom 1990, 2009, 2010) elevated the sophistication of the analysis of common property management considerably by developing a multi-variable model of so called social-ecological systems. The management of resources pertains most often various aspects of an economic, social, ecological and technical kind. All these aspects are studied by different sciences, but are mostly not connected into one holistic approach on resource management. Ostrom's framework of social-ecological systems (SES) attempts to cope with this multi-disciplinary reality (see Figure 2.3).

A SES consists of a network of interactions between four subsystems: (1) the resource system (RS) (e.g. a national park), (2) the resource units (RU) (e.g. trees, shrubs, wildlife), (3) the users (U) (tourists, natural scientists, lumber companies) and (4) a governance system (GS) (e.g. the federal government). Successes, failures and evolutions of the SES should be explained by second level variables which have an impact, first on the subsystem to which they belong, second on other subsystems of the SES through all kinds of interaction. Examples of such second-level variables are:

- For the resource system: the size of the system (surface)
- For the resource units: the mobility of the units
- For the governance systems: top down government or bottom up self-organization
- For the users: the mobility of the users

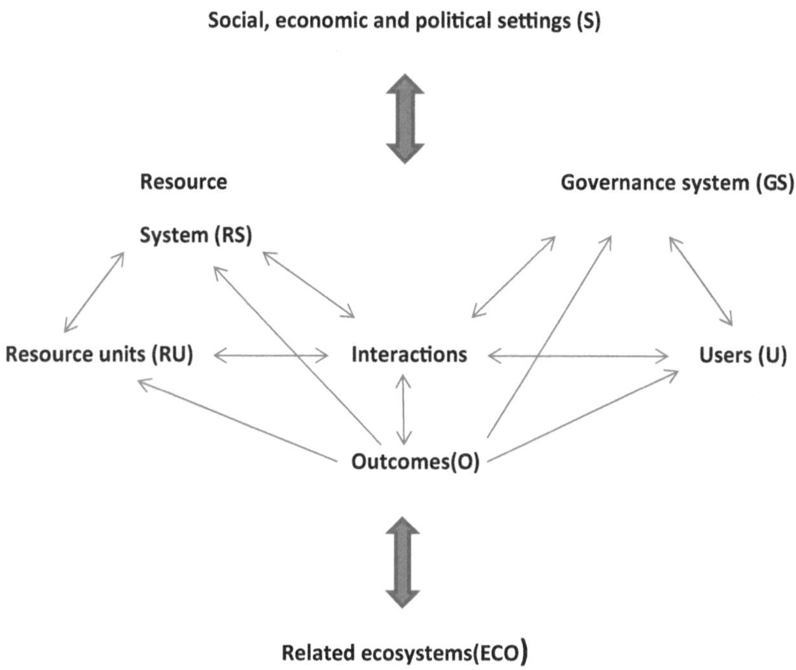


*Figure 2.3* Ostrom's social-ecological systems

Research on various SES has pointed out several robust correlations between these second level variables and outcomes concerning successful self-organization.

For instance concerning size of land-related resource systems: the larger the size the less likely that the commons will be self-governed (too high monitoring costs, heterogeneity of the users). Very small territories however do not generate substantial flows of valuable products and will not sustain a critical group able of self-governance. Moderate territorial size is most conducive to self-organization.

For instance the variable of productivity of a resource: this variable has a curvilinear impact on the capacity of self-organization. When the resource has a very low productivity due to exhaustion or has a very high productivity due to abundance self-organization is unlikely. When the users perceive the problem of imminent resource scarcity self-organization becomes likely.

For instance the variable of predictability: users have to be able to predict the impact of rules and governance on resource productivity. Often the system dynamics do not allow for some predictability. Some fishery systems for instance approach mathematical chaos. Unpredictability on a small scale may lead users to merge at larger scale.

For instance the variable of users' mobility: the higher the mobility the less likely self-organization. Concerning the variable of number of users it is clear that high numbers increase the chances of heterogeneity which can impair self-organization. On the other hand, a high number may be necessary to mobilize sufficient labour resources to exploit the resource.

For instance the variable of human/social capital: the presence of influential leaders and college graduates, who are respected as social leaders, strengthens the likelihood of effective self-organization.

For instance the variable collective autonomy: when the group of users is allowed to make its choices autonomously, its leads to a more effective defence of the resources against invaders then when the group is placed under administrative subordination, which can lead to high transaction costs.

In general Ostrom warns again blue print solutions neglecting important side variables by which they result in unintended negative consequences. For instance:

> the total allowable catch quotas for the west coast of Canada led to widespread dumping of unwanted fish, misrepresentation of catches and the closure of groundfishery in 1995. To remedy this initial failure, the government reopened the fishery, but divided the coastal area in to more than 50 sectors, assigned transferable quotas, and required that all ships have neutral observers to record all catches.
>
> (Ostrom 2009: 421–422)

9 **Common property: freedom to pool, freedom of exit.** Individual freedom to pool properties and individual rights to exit are no issues in collectivistic legal systems in which pooling and eventual exiting are framed into a command economy. Within traditional legal systems these rights are rather exceptional as these systems are based on logic of group rights. These rights are however central within the private law of all countries which adopted the individualist principles, which are historically underlying civil as well as common law traditions.

From a legal-economic viewpoint freedom to pool (or not to pool) should be endorsed in principle. As was already stated, pooling properties involve benefits (less exclusion costs, economics of scale) as well as costs (information, negotiation, monitoring costs). The level of these costs is however not written in the stars, but depends, at least partially, on the subjective evaluation by the owners, waging an eventual pooling. As knowledge on economic data is dispersed across the individual agents in society (Hayek 1945), it would be inefficient to leave the decision about pooling to third parties such as government authorities. These third parties would lack the relevant information to make efficient decisions about pooling or not pooling.

The counterpart of the freedom of pooling is the freedom of a co-owner to leave the common property arrangement. A right to exit concerns first the person of the co-owner himself. Coercing individuals to stay physically within the premises of the commons and/or to work for the commons would obviously violate personal freedom and would be tantamount to slavery. Also from an economic point of view personal freedom should be respected as a human right as individuals value their own freedom and labour capacities the highest. Allocating these to a third party (the state, a slave owner) would be inefficient as the individual would buy back his freedom and labour capacity which leads to a waste of transaction costs (Posner 1983).

Another question however concerns the share of the exiting commoner into the pooled assets. Is she/he allowed taking his/her share out of the commons or not? The answer is not evident as the exit can result in negative spillovers to the other commoners. Basically there are three ways to leave and/or to end the commons:

1) The exiting commoner transfers his/her share to a third person. This may trigger an externality problem in cases where the commons involve cohabitation and cooperation among the commoners. The qualities of the substituting member may be of that kind that the other members would never have him/her allowed into the original establishment of the commons.
2) The exiting commoner takes his/her asset, brought in into the commons, physically out of the commons. This is of course only possible with mobile goods, and not with land. Also in this case the exit may cause negative spillovers. The asset, taken out, can have a complementary character towards the other assets in the commons. As a consequence the exit may disrupt the functioning of a chain of different components. It is also possible that it is difficult or even impossible to find a functioning substitute for the asset taken out.
3) The exiting commoner ends the indivisibility of all the assets of the commons. The assets are sold on the market and the commoners receive their counterpart in money. Also this way of exiting can create negative spillovers. The remaining commoners are faced with a forced sale of their shared assets. It is possible that their willingness to sell was higher than the market price they will receive at the liquidation of the commons.

Such problems can be anticipated by contractual provisions in the initial contract of co-ownership. The Civil Code of Belgium for instance provides on one hand that co-owners may always ask to end the indivisibility of the co-ownership (art. 815 CC, 1°)[11] but provides on the other hand that co-owners may ban exiting during a renewable period of maximum five years (art. 815 CC, 2°). In this way co-owners are able to limit to a certain extent the negative

11 The Belgian Supreme Court in civil and criminal matters (Cassation Court), however, narrowed down considerably the scope of this article. Indivisibility can only be asked when the co-ownership is the consequence of inheritance. In cases of contractual co-ownership the parties may decide freely about the duration of the co-ownership arrangement.

spillovers, triggered by a sudden exit. The question however remains whether it would be efficient to allow a ban of exiting for longer periods, even at perpetuum. The further advanced into the future, the more difficult it is to predict the balance between benefits and costs of remaining in or exiting the commons. Putting some limits on the period of an exit ban may be defendable from a soft paternalistic point of view. Such paternalism would however impair the benefits from learning curves in society. By allowing the parties to freely negotiate exit bans, accidents with too long exit bans will certainly occur. Other parties, and a fortiori involved professionals (lawyers, notaries), will learn from these accidents and warn reckless parties to be careful with long exit bans. Finally, it should be clear that exit bans should not be extended to the heirs of commoners, as they were not part of the initial agreement, founding the co-ownership.

10 **Exceptions to freedom to pool and not to pool.** Even in liberal legal systems some exceptions are accepted on the freedom to pool or not to pool. Civil as well as common law provide two cases in which individuals can be coerced to pool assets, i.e. the party wall and, more important apartment co-ownership.

A party wall is a wall erected on the borderline of a land parcel. A party wall can be made coercively common. The Civil Code (art. 661 CC) provides that the initiative for making common the wall has to be taken by the neighbouring owner. He has to ask that the wall be made common in exchange for a compensation, for which the tariffs are fixed. According to civil case law also the owner, on whose land the party wall is erected, can take the initiative to make the wall common. When the neighbouring owner uses the wall in a way which can be qualified as possessory (for instance building against it) then the first owner can also ask that the wall has to be made common in order to make the neighbour pay for that use.

From a legal economic viewpoint both rules make sense. The first rule avoids that the neighbouring owner would make duplicate efforts and costs by building two adjacent walls. By making the wall common the neighbour can use the wall and can avoid the costs of building a wall him/herself. The second rule prevents free ridership from the side of the neighbour. When neighbours could use freely the wall of their neighbours without paying for it, builders could refrain from building a wall at all or would build it at some distance beyond the border line. This could lead to difficult negotiations as the neighbours are in a bilateral monopoly situation towards each other. The possibility of making the wall common in a coercive way (see below Chapter 5, ‘a private taking’; Bouckaert and De Geest 1995) precludes such a possible stalemate.

In apartment buildings some parts, such as the lobby, the elevator, the staircase, the roof, are built for the common use by the inhabitants of the apartments. As stated before, common pool resources are not necessarily under a legal regime of common property. This is also the case for the common use parts in an apartment building. These parts could be owned by for instance the corporation which built the apartments or one of the owners of an apartment. In most legal systems however, the law imposes a co-ownership regime of the common use parts by the owners of the private apartments. The co-owners have a share in this co-ownership according to the number of apartments, the size and value of the apartments they own in the building. According to their share the maintenance and investment costs of the common parts are apportioned to the individual owners. The decisions are made by a board of co-owners, sometimes deciding by unanimity, sometimes by a qualified majority, sometimes by simple majority. Often this board delegates the administration and investment policy of the common parts to specialized companies.

From a legal-economic viewpoint the mandatory character of the co-ownership regime on common parts in apartment buildings can be justified in order to avoid strategic behaviour by the common parts-owner. If some agent, other than the board of co-owners, retains the ownership on the common parts he is able to extort the inhabitants of the apartments. Through his monopoly position he can block the access to the apartments, he can block necessary repairs to the roof, outside walls, the elevator and so forth. This position is a bilateral monopoly as apartment inhabitants are not able to run to competing agents offering similar services for the common parts. By putting the common parts under a co-ownership rule, such problems can be avoided.

The law on apartment's buildings or the co-ownership contracts on them also provide for different majorities according to the kind of decisions that have to be made by the co-ownership board and regulations on the behaviour of users of the common parts. Through an analysis of several co-ownership contracts and co-ownership laws De Geest (1992) develops an economic explanation for the choice between different majority rules. Within an apartment building a lot of services and decisions have a public good character. For instance the use of a staircase is non-rival and non-excludable (or at least difficult to exclude). Decisions which are ex ante determinable, such as for instance all costs which are directly related with the standing of the building and which cannot be altered, have however rather a club-good character. They are known at the moment of the negotiation of the initial contract. As a consequence, would-be owners can integrate information about these costs in their decision to join or not to join the 'co-owners-club'. Consequently for this type of decisions unanimity rules or qualified majority rules are currently provided. Other decisions are not ex ante determinable, such as for instance the costs of conservation acts or adaptation to the evolution of building styles. For such decisions decision- costs[12] could be very high, so that simple majorities are to be preferred. Apartment-owners have votes according to the value of their property in the building and not a one man-one vote-system.

12 In the model of Buchanan and Tullock (1962) decision costs relate to the costs of reaching the required majority or unanimity. The higher the requirement, the higher the decision costs. The counterpart of this cost-category are the external costs, i.e. the costs of the decision which are externalized to the group which did not agree with it. The lower the requirement, the higher these external costs. Under a unanimity rule these costs are evidently zero (Buchanan and Tullock 1962: 62–68; Mueller 1989: 53)

This can be explained as a way to have a stronger and more relevant preference revealing.

## 2.2 Case analyses

### *1.* Abbahall Ltd v. Smee; *Court of Appeal Civil Division, 5, 12 December 2002; [2002] EWCA Civ 1831*

A **Facts and legal sources.** Abbahall Ltd and Smee are both owners of a house in London. Abbahall Ltd owns the ground floor while Smee owns the first and the second floor ('a flying freehold'). The second floor comprises only a living space created in the attic of the rooftop. Abbahall Ltd rents the ground floor to Mr. Patinson. Since the beginning of the 1990's the roof has fallen into disrepair due to the neglect of Smee. On 1 November 1994 Abbahall Ltd obtained from the county court an injunctive order to enter the flat of Smee to carry out the necessary repairs to the roof to render it safe, sound and watertight. The order was silent on the cost distribution. Abbahall Ltd sought to recover from Smee the total costs of the repair (£7,255) and the costs of further repairs, as assessed in an expert report (£23,617.50). In a court order, Judge Cotran decided that Smee had only to contribute one-fourth of the costs and Abbahall three-fourths of it. He assessed the necessary future costs at £13,800. Abbahall Ltd appeals to the Court seeking to recover the full costs of the repairs.

Principles of nuisance law, applicable to this case, have been developed in the cases *Goldman v. Hargrave* [1966] 2 All ER 989, 1967, *Leaky*'s case [1980] 1 All ER 17, 1980 and *Holbeck Hall Hotel Ltd v. Scarborough BC* [2000] 2 All ER 705–722,2000.

B **Claims and defences.** Abbahall claimed and obtained from the county court an injunctive order to enter the flat of Smee and make the urgent repairs to the roof. In a later claim he asked Smee to pay the whole repair based on the following considerations: (1) Smee is the owner of the roof; (2) she committed a public nuisance by letting fall the roof into disrepair; (3) she paid a low price for the flat; (4) she acquired the flat through adverse possession and prescription. Smee at the contrary claims that Abbahall Ltd has to pay based on the following considerations: (1) she is under no duty to pay because Abbahall Ltd is a mere reversioner and does not live in the house; (2) her neglect was just an omission and not a commission; (3) the circumstances of the case indicate that she has no duty to pay. After the decision of Judge Cotran she claims the maintaining of his decision (the one-fourth/three-fourths division of the costs). Her consideration in this was that she was under no general duty to do the repair but '*to do that which is reasonable in all the circumstances, and no more than what, if anything is reasonable to prevent or minimise the known risk of damage or injury to one's neighbour or to his property'*.

C **Sentence and considerations.** The appeal of Abbahall Ltd is allowed and the court decided a sharing of the costs on a fifty-fifty base. The court of appeal rejects the consideration of Judge Cotran that Smee has to pay a smaller part because she has a low income. The court analyzes, on the base of the quoted cases and the opinions in it, the extent of the duty of a landowner, faced with the prospect of a risk of damages to the property of his neighbour. The existence of a duty of a land occupier depends on his knowledge of the hazard, his ability to foresee the damage, his ability to abate it. What is reasonable to expect from him depends on the individual circumstances of the case. An owner with a small property, who perceives a large hazard from his property, endangering the properties of his neighbours, is not under the same duty as a large owner. The small owner has for instance fulfilled his duty when he would have prevented the neighbour and have proposed to him a cost sharing according to his means. The extent of the duty depends also on the financial resources of the owner. This does not imply that the court has to make a detailed search of the financial means of the defendant, but only a broad assessment of it.

When applying these considerations to the specific situation of a flying freehold, such as in this case, common justice and reasonableness indicates that the parties are under a duty of cost sharing. Both parties derive a benefit of the costs of the repair of the roof. It is fair that both parties contribute. As the benefits are according to a rough assessment more or less equal also the cost sharing should be at 50/50.

The argument that also the means of the concerned parties, in this case of defendant Smee, have to be taken into consideration for assessing the contribution is rejected by the court. Although the means argument is accepted in the quoted case law as a possible consideration, case law is far from compelling in this matter, as it is stated that a means argument 'might' be considered or can be 'possible'. Accepting the means argument could however lead, under certain circumstances, to some kind of injustice. The hard working inhabitant would be then under a duty of paying a larger share than somebody who prefers to live on lower revenue. If the defendant claims that she cannot pay the repairs because she is living from social benefits and if she chooses to live in a flat with a roof, common also to a neighbour, there is no reason why this choice would diminish her liability and increase that of her neighbour, even being more solvent.

D **Economic analysis.** From a legal-economic viewpoint the roof and the repairing of it have the characteristics of a public good. When one of the owner repairs it, positive externalities for the other party are generated. When Smee repairs the roof she cannot exclude Abbahall Ltd and its tenant to enjoy it. On the other hand, letting fall it into disrepair generates negative externalities on the other party. Moreover, both parties are caught into a situation of bilateral monopoly. Abbahall Ltd for instance cannot run to a competing roof-provider. It is condemned to 'buy' the roof-service from Smee.

Different institutional arrangements for the concerned parties will generate different outcomes in terms of efficiency. The outcomes of two possible and also current institutional arrangements are analysed

1) *The roof is exclusively owned by the occupier of the flying freehold, Mrs. Smee in this case*: as there is a bilateral monopoly Smee can behave strategically and play hold up towards Abbahall Ltd. She can use her monopoly position in order to extort from Abbahall the highest possible contribution. This can lead to a complete breakup of the negotiation and to the further decay of the roof. This could lead to much higher costs in the long term and to danger for by passers on the street. To conclude: this arrangement involves a risk for a highly inefficient outcome
2) *The roof is under co-ownership by both parties*: In this case the decision for the repairs has to be made by both and the costs have to be shared by both. Whether a decision can be made and which decision will depend on the distribution of the votes and the majority requirement. A 'one man one vote'-rule can lead to a stalemate in this case, strategic behaviour from both sides and the same inefficiencies as under the first arrangement. In civil law countries (De Geest 1992) votes are apportioned according to the value of the apartment and for acts of mere conservation a simple majority is required. Consequently, only when the value of the apartments would be exactly equal again a stalemate could be possible. In all other cases, one of the two parties will have a majority. Will this lead to efficient outcomes? Under efficiency here is understood Pareto-efficiency, that is, all the outcomes in which the position of one party cannot be improved anymore without worsening the position of the other.

   Both parties have a willingness to pay for the repairs ($P^1$, $P^2$). According to the value of their apartment they have to pay a share of the total cost ($C^t$, $C^1$, $C^2$ and $C^1 + C^2 = C^t$).

   When ($P^1>C^1 \wedge P^2>C^2$) both parties will be in favour of the repairs. When ($P^1<C^1 \wedge C^2<P^2$) both parties will decide against the repairs. In both cases the outcome is evidently efficient.

   The problems arise when the relationship between willingness's to pay and costs is asymmetric. Suppose the first party has the highest value apartment and consequently the majority. When ($P^1>C^1 \wedge P^2<C^2$) then the first party will decide in favour of repairs and compel the minority party to pay its share, although this means a loss for this party. When the gain of the majority party ($P^1$-$C^1$) is larger than the loss of the minority party ($C^2$-$P^2$) then the outcome will be Kaldor-Hicks-efficient but not Pareto efficient, as the minority party loses. When the gain of the majority party ($P^1$-$C^1$) is smaller than the loss of the minority party ($C^2$-$P^2$) then the minority party can try to bargain with the majority party and make a side payment in order not to repair. This will lead to an efficient outcome, but this is not guaranteed as both parties are in a bilateral monopoly situation.

The gain can however also lie with the minority party and the loss with the majority party $P^1<C^1 \wedge P^2>C^2$). In this case the majority party will decide not to repair. When the loss for the majority is higher than the gain for the minority party, the outcome is again Kaldor-Hicks-efficient. When the loss of the majority party is smaller than the gain of the minority party, again this latter party can offer a side payment to make the repairs anyway. Again this is not guaranteed due to the bilateral monopoly situation.

As a result this institutional arrangement will lead in a majority of cases to an efficient outcome. Sometimes this efficiency is only a Kaldor-Hicks one. In other cases the efficient-outcome is not guaranteed but depends on the willingness of both concerned parties to negotiate and to share the gains of exchange. Compared to the first institutional arrangement the chances for an efficient outcome are much larger with co-ownership and proportional cost-distribution.

The court however cannot impose a general and mandatory regime of co-ownership. This is a prerogative of the legislator. As a consequence the judge has to attempt to mimic in his decision the efficient outcome of a negotiation between parties not hampered by transaction costs and strategic behaviour problems. De Geest (De Geest 1992: 309–310) points to the costs of such a substitution of a party's decision by a judicial decision. Courts may lack the necessary information about costs and benefits of the concerned measures, as they do not live in the house. For conservation costs this informational inferiority of the judge is less acute because conservation is a necessary matter for the basic quality of living in the house, so that we can assume that the parties would agree with these measures.

The first decision on the injunctive order by the county court is certainly efficient. It allows the party, which has the highest willingness and capacity to pay to take the most urgent measures. As also the other party will largely benefit from this measure, we may assume that parties not hampered by transaction costs and not tempted by strategic behaviour would have agreed.

The second decision by the court of appeal about the 50/50 sharing of the costs can be criticized from a legal-economic point of view. The 50/50 distribution is of course an easy solution but not therefore the most correct one. A more accurate assessment on the respective values of both apartments would have allowed also a more correct apportioning of the costs.

Finally, the court of appeal rejected the means-based apportioning as was decided by the county court. It is very unlikely that co-owners would distribute costs in the apartment building according to the means of the inhabitants. Although many people are ready to redistribute voluntarily parts of their revenue and fortune, they certainly would not like this to do on a random base such as inhabiting the same apartment. In so far as efficiency, understood as the assumed preferences of the parties, is the norm, a means based apportioning has to be rejected. Of course one can suggest that the court can apply a means based test in order to preserve distributive justice in society. From a legal economic point of view also this would be inefficient. The general order of private law is not adequate in order to organize distributive justice, as judges do not control the agenda of the cases, submitted to them.[13] Distributive oriented case law would by this always result in random distribution. At the contrary, political power has agenda control and can set up well-purposed mass-distribution schemes such as through welfare, social security, social housing programs, taxation and so forth.

E **Economic evaluation of the decision.** The decision of the county court to allow an injunctive order and the decision of the court of appeal to apportion the costs among the parties can be sustained from a legal economic viewpoint. The cost-sharing of 50/50 is however too rough and could have been more accurate through a minimal but effective value-assessment of the apartments. Even when the final decisions reflect more or less sound economic intuition, the considerations of the court do not. The court attempts to base the liabilities of the parties on the case law of private nuisance and landowners' liability. This leads to very unclear criteria with no convincing logical connection to the final decisions.

### *2.* R (on the application of Beresford) v. Sunderland City Council; *Court of Appeal Civil Division [2001] EWCA Civ 1218 All ER, 870*

A **Facts and legal sources.** The case concerns the use rights on an open space of land, close to the centre of the town of Washington, one of the towns of the Sunderland metropolitan area. The land, known in the town as the Sports Arena, is situated between the urban centre and a larger park area, the Princess Anne Park. In 1973 the area was included in the New Town Plan as parkland/open space/major playing field. The city council placed banks on the north, west and south side of the area, enough for 1,100 people to be seated and a non-turf wicket for cricket. Throughout a period of more than twenty years the grass was kept cut in the area by the owner, the Washington Development Corp (WDC). In a Board Paper of the WDC, drafted in 1977, it is stated that during the interim period, i.e. before a sport complex could be provided, the area could be used for recreational sporting use and other activities such as jazz band parades, displays and sporting events. After a transfer to the Commission for the New Towns and a transfer back to the City Council, a planning permission was granted on 19 November 1999 for the

13 This is, according to Richard Posner, one of the reasons why common law judges tend to be efficient in their decisions. Since they have not, as politicians do, the power to organize massive redistribution they have to earn social respect through making law more efficient (Posner 1983)

erection of a college of further education. On 18 November 1999 the appellant, Mrs. Pamela Beresford, together with three other local residents, submitted an application for the area to be registered as a town green according to the Commons Registration Act of 1965. The concerned commission of the city refused the application on the ground that the use which had been made by the inhabitants during twenty years was not 'as of right' but was based on an implied permission by the owner to use the land. This implied permission was sufficient to defeat the claim that there had been a use 'as of right'. The appellant challenged that decision by judicial review.

As a legal source there is in the first place the Commons Registration Act of 1965. According to this act citizens can apply for the Registration of land as a Commons or as Town and Village Green. Such a registration is possible when citizens used the land 'as of right' for sports and pastimes for not less than twenty years.

Concerning the question whether an implied permission by the owner can defeat a claim of use 'as of right' case law on the interpretation of the Prescription Act of 1832 is relevant, such as *Ex P Sunningwell Parish Council [1999] 3 All ER 385* and *Gardner v. Hodgson's Kingston Brewery Co. Ltd [1903] AC 229*.

B **Claims and defences.** The claimant, Mrs. Pamela Beresford challenges through judicial review the refusal of the licensing committee to register the concerned land as commons. She considers that the use, the public made of the area 'Sports Arena', was 'as of right' according to the Prescription Act of 1832. The 'as of right' use can only be defeated by an explicit permission, which is lacking here. The decision of the licensing committee was legally flawed because it advanced irrelevant considerations such as the consideration that the site was publicly owned and that it was adjacent to Princess Anne Park.

The defendant, the Sunderland City Council, wants the decision of the committee to be maintained and considers that an implied permission is first, sufficient, and is second, clearly present as it appears in many acts of the city, the public owner

C **Sentence and considerations.** The court dismisses the appeal by which the committee's decision is maintained. Based on the mentioned case law on the meaning and application of the Prescription Act the court argues that a prescription through a twenty years' use can only be established when *'nec vi, nec clam, nec precario'* (not through violence, theft or on the base of consent). The fact that the consent is not explicitly made in a special act is not relevant. Through its provisional investments and maintenance (seating, cricket, grass cutting, etc.) the owner clearly did not acquiesce in the use made by the public, but gave it a permission to enjoy the area during the interim period, before making its planned definite investments. The court also denies that the consideration of the committee, i.e. that the area was publicly owned, was irrelevant. The court argues that there is a link between the public character of the use and the public quality of the owner. Because the owner is a public authority he has the competence and the task to open the area for the public. The fact that the other consideration was indeed irrelevant does not affect the legality of the decision of the committee.

D **Economic analysis.** In this case the decision of the court will affect the allocation of the land, known here as Sports Arena: either the land will become a commons for the inhabitants or it will be used for the erection of a college for educational purposes, such as planned by the City authorities. From a general economic point of view efficient allocation is best guaranteed by a market process. Parties bid up with prices and the asset is allocated to the highest bidder. The highest bidder is the agent expecting the highest utility of the asset. This market process may, however, eventually fail for land, which is, technically or socially seen, fit for an open and common use by the public (e.g. through its location, the (low) quality of its soil, historic use by the public). As the commons is open for the general public, free riders' attitudes may appear when the land is offered for sale (e.g. in an auction organized by the city authorities). A substantial part of the citizens-future users may bet on the willingness of the others to pay and enjoy later a free ride. By this the bid for public use may fall short and the land could be allocated for another use, a use in which all gains can be internalized by the bidder-future user. Making abstraction from the free riders' problem, it could be that the total willingness to pay for the common use is higher than that for all competing uses, but this willingness to pay does not materialize into an effective payment precisely due to the mentioned problem.

This potential market failure may explain, ergo justify, why other procedures are provided in the law to allocate land for common use. One of them is Section 22(1) in the Commons Registration Act of 1965 providing that a common use 'as of right' for not less than twenty years can result in a registration as a commons. This type of acquisition may be interpreted as a proxy for a market process. The continuing and uninterrupted practice of use by a large group during a long period signals a strong use value among the general public. The fact that the real owner of the concerned land does not react to that practice and acquiesces in it signals at the contrary a low valuation from his side. From a legal economic point of view the optimal length of the prescription period is determined by several costs variables: the longer the prescription period the higher the costs of uncertainty, the costs of inefficient investment and the costs of preserving evidence; the shorter the prescription period the higher the protection costs for the owner (Depoorter 2010: 187). The length should be at that point where the sum of these costs is the lowest. It is difficult to find out whether the twenty years' period, provided by Section 22(1) Commons Registration Act is the efficient one, as this would require complicate assessments of the mentioned costs. It is however more likely that the period is rather too long than too short from a cost perspective. Prescription periods are often fixed in older legislation, such as for instance the Code Civil in France (1804) and the Prescription Act of 1832 in England and Wales. In the age of these laws means of communication were much less developed than now. As a consequence it was more difficult for an owner to check whether his land was taken into adverse possession. By fixing the period rather short protection costs would have been tremendously high. This all has changed. It is much easier for an owner to check whether somebody uses his land adversely and to stop this possession. As a consequence much shorter prescription periods are probably more advisable.

Case law also provides that consent by the owner vitiates the prescription and defeats the use 'as of right'. A similar rule holds in civil law: in cases of 'detention', for instance, a lord-tenant-relationship, prescriptive acquisition is impossible. Also this can be sustained from a legal economic point of view. If, *a contrario*, prescription was possible by a contracting party such as a tenant or a permitted user, contracts with terms longer than the prescription period would become impossible as the owner would lose his property or other interests with the elapse of that period. By this many contracts, which could be to the mutual benefit of both concerned parties, would be driven out of economic interaction.

A last question discussed by the court concerns the form of the permission, which defeats use 'as of right': should the permission be explicit or could it be derived implicitly from acts of the owner. From a legal economic point of view it is sufficient that the signalling of the will of the concerned party is beyond any doubt. It has to be clear that the parties are in a consensual relationship, in this case one based on a unilateral permission, because this signals at its turn the mutually beneficial character, for the public owner on one side, for the practicing public on the other side. Requiring an explicit permission, for instance by written acts and deeds, is not necessary and increases transaction costs. By deciding in favour of an implicit permission the court avoids wasteful transaction costs in future similar cases.

E **Economic evaluation of the decision.** From a legal-economic point of view the decisions reached by the court can be sustained. The rule that a permission defeats 'as of right' prescription reflects economic common sense. The opinion that permission does not need to be explicit saves transaction costs in society. The considerations, which are on the base of these decisions, would however be different in legal economics. Whereas the court develops mainly arguments of authority (case law and legislation) legal economics would rather advance substantial economic reasons.

### 3. *Sentence Arbitrale 23 octobre 1986 (Arbitral Decision 23 October 1986), Revue du Notariat Belge, 1988, 349–356*

A **Facts and Legal Sources** In 1966 an apartment building of five storeys with twenty three apartments was erected in Etterbeek-Brussels. On 26 December the agreement (Basic Act according to Belgian law) between the owners of apartments in the building was signed. Garage boxes are provided in the basement of the building. The basement is partially overarched by the building itself, partially by terraces and a garden, stretching in front of the building.

Since ten years water infiltration occurs in some of the garages and the open spaces used for turning the cars. An expert report states that the porosity of the concrete pavement in top of the basement is causal to the water infiltration. The claimants, co-owners also owning a garage box, filed suit for the Brussels first instance court against the architect and the construction firm for damages on the base of the ten-years-liability for architects and constructors. They also claim that the defendants, co-owners not owning a garage box, have to contribute to the repair and maintenance costs of the roof of the garage because this part is common and consequently all co-owners have to contribute. The co-ownership agreement provided that litigation about the terms and the execution of the agreement has to be submitted to arbitration. An arbitration agreement was drafted and signed on 8 October 1985.

The main legal source here is the agreement between the co-owners, drafted in a notarial deed, the Basic Act, according to art. 577 bis of the Belgian Code. Such a Basic Code is more or less the constitution of the apartment building and the relationships between the co-owners. The Basic Act provides the list of the common parts, the regulation of the use of these parts, the procedures and the majorities to decide about the maintenance and repairs of the common parts and the sharing of the costs.

Article 1 of the agreement of this building provides that changes in the real status of the building have to be decided by unanimity among the co-owners. Article 7 lists the common parts (the land on which the building stands, the foundations, the walls of the facades, the fences, the roof, the pipes for water and gas provision, the basement, the central heating installations, the sewerage, the garbage rooms, etc.). Additional to this list article 7 states that in general all parts not affected by exclusive private use are assumed to be common.

B **Claims and defences.** The claimants, namely, the co-owners also owning garages, demand that the co-owners not owning garages also contribute to the repairs of the roof of the garage. According to them the co-ownership agreement provides that the roof of the garage forms an integral part with the rest of the building and is by consequence common to all owners. The defendants reply that the roof of the garage is exclusively servient to the garage owners. As a consequence only the garages owners should pay for the repairs and maintenance of the roof. They also mention that a separate account is already provided for the costs, exclusively related to the maintenance of the garages. These costs are borne only by the owners of these boxes.

C **Sentence and considerations.** The arbiter decides that the roof of the basement is an integral part of the building and is consequently common to all co-owners. Also the co-owners, not owning a garage box, will have to contribute to the repairs. The decision is based on the agreement. This agreement provides that parts which are not affected by exclusive private use are considered to be common. This is the case for the roof of the basement. The consideration of the defendants that the building should be conceived as composed by two blocks, one for habitation and one for garages and that the common parts in the second block are only common to garage owners, does not find any support in the agreement. The arbiter is also not convinced by defendants' consideration of the separate account. Such a specific arrangement does not change the real status of the parts of the building and the ensuing distribution of the costs.

**D** **Economic analysis.** Making abstraction from the provisions of the co-ownership agreement, economic rationality suggests that agents, enjoying benefits of a service, should also cater for the costs of it. This benefit-cost link stimulates agents to use resources efficiently. When benefits of use are linked with the cost of use, agents will only use up to that level where the marginal costs of use become equal to the marginal benefits. When this link is failing users are able to externalise the costs of their use to other agents, which stimulates inefficient levels of use. Such externalization can be eliminated or limited through negotiation and agreements, but this latter generate transaction costs, which may be prohibitive for an efficiency enhancing agreement.

Applying this economic rationality principle to this case would imply that garage owners would have to cater for all the costs which are exclusively linked to the use of the garages while co-owners non-owning a garage box would be exempted from these costs. Otherwise garage box owners/users would be tempted to make unnecessary costs because these are shifted partially to the non-owners and non-users of the garage boxes.

Before checking whether this principle was applied correctly in this case, a more general question should however be raised, that is, which institutional settings are conducive to the promotion of the mentioned economic rationality. In the case of co-ownership relationship one has the choice between either endogenously generated ex ante arrangements or exogenously imposed ex post-interventions. In the first case one relies on the supposed economic rationality of the co-owners, who will anticipate the problems by including benefit-cost linking devices in their arrangements. In the second case such reliance is (totally or partially) absent and reliance is put in external authorities, such as the court, which is supposed to correct failures in the arrangements and to impose ex post economic rationality inducing solutions.

In the case under discussion, the arbiter opted for the first solution by relying entirely on the terms of the agreement. Although the decision of the arbiter was based on a strict legal principle, i.e. respecting the will of the contracting parties, there are also economic considerations in support of this decision. As mentioned earlier (see earlier, this chapter, 9. Common Property: freedom to pool, freedom of exit) the freedom to pool properties in a commons and to determine the rules of the commons finds support in the Hayekian economic theory of dispersed knowledge. Freedom to pool allows the individual parties to use their own concrete knowledge to find out that commons' arrangement which will suit their aims and interests the best. To be efficient, ex post interventions by the judge involve high information costs. Moreover, the possibility of such interventions may lead to strategic behaviour of the parties and foster instability in the relationships among the co-owners. Such ex post interventions are only justifiable in exceptional circumstances such as apparent gaps in the agreement, problems of interpretation, fraud in contracting.

A closer look to the provisions in the agreement confirms the economic viability of the choice of the arbiter.

First, the existence of a separate account for the garage box owners suggests that the co-owners were well aware of the benefit-cost link for these owners. Although the details about the costs covered in this account are not known, one can suppose that the garage box owners were obliged to pay for those costs, which were exclusively linked to the use of these boxes.

Second, the roof of the basement and the garden above it, are not exclusively useful for the users of the garage boxers. The garden embellishes the building as a whole while the repair of the roof of the basement increases the value of the building as a whole. The increase of the value of the whole building benefits all the owners of an apartment included also the owners not owning a garage box, because all owners also own a share in the common parts of the building. By increasing the value of these common parts they also increase the market value of their private property for their private property includes their private apartment plus their share in the common parts. Potential purchasers of apartment not only look to the state of the private apartment but also to that of the common parts.

The arrangement among the co-owners seems to reflect basic economic rationality and constitutes an empirical-casuistic proof of the economic viability of the freedom to pool-principle.

E **Economic evaluation of the decision.** The arbiter strictly followed the contractual provisions in the co-owners' arrangement. Because the following of such arrangements in most circumstances is economically viable, the decision of the arbiter is also. Some more explicit awareness about the economic rationality of principles such a freedom of contract and freedom to pool, would however strengthen the respect for these principles in case law and prevent courts to intervene too frivolously into the parties' arrangements.

### *4.* **Matter of Levandusky v. One Fifth Ave.** ***Apt. Corp.; Court of Appeals of New York, April 5, 1990; www.courts.state.ny.us/reporter/archives/levandusky_one.htm***

A **Facts and legal sources.** The plaintiff Ronald Levandusky is an owner-tenant of an apartment in a residence called One Fifth Avenue NYC. In 1987 he wanted to enlarge his kitchen area by realigning the steam riser of the kitchen. In the proprietary lease of Levandusky it is stated that there will be no alteration to the water, gas or steam risers or pipers without prior consent of the Board of the Residence Corporation. On the plan of the works in the apartment, submitted to the Board, no change on the steam riser is shown. In a meeting in March 1988 the Board approves the submitted plan. In the late spring of 1988 Levandusky tells an agent of the Board about his plan to realign the steam riser. This agent informs the Board. In a report drafted by an engineer-expert it is mentioned that the relocation of the steam riser is feasible but that this involves a risk of causing problems to the old piping system. In June 1988 the Board decides that no relocation of the steam riser is permitted. In a second meeting the Board also votes to deny a modified plan by Levandusky. Despite these decisions Levandusky hires a constructor to sever and to jog the steam riser. In May 1988 the Board orders Levandusky to stop the works. Levandusky then commenced proceeding on article 78 of the *Civil Practice and Law Rules of New York* asking to annul the order. The Supreme Court first grants the petition of Levandusky on the ground that the jogged pipe did not cause any damage and considers the order of the Board as arbitrary and capricious. On reargument, the Court withdrew its decision, dismissed the claim of Levandusky and ordered him to restore the riser in its original position. According to the Supreme Court the standard of the business judgment rule precluded any revision of the Boards' decision. Levandusky appealed against this decision. The Appellate Division was divided on the issue. The majority restored the original decision in favour of Levandusky while the minority considered the Boards' decision to be within the scope of the business judgment rule.

The legal basis of Levandusky's claim is art. 78 of the *Civil Practice Laws and Rules of the state of New York.* This article provides relief against a body or officer (1) for failing to perform a duty enjoined upon it by law, (2) for proceeding without or in excess of jurisdiction and (3) for making a determination which was in violation of lawful procedure, affected by an error of law or was arbitrary and capricious or an abuse of discretion. The expression 'body or officer' has a wide meaning: it includes also boards of administration of private companies and, as is the case here, board of a condominium or cooperative corporation.

Important case law refers to the standard of judicial review concerning decisions of boards of corporate bodies. Case law is however quite divided on this issue. The business judgment rule, which leaves a wide discretion to the deciding bodies is endorsed by *Auerbach v. Bennett, 47 NY2d 619,629* and other concurring cases. The reasonableness test, giving a wider scope of review to the court, is endorsed by *Amoruso v. Board of Managers, 38 AD2d 845* and other concurring cases.

B **Claims and defences.** Levandusky asks the maintenance of the annulation of the order to stop works, as was decided by the Appellate Division. The board decision was unjustified because the works apparently caused no harm to anyone. The Board at the contrary asks the confirmation of its order to stop as was decided by the Supreme Court. According to the Board their decision is within the scope of their discretion and is, moreover, rational as it is based on an engineer-expert report.

C **Sentence and considerations.** The Court of Appeal dismisses the demand of Levandusky and reconfirms the order to stop the works, as decided by the Board and confirmed by the Supreme Court. In the opinion of Judge Kaye the decision finds its ground in the business judgment rule. According to this standard all decisions which are in furtherance of the purpose of the cooperative are beyond any judicial review. Courts have to respect the autonomy of these governing bodies for they are close to the problems, have most information on it and are consequently best placed to take the right decisions. In the opinion of Judge Titone however not all decisions of a board should be matched by the same standard. As far as mere internal business decisions are concerned, the standard of the business judgment rule is appropriate. When however questions concerning the application of legal rules and the rights of the individual tenants are concerned the more restrictive rule of art. 78 of CPLR should be applied. The court has to check whether the decision was not arbitrary or capricious. According to Judge Titone this latter was not the case so that his final decision is concurrent with the one of Judge Kaye.

D **Economic analysis.** From a legal-economic point of view the efficiency problem appears in this case on a double level. The first level is a level of decision: was the decision of the Board to deny to Levandusky the right to change the position of the steam riser efficient or not. The second level is a level of institutions: is it efficient to allow external authorities such as the court to review and eventually change the decision of the board or should we leave this entirely to the discretion of the Board?

Concerning efficiency on the first level, it appears from the report of the engineer-expert that the change of the location of the steam riser may affect the rest of the pipe system. In economic terms this action will have negative side-effects to the other owners-leaseholders in the building. The action may thus be inefficient, i.e. when the costs imposed by this action to the other owners-leaseholders are higher than the benefits of it for Levandusky. It might be for instance possible that the nuisances caused through the pipe-system have a negative impact on the value of the other apartments while this negative impact is not compensated by the increase of value on the apartment of Levandusky.

Of course, an inefficient decision by the Board can be corrected by a Coasean market process. Suppose that the Board denies the concerned action to Levandusky and suppose that the benefits of the action for Levandusky are significantly higher than the costs for the other owners. In this case Levandusky will make an offer to 'buy' the permission from the other owners. As the willingness to pay is higher than the willingness to sell, a deal will be made and Levandusky will get his permit, which is the efficient outcome. Suppose at the contrary that the costs of the other owners are significantly higher than the benefits for Levandusky. In this case the latter won't get the permission because the willingness to pay is lower than the willingness to sell, which is again the efficient outcome. Suppose that the Board grants Levandusky the right to carry out the concerned action and that the costs for the other owners are significantly higher than the benefits for Levandusky. In this case the other owners will make an offer to Levandusky to abandon his plans. A deal will be struck, as the willingness to pay is higher than the willingness to sell, again an efficient outcome. When at the contrary the benefits are higher than the costs Levandusky will not abandon his plans and carry out his plans, which is again an efficient outcome. The former analysis illustrates Coase's theorem: at the condition that transaction costs are not prohibitive, it does not matter to whom the initial rights are allocated, and the outcome will be always efficient.

The initial rights have, however to be allocated, in this case by the Board as the executive body of the community of co-owners of the residence. Deals among the co-owners involve evidently transaction costs. The participants in the deal have to assess their costs and benefits (information costs), the deal has to be negotiated (negotiation costs); there is the probability that the deal is not respected which may lead to further legal action, ergo litigation costs. There might be, moreover, additional obstacles such as free riders' attitudes when the co-owners have to 'buy' away the concerned action. There might be problems of anti-commons when Levandusky has to buy the permission from the other owners. The initial allocation, to be made by the Board, will enhance efficiency when the transaction costs for an eventual correcting shift of the right, are the lowest. To allocate the right to the co-owners and not to Levandusky is probably the most efficient decision from a Coasean point of view. The risk of free ridership, when a large community of co-owners have to coordinate and to pool an amount to buy away an initially granted permission to Levandusky, is probably higher than the risk of anti-commons problems when Levandusky has to acquire the permission from the other co-owners. Whether the Board had intuitively this Coasean reasoning in mind when taking the decision, is difficult to know. From what is known from the case, the decision of the Board seems to match the requirements of economic efficiency.

Concerning efficiency on the institutional level, one has to refer, as in the former case, to the problem of the use of dispersed knowledge, as analysed by Friedrich von Hayek. As it is difficult to aggregate perfectly dispersed knowledge, it is efficient to give decision power to the level which is the closest to the problem area. In this case this is the Board. In the analysis about the efficiency of the Boards' decision the assessment of the risks of free ridership and anti-commons' problems are crucial. Such an assessment is only possible by an instance who knows well the preferences and the character of the involved players. There is no doubt that the Board has in this respect a huge advantage to the court.

The business judgement rule, endorsed by substantial case law and also adopted in this case, seems to reflect this Hayekian concern. Courts should only meddle in Boards' decisions when their decisions are clearly illegal, fraudulent or obviously 'capricious or astucious'. For all these cases, the burden of proof is on the party, acting against a Board's decision. For normal managements' decisions the court should not substitute itself to the Board. When one adopts on the other hand 'reasonabless' as a review standard, the risk is high that the court will substitute its view on what is reasonable to that of the Board.

E **Economic evaluation of the decision.** The decision of the court to follow the decision of the Board is certainly sustainable from a legal-economic perspective. The business judgment rule reflects a deep economic concern, namely, to maximize the use of knowledge, present into society. By this, courts have to focus on what they are best able to do: applying the laws and regulations, avoid fraudulent decision-making and decisions which favour clearly one party and are in conflict with the fiduciary duty put on a body like the Board. The court should avoid however to play manager of the residence because for this it is ill equipped.

## *5.* Indian Oil Corp Ltd v. Greenstone Shipping. *The Ypatianna; Queen's Bench Division (Commercial Court, 18 March 1987; [1987] 3 All ER QBD, 893*

A **Facts and legal sources.** On 29 November 1980, the Indian Oil Corp Ltd chartered the vessel 'The Ypatianna' for a carriage of 75,000 tons of crude oil from the Russian port Novorossiysk to the Indian port of Madras. The owner of the vessel is Greenstone Shipping SA, operating under the law of Panama. At the moment of the loading in Russia the vessel was carrying a residue of crude oil from previous voyages to Iran and Indonesia.

According to the bill of lading, dated 26 December 1980, 69,276 metric tons of Soviet export blend had been shipped in Novorossiysk.

The bill of lading further indicates that at the moment of loading:

- The cargo tanks contained 13,262 barrels (5,528 from Iran and 7,734 from Indonesia) including also ballast water
- The deep tanks contained 2,371 barrels

The total loading in Russia amounted to 508,000 barrels. The total load of the ship was about 523,000 barrels.

In Madras 503,896 barrels of crude oil were unloaded plus 6,229 barrels of water.

9,545 barrels remained within the ship.

The claimants (i.e. the receivers – The Indian Oil Corp Ltd) filed a claim to arbitration. An arbitration clause was provided in the bill of lading. The claimants introduced

(1) A smaller claim for the shortage of delivery in Madras, revealed by comparing the bill of lading (507,977 barrels) and the actual discharge (503,896 barrels). The arbitrators allowed this claim but deduced from the total of the barrels a tolerance of 0.55 percent and awarded damages for only 1,287 barrels.
(2) A larger claim for the remaining crude oil in the vessel (9,545 barrels). The claimants consider this residue as their property as it was mixed with 'their' oil and claim an amount of US$388,000 in damages.

The legal sources concerning the mixture of goods are mainly found in case law. The Institutes of Justinian in Roman law state that a mixture of goods does not alter the initial property rights and that each owner has an '*actio in rem*' to retake his part from the mixture (Just Inst II, 1, 28). According to the main trend in English case law the whole of the mixture should be awarded to the innocent party, which was the victim of a mixture, originating from fraud or negligence by the other party. In cases of accidental and inseparable mixture however the whole should be split according to the proportion of the initial inputs: *Lupton v. White (1808 15 Ves 432 [1803–13] All ER* 356), Blackstone's Commentaries on this case (2 Bl Com, 17th edn,1830,404–405), *Cock v. Addison* (1869) LR 7 Eq 466, *Jones v. De Merchant* (1916) 28 DLR 561.

B **Claims and defences.** The receivers (Indian Oil Corporation) appeal against the decision of the arbitrators. They claim that all crude oil, remaining in the vessel after the discharge in Madras (9,545 barrels), became their property through the mixing with 'their' oil, charged in Russia. They do not however claim a physical restitution of this oil, but a compensation for it, an amount of US$388,000. According to the receivers the mixing was due to the negligence of the defendants (the Greenstone Shipping Company), which charged the Russian oil on top of the residue of oil from former voyages. The receivers also advance that there was no consent at all from their side to the mixing of the oil. As a result the rule applies that the innocent party in case of mixture by negligence should become owner of the whole. The defendants argue that the loading on top is a custom in the practice of oil carriage. Consequently there is no negligence on their behalf and the total mix of the oil should be divided among the two parties according to the proportion of their input. As a consequence, the receivers are entitled to the quantity they loaded in Russia, while they remain entitled to the residue in the ship. Therefore the claim for compensation fails.

C **Sentence and considerations.** The court dismisses the appeal. According to older English case law (see before under A.) the innocent party, which became the victim of a fraudulent or negligent mixing of its goods with the goods of the guilty party, should become entitled to the whole. This way of punishing the guilty party was considered as an effective preventive means to avoid involuntary mixing of goods. This rule dates however from times of illiterate people and ineffective means of providing evidence. The legal consequence of awarding the whole to the innocent party could constitute a gross injustice. Suppose the input in the total mix from the innocent party is only 10 percent. Applying the mentioned rule would imply that the guilty loses 90 percent of the total mix, which could mean a sanction in overkill. The court does not feel itself bound by this old fashion rule. Although it is clear that the parties did not consent explicitly to the mixing, the practice of loading on top may be a part of the customs in the oil transportation sector. As a consequence it is not established that the defendants acted in this through negligence. The larger claim cannot be awarded and the court confirms the decision of the arbitrators, who only awarded the smaller claim.

D **Economic analysis.** By the mixing of two inseparable substances, owned by two different agents, a situation of an involuntary commons is established. Without any possibility of any exogenous enforceable intervention, the parties in the commons have to solve their eventual problems through negotiation. One party may prefer to divide the mixed whole, while the other party does not. The parties may agree on the division but do not agree on the proportion to which they are entitled. As parties are clearly involved in a bilateral monopoly situation, strategic behavior attitudes may block any solution so that the parties are locked into a suboptimal situation. From a legal-economic point of view the possibility of an intervention by an outsider, such as a court, in order to unlock such a situation is consequently justified.

In order to discuss the most efficient measures, courts may eventually take, it is crucial to distinguish between (1) voluntary mixing, (2) mixing by accident and (3) mixing resulting from fraud or negligence.

In the first case the mixing of substances is the result of consent of the two concerned owners and should be economically efficient as it is considered mutually beneficial. Valuations may change, however, and both parties or one party may prefer to end the commons situation and split the whole. As both parties are in a bilateral monopoly position and strategic behavior may occur, a decision from the court may be necessary in order to determine how and when to split and which proportions will accrue to each party. The most efficient rule seems to be the split proportional to the input even when this could lead to a loss for one party and a gain for the other due to the change in quality of the substances. The absence of a consensual arrangement about an eventual split allows the assumption that both accepted the risk of a change of quality as a result of the mixing. Mere proportionality is consequently the closest proxy for a consensual arrangement. In addition this rule saves on costs of administration of justice, as judges do not have to assess the changes in quality of the substances.

In the second case the mixing happened as a result of an event beyond the will of the concerned owners ('by an Act of God'). Otherwise than in the former case the parties did not assume the risk of mixing but are involuntarily submitted to it. When substances differ significantly in quality the court should take this into account and compensate the losing party by either deviating from the proportion of the input or by awarding a monetary compensation.

In the third case the mixing is the result of harmful behavior by one of the owners. Through fraud the other party is seduced to do or to allow things it wouldn't do or allow when honestly informed. In the case of mixing by negligence the guilty party acted without due care or to put it in economic terms, on a prevention level which was lower than the expected accident costs. In both cases the outcome is inefficient.

Concerning harmful acts the focus of legal economics is more directed on ex ante prevention than on ex post compensation. The Justice Learned Hand formula for instance (Landes and Posner 1987) holds that in cases of negligence damages should be awarded to the victim when the prevention costs, spent by the injurer are inferior to the expected accident costs (i.e. the costs of damage multiplied with the probability of the accident). Courts should follow this formula in order to stimulate an optimal prevention level in society. Decisions of the court in cases of fraudulent or negligent mixing should therefore be directed at discouraging such acts of mixing. Following the economic theory of crime and punishment, developed by Gary Becker (Becker 1968), potential candidates for fraudulent or negligent mixing will be deterred from such acts when the costs of their harmful acts exceed the benefits of it. Assuming risk neutrality the costs of crime consist of the costs of a conviction (fine, imprisonment, damages, etc.) multiplied by the apprehension rate for this kind of acts. As these harmful acts have a victim and as the injurer is mostly known, i.e. the person who mixed the substances, the apprehension rate will be rather high. As a consequence there is no need to increase the compensation to the innocent party with substantial punitive damages or with criminal sanctions. A full compensation of the innocent party (*restitutio ad integrum*), eventually increased with some punitive damages must be sufficient to deter such acts.

Consequently, in cases where the proportion of the input is known the court should award to the innocent party the quantity of its input, eventually increased with a compensation for quality loss, and some punitive damages. In cases where the proportion of the input is not known, the court should award to both parties 50 percent of the total, again added eventually with compensation to the innocent party for quality loss and some punitive damages. Under total ignorance about the proportions of the input a 50/50 percent split is the closest proxy to the real one when taking into account all possible distributions. When the disappearance of all evidence about the proportions of the input is the result of a fraudulent act the punitive damages have to be increased substantially in order to deter such frauds in the future.

The prevailing rule in English case law providing that the innocent party is awarded the whole mixture in case of fraudulent or negligent behavior by the other party is not sustainable from a legal economic viewpoint. This rule makes the legal consequence of fraud or negligence dependent on an exogenous given, i.e. the proportion of the input. When the input of the guilty party was very minimal, let us say, 10 percent, then the sanction for its fraud or negligent is light, probably too light from an economic 'Beckerian' perspective. When the input of the guilty party was very high, let us say 90 percent, then the sanction may be exaggerated. Such sanctions are may be effective from a preventive perspective, but may undermine the sense of justice and the popular support for the justice system. Moreover such an exaggerated sanction implies also overkill in compensation for the innocent party. This may trigger incentives of provocation. A party may provoke a mixture under such circumstances that it looks like fraudulent or negligent on behalf the other party in the hope to get a disproportional compensation.

In his opinion, Judge Staughton, labelled this rule as outdated and linked with circumstances from a remote past such as an illiterate population and primitive means of evidence. In such circumstances a brutal rule, such as this one, may be the best solution. In our times however, more and more precise evidence, especially written one, is available so that the responsibility of the parties in the fraudulent or negligent mix and the initial proportion can be better established. This allows also more fine-tuned sanctions such as the ones mentioned earlier. The opinion of Judge Staughton is similar to the analysis of Richard Posner (Posner 1983) on the evolution of tort law. The prevailing of strict liability in primitive societies can be explained, at least partly, by the enormous difficulties to provide evidence on possible negligent behavior of the parties (low density of population, absence of witnesses, no written evidence, no recording of acts, etc.).

E **Economic evaluation of the decision** The decision of the court to dismiss the appeal against the decision of the arbitration committee can be sustained from a legal economic point of view. It is not proven that the defendants acted fraudulently or negligently as 'loading on the top' seems to be a general practice in the oil carriage business. As a result the rule in English case law about fraudulent of negligent mixing is not applicable in this case and awarding a compensation for the whole residue would not be justified. Also the opinion of Judge Staughton that the rule of English case law (100 percent to the innocent party) is obsolete and that even when there would have been fraud or negligence into play, the rule should not be applied, can be sustained from a legal economic point of view. The opinion of Judge Staughton was however incomplete as the opinion did not state what kind of rule should be in place of the older obsolete rule. In the former paragraph it is argued that rules and sanctions should have a sufficient preventive impact and that beyond a mere split according to the proportion of the inputs also punitive damages should be envisaged.

## Cases


*Abbahall Ltd v. Smee; Court of Appeal Civil Division, 5,12 December 2002; [2002] EWCA Civ 1831*

*Matter of Levandusky v. One Fifth Ave. Apt. Corp.; Court of Appeals of New York, April 5, 1990; www. courts.state.ny.us/reporter/ archives/levandusky_one.htm*

*Indian Oil Corp Ltd v. Greenstone Shipping. The Ypatianna; Queen's Bench Division (Commercial Court, 18 March 1987; [1987] 3 All ER QBD, 893*

*R (on the application of Beresford) v. Sunderland City Council; Court of Appeal Civil Division [2001] EWCA Civ 1218 All ER, 870*

*Sentence Arbitrale 23 octobre 1986 (Arbitral Decision 23 October 1986), Revue du Notariat Belge, 1988, 349–356*

## Bibliography

Acheson, J.E. (1979) 'Variations in Traditional Inshore Rights in Maine Lobstering Communities', in R. Anderson, ed. *North Atlantic Maritime Cultures*, de Gruyter, New York

Becker, Gary S. (1968) 'Crime and Punishment. An Economic Approach', *The Journal of Political Economy*, Vol. 76, 169

Boesen, Jannik, Birgit Storgard Madsen and Tony Moody (1977) *Ujamaa-Socialism from Above*, Scandinavian Institute of African Studies, Uppsala

Bouckaert, Boudewijn R.A. and Gerrit De Geest (1995) 'Private Takings, Private Taxes, Private Compulsory Services: The Economic Doctrine of Quasi-Contracts', *International Review of Law and Economics*, Vol. 15, 463

Buchanan, James M. and Georges Tullock (1962) *The Calculus of Consent: Logical Foundations of Constitutional Democracy*, The University of Michigan Press, Ann Arbor

Casari, Marco (2007) 'Emergence of Endogenous Legal Institutions: Property Rights and Community Governance in the Italian Alps', *Journal of Economic History*, Vol. 67, 191–226

Conquest, Robert (1986) *The Harvest of Sorrow: Soviet-Collectivisation and the Terror-Famine*, Oxford University Press, Oxford

De Geest, Gerrit (1992) 'The Provision of Public Goods in Apartment Buildings', *International Review of Law and Economics*, Vol. 12, 299–315

de Jasay, Anthony (1989) *Social Contract: Free Ride. A Study if the Public Goods Problem*, Oxford University Press, Oxford

Depoorter, Ben (2010) 'Adverse Possession', in Boudewijn Bouckaert, ed. *Property Law and Economics*, Edward Elgar, Cheltenham, 183–190

Ellickson, Robert C. (1993) 'Property in Land', *The Yale Law Journal*, Vol. 102, 1317–1398

Field, Barry C. (1985) 'The Optimal Commons', *American Journal of Agricultural Economics*, Vol. 67, no. 2, 364–367

Foldvary, Fred (1994) *Public Goods and Private Communities: The Market Provision of Social Services*, The Locke Institute, London

Hayek, Friedrich A. (1945) 'The Use of Knowledge in Society', *American Economic Review*, Vol. XXXV, no. 4, 519–530

Higgs, Robert (1996) 'Legally Induced Technical Regress in the Washington Salmon Fishery', in L.J. Alston, Thrainn Eggertson and Douglas North, eds. *Empirical Studies in Institutional Changes*, Cambridge University Press, New York

Jodha, N.S. (1985) 'Population growth and the decline of common property resources in Rajasthan, India', *Population and Development Review*, Vol. 11, no. 2, 247–264

Landes, William and Richard A. Posner (1987) *The Economic Structure of Tort Law*, Harvard University Press, Chicago

Mueller, Dennis C. (1989) *Public Choice II*, Cambridge University Press, Cambridge

Ostrom, Elinor (1990) *Governing the Commons: The Evolution of Institutions of Collective Action*, Cambridge University Press, Cambridge

Ostrom, Elinor (July 24, 2009) 'A General Framework for Analyzing Sustainability of Social-Ecological Systems, *Science*, Vol. 325, 419–422

Ostrom, Elinor and Charlotte Hess (2010) 'Private and Common Property Rights', in Boudewijn Bouckaert, ed. *Property Law and Economics: Encyclopedia of Law and Economics*, Edward Elgar, Cheltenham, Vol. 5

Posner, Richard (1983) *The Economics of Justice*, Harvard University Press, Cambridge, MA

Robert MCC Netting (1981) *Balancing on an Alp: Ecological Change and Continuity in a Swiss Mountain Community*, Cambridge University Press, New York

Smith, Henry (2000) 'Semi Common Property Rights and Scattering in the Open Fields', *Journal of Legal Studies*, Vol. 29, 131–169

Stahl-Role, Silke (March 2000) 'Transition on the Spot: Historicity, Social Structure, and Institutional Change', *Atlantic Economic Journal*, Vol. 28, no. 1, 25–36

Tairako, Tomonaga (2016) 'A Turning Point in Marx's Theory on Precapitalist Societies – Marx's Excerpt Notebooks on Maurer in Mega IV/18', *Hitotsubashi Journal of Social Studies*, Vol. 47, 1–10

Tracht, Marshall E. (2000) 'Co-Ownership and Condominium', in Boudewijn Bouckaert and Gerrit De Geest, eds. *Encyclopedia of Law and Economics Vol. II, Civil Law and Economics*, Edward Elgar, Cheltenham, 62–89

# 3 Nuisance

## 3.1 Nuisance in the economic theory of law

1 **Nuisance law: historical and comparative context.** All documented legal systems encompass rules and remedies dealing with interferences in the rights on land use, other than dispossession and physical invasion (trespass). In Roman law the '*actio negatoria*' was used as a remedy for such interferences. Originally the scope of this action concerned the denial of interfering activities for which a servitude was necessary, but as servitudes could be established for nearly all type of activities, the '*actio negatoria*' developed in practice as a remedy for enjoining all kind of interferences in the rights of the landowner (Van Es 2005: 15–90).

Also within the doctrine of **European continental law** the '*actio negatoria*' evolved from an '*actio de servituto*' to an '*actio de dominio*' (Van Es 2005: 93–139). This remedy was integrated in several civil codes on the European continent, although in very varying ways.

In the German BGB for instance the remedy (§1004 BGB) was considered as a proprietary one ('*rein dinglicher Anspruch*') and was for this reason separated from the tort law section in the BGB (§823 BGB), but in German case law often also damages were awarded instead of injunction ('*Beseitigung*') by which it comes close to tort remedies (Van Es 2005: 165; Ott and Schäfer 2008: 46–50).

In the Dutch Civil Code a specific nuisance remedy is provided but it is limited to the relationship between owners of neighbouring estates. Nuisances from other sources are qualified and treated as torts (Davids 1999: 18–20).

The French Civil Code, adopted in many countries, does not provide a specific rule or remedy for nuisances. In case law nuisance was however considered as a specific category of harm infliction, separate from tort and linked with art. 544 Civil Code, defining the scope of property. The remedy, connected with this article, involves a strict liability, but does not always provide for compensation of the damage. Only when the damage stretches beyond the threshold of 'normal disturbances of neighbourhood' it can be recovered by this remedy. When the plaintiff is however able to prove that negligence on behalf of the defendant was causal to the damage, the threshold of 'normal disturbances of neighbourhood' does not count (Sagaert 2014: 230–272).

Finally, in many continental European countries a nuisance can be qualified as an 'abuse of right', in which case the plaintiff has to show that the harmful activities of the defendant were, although within the limits of his rights, driven by an intent to harm the plaintiff or were without any benefit for the defendant (Sagaert 2014: 226–229).

English common law distinguishes between private and public nuisance. The first concerns interference within the rights of a specific land owner. The second harm to a wider category of the general public. Borrowing from the principle of Ulpian '*sic utere tuo ut alienum non laedas*' early English precedent law developed an action of strict liability for the land owner who suffered from a legal injury ('*iniuria*') from activities of neighbours. The William Aldred's case constituted a land mark decision in English nuisance law. In this case the availability of the remedial relief of nuisance was extended beyond the group of owners of a freehold estate. Additionally, this case also addressed the problem of the social utility of the activity as a possible defence against injunction (Smith 1995: 680–686). During the first half of the nineteenth century, nuisance was considered by American common law as a strict proprietary remedy always leading to an injunction. Later this strict position was abandoned by the introduction of the 'reasonableness'-criterion. The 'reasonableness'-test considered further elements such as the nature of the activity, the character of the neighbourhood, the 'hypersensitivity' of the plaintiff and the defendants' motive (Swanson and Kontoleon 2010: 162). The proprietary character of nuisance was further undermined by abandoning the strict link between nuisance and injunction and by allowing damages as a remedy. The landmark case in this respect is *Boomer v. Atlantic Cement Co.* in which injunctive relief was made conditional on the payment of damages by the victims. The court considered that the social benefits of operating the factory were too important to shut it unconditionally down. On the other side, the harm caused to the plaintiff, was not of the kind that a property owner should bear without compensation (Singer 2001: 107).

2 **Nuisance: Pigou and Coase.** Arthur Pigou and his school of welfare economics integrated the phenomenon of interferences into property rights within the framework of economic sciences under the notion of (negative) externalities. An agent, interfering into the property rights of another, imposes a social cost on him/her. By this a divergence between private and social net product will arise causing efficiency problems within the economy. To bridge this divergence Pigou advocated a policy of taxation in order to eliminate inefficient activity levels. In 1960 Ronald Coase published his essay 'The Problem of Social Costs' (Coase 1960) in which he discusses several nuisance cases. *Sturges v. Bridgman*, one of these cases, concerns a dispute between two neighbours, a physician and a confectioner. The physician had moved next door to the confectioner, who produced sweets for sale in his kitchen for many years. The physician constructed a small shed for the purpose of his

practice. The physician sought an injunction to stop the noise produced by the confectioner. The injunction was granted and the defence of 'coming to the nuisance' rejected. Classical lawyers would qualify this case as a unilateral intrusion by the confectioner into the legal domain of the physician, while Pigou would qualify this as a negative externality, a social cost unilaterally imposed on the physician. Not so Coase. According to him the problem here is not unilateral but reciprocal. The activity of the confectioner imposes a cost on the physician, but the fact that the physician moved close to the confectioner, thereby threatening the viability of his activity, imposes a cost on the confectioner too. As a result, the problem here does not concern a unilateral imposition of costs but the question which of the two conflicting uses is the most efficient: the one of the confectioner or the one of the physician. If there were no transaction costs, the problem would solve itself however, without any intervention of a third party (the court, a regulatory agency, etc.). Suppose that the profit of the confectioner's activity is 100, while that of the physician is 120; then the physician would pay between 100 and 120 to the confectioner to stop or to move. In the opposite case the confectioner would pay the physician to stop or to move. Transaction costs are however often prohibitively high to block such efficiency enhancing deals, which necessitates the intervention of courts and regulators to allocate resources efficiently. Transaction costs can be prohibitively high due to sheer numbers of involved parties, but also due to strategic behaviour such as free ridership and extortion attitudes in bilateral monopoly situations.

The contribution of Coase implies two remarkable shifts within the approach of nuisances. To start with the most acknowledged one: in contrast to Pigou, Coase perceives potential inefficiencies not in the occurrence of externalities as such, but in the occurrence of transactions cost, imposing effective barriers to negotiate away inefficient externalities. As a consequence, legal or regulatory intervention depends on the level of transaction costs, not on the occurrence of externalities.

The second shift, however less acknowledged, concerns the reframing of nuisance settings from a unilateral event to a reciprocal cost relationship. This reframing presupposes in fact a hypothetical elimination of the property borders between the involved parties and the approach of the concerned estates as one economic resource. To refer to *Sturges v. Bridgman*, abstraction is made of the legal borders between the estate of the physician and the one of the confectioner and both estates are hypothetically considered as one resource, about which the question which of the two incompatible uses, that is, observing patients or making candies, is the most efficient, must be solved. Such an approach runs obviously against the basic intuitions of classical lawyers, starting ex ante from the legitimacy of property borders and the ensuing framing of the situation as a unilateral infringement of a property right. Or, to qualify it in Pigouvian terms, as a unilateral externalization of costs. As we will discuss later, the approach of Coase marks a profound shift from an exclusion regime of nuisance to a governance regime of nuisance (see later in this chapter, the section on "Smith: exclusion and governance regimes").

3 **Calabresi and Melamed:** the nuisance is remedied either by injunctive relief or by awarding damages. From a strict proprietary logic injunctive relief should be the appropriate remedy, but this logic has been abandoned in case law in favour of a more eclectic approach in which the choice between injunction and damages has been made dependent on various social and economic considerations. In one of the most cited law and economics-articles 'Property Rules, Liability Rules and Inalienability: One View of the Cathedral' Calabresi and Melamed (Calabresi and Melamed 1972) elaborated an explanatory and normative theory on the choice between these remedies. They perceive in the law two thoroughly different ways to protect entitlements (by which they mean all kinds of legally protected interests). Entitlements can be protected by what they call a property rule. In this case nobody is allowed to use the protected resource without the consent of the entitled party. In case of violation of an entitlement protected by the property rule, the injurer can be submitted to various sanctions such as injunction, punitive damages and criminal sanctions. Entitlements can be protected only by what they call a liability rule. In this case the use of the protected resource is 'allowed', however under the condition the injurer compensates the entitled party for the damage. The choice legal systems make (or should make?) between these two remedies depends on cost considerations. Calabresi and Melamed perceive two cost categories, decisive for the remedial choice: transaction costs and the costs of administration of justice. When transaction costs are low resources will easily shift towards the most efficient user. In this case resources should be protected by the property rule. Take the case of goods for sale in well-organized markets. Due to competition and market prices consent is easy to obtain so there is no need to release the condition of consent by the entitled party. When transaction costs are high resources do not shift easily to the more efficient user. In this case it may be better to allow a more efficient user to use the good without the consent of the entitled party but require an ex post full compensation of that party. Take the case of an ambulance with a dying patient which can take a shortcut to the clinic by using a private way. It is utterly efficient to use that way but transaction costs to reach the owner may be prohibitive. In this case the liability rule should apply by allowing the ambulance to use the private way and to grant damages (if any) ex post to the owner. The costs of administration of justice concern mainly the difficulty to assess the damages 'correctly'. From an economic point of view damages are assessed correctly when 'the indifference principle' has been matched: the victim should not be able to choose between the lost good and the compensation because they are perfectly equal in value. Whether the indifference principle can be matched or approached depends on the type of damage. Rather easy for market goods, less easy for unique goods, difficult for physical harm, very difficult for lethal harm. As a consequence, difficult to assess resources are better protected by the property rule, easy to assess ones qualify better for protection by the liability rule.

As did Coase, also Calabresi and Melamed depart from the classical legal perception of property and the strict proprietarian character of the nuisance remedy. What they call 'property rule' has little to do with the traditional '*in rem*'- character of property rights, but is rather reduced to a protection modus of whatever entitlement, even entitlements which should be labelled as mere contractarian ones within the classical legal categorization (Merrill and Smith 2001: 381). Applied to nuisance cases the choice between injunctive relief and damages should depend on the two cost categories. As nuisance cases show often the frame of a bilateral monopoly, strategic behaviour will often preclude efficient bargaining. This points to the application of the liability rule and the awarding of damages as the sole remedy. Often however nuisance may affect typical sets of values, difficult to assess monetarily (silence, enjoyment of nature, environmental harmony). This points to the application of the property rule and injunction, for it allows the victims to assess for themselves the damage and the required compensation (Polinsky 1979: 40).

4 **Smith: exclusion and governance regimes.** The approaches of Coase and Calabresi and Melamed created a wide intellectual and terminological gap between classical lawyers and law and economics-scholars. Coase's framing of nuisance cases as reciprocal relationships and joint causation runs flatly against the age old legal perception of nuisance as a unilateral interference into somebody else's legal domain. The use of terms such as property rule and liability rule is so different from the classical legal one that it leads inevitably to a lot of misunderstanding between the two intellectual worlds. Smith bridges this gap by providing again economic legitimacy to the classical legal view of property as a specific 'in rem' right, opposed to contractual rights and other kinds of 'entitlements', and by developing a theory to explain why sometimes a mere proprietarian approach and sometimes a rather liability approach is followed in legal tradition and in case law (Smith 2004). Legal remedies to protect property rights can be ranged on a continuum between what Smith calls an exclusion regime and a governance regime. Under the exclusion regime property is regarded as a legal domain, protected against interferences from the rest of 'the world' ('erga omnes'). Legal disputes about interferences into property rights are treated on the base of the rough informational variable whether the interferer crossed the border of the legally protected domain of the right holder or not. No questions on the most efficient user or use should be raised. The exclusion regime relies in fact on a kind of delegation to the owner: it is up to him/her to decide about the most efficient use of the resources, falling within the confines of his domain. Outsiders are preliminarily disqualified as candidates for more efficient use, unless of course with the consent of the owner. The remedy of trespass clearly falls under this regime. In trespass cases the court investigates whether the defendant crossed the border or not and in case he did awards sanctions which can go far beyond damages as mere compensation. In *Jacque v. Steenberg Homes Inc.* the Wisconsin Supreme Court upheld a jury award of punitive damages

of $100,000 for a trespass case in which the jury had awarded nominal compensatory damages of only one dollar (Smith 2004: 983). In the same line Parchomovski and Stein advocate typical sanctions for trespass going far beyond mere compensatory damages such as a 'propertized' damage, by which the trespasser has to pay a compensation equal to the owner's pre-trespass asking price (Parchomovsky and Stein 2009: 22). Under a governance regime the central question is about the efficiency of incompatible use of one resource or within one resource area. The court does not raise the question whether a border has been crossed or not, but investigates in which way and by which remedy it will stimulate the most efficient use of the involved resources. It can for instance limit the remedy to mere damages with the expectation that only efficient uses will survive because only such activities realize a social benefit that is higher than its social cost. By imposing damage compensation only such activities will survive. Tort law cases clearly pertain to the governance regime. Either the court awards always damages when there is an interference (strict liability) knowing that the uses with a higher-than-its-social cost-value will continue, or the court can be more selective and only grant damages when the prevention costs of the interference were ex ante lower than the expected accidents costs (*Learned Hand* – negligence liability).

The legal remedy of nuisance is however more difficult to classify on the exclusion-governance continuum. Smith considers this remedy as a legal hybrid in which sometimes the exclusionary element dominates, sometimes the governance element. To explain the choice for one of the two regimes Smith relies on the notion of information costs as the main variable. In order to make plausible decisions on the use of resources courts may be confronted with high information costs. An exclusion regime relieves them of costly searches and balancing on the efficiency rates of the concerned uses. As a consequence it is plausible to depart from the assumption that in cases in which the result of efficiency balancing seems quite plausible ex ante, courts will relieve themselves from costly efficiency research and rely on the simple on/off approach proper to the exclusion regime. In cases where such plausibility is not at hand courts will rather apply the logic of a governance regime and proceed to efficiency balancing. Smith analyzes different trends in nuisance case law and observe a systemic compatibility with their main assumption.

In nuisance cases of substantial harm ('nuisance per se') courts consequently apply an exclusion logic because the nuisance is so harmful that it precludes multiple uses so that it makes no sense to engage in costly searches about the efficiency of incompatible uses.

Location and physical invasion remain decisive in case law to decide about the existence of a nuisance. Courts remain reluctant to recognize for instance aesthetic disturbances (e.g. ugly building) or moral disturbances (e.g. public nudity) as a nuisance because other than tangible harm, such disturbances are difficult to meter and involve huge information costs for the courts.

The neighbourhood test, requiring courts to look for the proper toleration-threshold in accordance with the neighbourhood context, seems to point rather into the direction of a governance regime. The neighbourhood-principle has however probably more to do with the element of mutual beneficial forbearance. In a residential neighbourhood families have a similar life cycle and produce similar types of disturbances during each phase (young children crying, older children playing loud music, teenagers with noisy motorcycles on the street, etc.) of their life cycle. If the phases of the life cycles of the families in the neighbourhood would be synchronic, no complaints about recurrent disturbances would go to court because each complaint would trigger a retaliating counter-complaint about a similar disturbance coming from the plaintiff. Complaints and counter-complaints would neutralize each other. By not suing for such nuisances the families would avoid the involved costs of administration of justice. In real life the phases of the different life cycles of families in residential neighbourhoods are diachronic however. Families in a quiet phase would sue families in a roaring phase, which leads to long term inefficiency due to the transactions costs and costs of administration of justice involved. As a consequence it is efficient to apply a neighbourhood test and a threshold for 'normal' disturbances (Bouckaert and De Geest 1998)

5 **Coming to the nuisance.** Defendants in nuisance cases often invoke the 'coming to the nuisance' by the plaintiff. When the plaintiff moved to an area in which the nuisance was already present, the plaintiff, as the argument goes, accepted voluntarily the nuisance. *Volenti non fit injuria.* Moreover, the lowering of the quality of the location by the nuisance was probably already compensated by a price discount in the purchase or the renting of the concerned land. In *Bove v. Donner-Hanna Coke Co.* the plaintiff, Mrs. Bove, had moved into a factory district across the street of Donner-Hanna Coke Company. She claimed an injunction against the company for noise and air pollution. The court however stated:

She voluntarily moved into this district, fully aware of the fact that the atmosphere would be constantly contaminated by dirt, gas, and foul odors; and that she could not hope to find in this locality the pure air of a strictly residential zone. She evidently saw certain advantages of living in this congested center. This is not the case of an industry with its attendant noise and dirt, invading a quiet, residential district. This is just the opposite. Here a residence is built in an area naturally adapted for industrial purposes and already dedicated to that use. Plaintiff can hardly be heard to complain at this late date that her peace and comfort have been disturbed by the situation which existed, to some extent at least, at the very time she bought her property.

Case law is divided about the robustness of the argument of coming to the nuisance. In the already quoted case *Sturges v. Bridgman* for instance the physician moved his examination room adjacent to the workplace of the confectioner. Although he moved to the nuisance the court upheld strict exclusion logic and allowed an injunction in favour of the physician. Donald Wittman (Wittman 1980) discusses the coming to the nuisance argument from an efficiency point of view. In cases where the argument is endorsed, such as the mentioned *Bove v. Donner – Hanna Coke Company* case, crucial importance is attached to the question who was historically the first. The use by the historical first is considered as the benchmark for the later comers. Wittman however criticizes this criterion on efficiency grounds. Not the one who was historically the first, but the one who should have been the first should be the benchmark to solve such disputes. If it turns out that the use of the resource, the late comer is planning, is superior to the incumbent use in terms of production output, the judge should give prominence to the late comer and enjoin the incumbent user. As a consequence the decision should always be based on a utility comparison between the two competing uses. Wittman also points to a perverse effect of accepting the coming to the nuisance defence. Accepting this defence means that first comers establish a kind of easement allowing them to externalise beyond the confines of their legal domain. Analogous to homesteading procedures (Dean Lueck 1995) races will develop to be the first and enjoy the 'free easement'. As is the case with homesteading also races coming to the nuisance would lead to inefficient and premature establishing of such 'easements' (Wittman 1980). The efficiency approach of Wittman is however criticised by Roy Cordato (1998). Requiring the judge to proceed to an interpersonal utility comparison between the first comer and the later comer is a task impossible to fulfil because of the lack of an interpersonal utility standard. Although based on a different methodological approach, the argument of Cordato is parallel to the criticism of Smith on the Coasean approach in general (see earlier section on "Smith: exclusion and governance regimes"). According to Cordato the question of coming to the nuisance should be dealt with by a strict and stable application of the property logic. In this respect the notions 'first comer' and 'later comer' can be very confusing because by using them as the sole criterion abstraction is made from the underlying property situation. If the so called 'first comer' caused nuisance on the private property of someone else but the victim neglects to react, the so called 'first comer' enjoys a kind of free ride but does not establish a right unless a clear consent by the victim. If the victim sells his estate to a third party, she can claim again all rights which are inherent to the property right of that estate although she would be considered, according to the doctrine of coming to the nuisance, as a' later comer' who has to accept the nuisance, established by the 'first comer'. Often however a mere application of the property logic does not generate such an easy answer as nuisance issues are often complicated by zoning laws and environmental regulations giving polluters a right to pollute up to a certain level.

## 3.2 Case analyses

### *1.* Hunter and others v. Canary Wharf Ltd; Hunter and others v. London Docklands Development Corp *[1997] 2 All ER 426*

**A Facts and legal sources.** In 1990 the tower Canary Wharf (250 meters high and 50 square meters wide) was built in the London area of the Docklands. The tower is built about ten kilometres from the BBC television transmitter at

Crystal Palace and prior to the summer of 1989 television reception was good. Before, in 1981, the area of the Docklands was designated as an urban development area by statutory instrument pursuant to section 134 of the Planning and Land Act of 1980. An urban development corporation (the London Dockland Development Company; LDDC) was established and made the local planning authority. In 1982 the area was declared an enterprise zone with the effect that planning restrictions were eased for the development within the area.

In April 1991 a relay transmitter at Ballroom tower came into service to transmit into 'the shadow' and the plaintiffs' television were adjusted or replaced to receive the new signals between July 1991 and August 1992.

B **Claims and defences.** Inhabitants of the neighbourhood claim damages from the defendants (CW Ltd) in nuisance for interference over a period of years with reception of television broadcasts. They allege the interference to be caused by the building of the tower.

The same plaintiffs claim damages against the LDDC for the deposit on their properties of substantial quantities of dust, created as a result of the construction of a link road within the enterprise zone.

The defendant CW Ltd contends that interference in TV reception is not an actionable private nuisance, that he can rely on the statutory authority arising out of the statutory scheme under which the tower was built and because there had been a permission to build the tower, that the interference with TV reception is neither an actionable public nuisance and that the plaintiffs have no proprietary or possessory interest in the area.

C **Sentence and considerations.** The court of appeal, deciding on leave to appeal to the House of Lords raises several questions, relevant for the decision in this case.

First the question is raised whether interference with television reception is capable to constitute an actionable nuisance. The court, relying on the analogy with cases of loss of prospect, answers this question in the negative considering that city life would become virtually impossible when all interferences would become actionable.

Second the question is raised whether the defence of statutory authority is valid. The court is of the opinion that the planning act did not confer to the planning authority's immunity for nuisance. Consequently this defence does not hold.

Third, the court raises the question whether a proprietary or possessory link is necessary to have locus standi in nuisance cases. The court is of the opinion that a substantial link is necessary but that occupation of the property is sufficient for locus standi. The court refers to the general trend in nuisance law holding that it is not tenable to restrict the action to proprietary or possessory interests.

Fourth, the court raises the question whether the deposit of dust is capable of founding an action in negligence. The court is of the opinion that an action in negligence is only possible when the dust deposit is excessive and causes substantial costs to the plaintiffs. Non-excessive dust deposits are an inevitable incident of urban life.

## D Economic Analysis.

**D1 A problem of externalities.** The interference with the television reception is a clear case of a negative externality. By building the tower the receivers of television signals bear costs such as either foregoing television watching or installing additional reception devices (e.g. cable television). When these costs are higher than either the benefits the builder derives from the tower or the costs of prevention the builder can eventually take, the situation is inefficient. It is unlikely that such inefficiency can be eliminated through Coasean bargaining, as transaction costs may be prohibitive due to the large number of involved inhabitants in the neighbourhood and to possible problems of hold-up strategies. Coasean bargaining is further complicated by the question who is the externalizing agent. Is it the Canary Wharf Limited, the London Docklands Development Company or the Planning Authorities? As a consequence a decision of the court is required to decide whether the costs of the neighbours have to be internalized by awarding damages and by this give an incentive to agents with similar externalizing behaviour to avoid such behaviour, or whether such costs should not be internalized through court decision and by this give a signal to future victims not to seek compensation through the court system for similar cases.

**D2 The defence of statutory authorities.** From a law and economics point of view this is a question of definition of property rights. Did the Planning act award immunity for nuisance to the builders and the constructors of the road or not. In the case they did a taking occurred by diminishing the scope of the property rights (in the large sense, see before Chapter 1) of the neighbours. The question then arises whether the government should compensate the neighbours for these takings. One could argue that the takings are so minimal in comparison with costs of administration of justice, that a 'de minimis' rule would apply. Not compensating taking on the other side may increase a moral hazard-attitude on the side of the government by engaging in inefficient projects.

**D3 Are proprietary or possessory interests required for locus standi?** From a law and economics viewpoint all interests, which are institutionally protected should be considered as 'property rights' (or entitlements) in the broad sense. According to law and economic- scholars property rights in the broad sense should be ranged on a continuum from weaker (e.g. the property rights of the tenants) to stronger property rights (e.g. fee simple). As a consequence the division between proprietary and possessory interests on one side and other interests on the other side is not relevant to decide for locus standi.

## E Economic evaluation of the decisions.

**E1 Interference in television reception is not an actionable nuisance.** The main consideration for this decision concerns the context of city life. A lot of activities would become impossible if this type of nuisance would become actionable. From a law and economics viewpoint this decision can be sustained. Other than life on the country side, city life involves a large exposure to positive and negative externalities. Positive externalities such as the possibility of meeting many people, the proximity of commercial, cultural, administrative and economic centres. Negative externalities such as noise, dust, pollution and the unpredictability of the environment. As long as people consider the positive externalities to be outweighing the negative ones, they will continue to live within the city and leave in the opposite case. If all negative externalities of city life become actionable the evolution of city life will be halted and also the positive externalities of it will disappear. This unintended consequence for the surplus of the choice for city life makes society less wealthy, so less efficient.

**E2 No defence of statutory authority.** Because nuisance law is a general and widely known remedy and that we can assume that agents act 'in the shadow' of this law, an immunity exception should only be accepted when it is clearly and unambiguously stated in statutory law. The court adopted this view and did not read such immunity in the statutory law. In case the court would have read such immunity it should have considered whether this constituted a taking and whether this taking should be compensated. For this the court should have compared the cost of administration of justice, caused by the compensation, and the increase of moral hazard on the side of the government, caused by a non-compensation decision.

**E3 No proprietary or possessory interests are required for *locus standi*.** It is efficient to grant a *locus standi* to all inhabitants who have a certain property right (in the broad economic sense) on land and houses within the concerned neighbourhood. The inhabitants are the better information gatherers on externalizing behaviour from thirds. By not granting them a *locus standi* for nuisance they would be obliged to negotiate with other holders of interests, such as the holders in fee simple, to file a claim for nuisance, which would lead to additional transaction costs and possible suboptimal internalization.

## *2. Nuisance by noise of roosters. Tribunal Civil de Nivelles (Belgium), 31 Mars 1982, Revue Générale des Assurances et des Responsabilités, 1984, 10828*

**A Facts and legal sources.** The plaintiffs, Mr. Desmyter and Mrs. Geurs live nearby a farm, run by Mr. Laporte where roosters and chickens are kept. Mrs. Geurs pretended that she became ill by the noise, produced by the roosters. As a gesture of reconciliation Mr. Laporte offered to limit the number of the roosters to two during the illness of the plaintiff, while it was before one rooster for ten chickens, the usual proportion. Mrs. Geurs also invokes a medical certificate, stating that she needs to sleep eight to nine hours a night and also to have a siesta in the afternoon. Under Belgian law nuisances are actionable either as a negligence tort under art. 1382 Civil Code or as a strict liability tort under art. 544 Code Civil, involving disequilibrium in the exercise of property rights by imposing excessive charges to a neighbour.

B **Claims and defences.** The plaintiff, Mrs. Geurs claims that her illness is caused by the noise produced by the roosters and requests an interlocutory injunction against the roosters and damages for the medical expenses for her illness, pretended to be caused by the noise. The defendant, Mr. Laporte, replies that his farm is located in a very rural area, where chicken farming is common. Also the proportion of one rooster to ten chickens is the normal rule. He also refers to his gesture of reconciliation and denies that the noise of the roosters is of that kind that it would prevent the plaintiff to follow the prescription of the medical certificate.

C **Sentence and considerations.** In the sentence of the justice of the peace, against which the plaintiff appealed, the judge stated that the noise was not excessive taking into account the rural character of the area. He also pointed to the reconciliatory attitude of the defendant. As a consequence, both claims of the plaintiffs were dismissed. In appeal the court maintains the decision of the justice of the peace, stating that the harm to the plaintiff is not excessive but normal, considering the rural character of the area. The court also denies proof of the fact that the noise prevents the plaintiff to follow the sleep prescription of the medical certificate.

D **Economic analysis.**

**D1 Welfare economics.** According to a welfare economics approach this is a clear cut case of negative externalities, imposed by the chicken farmer Laporte to the neighbour Geurs. As a consequence, the number of roosters to chickens raised by Laporte might be inefficiently high. This is shown in Figure 3.1.

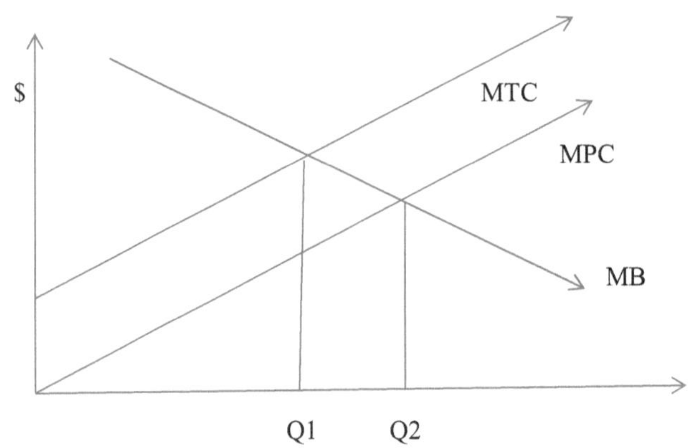


*Figure 3.1* Negative externalities

The upward arrows represent respectively the marginal private costs of the roosters-chickens of the farmer and the total marginal costs (including the ones incurred by the neighbour) of the farming. The downward arrow represents the marginal benefits of rooster-chicken-breeding. When only the private costs are envisaged then Q2 is the optimal (efficient) amount of rooster-chicken-breeding. When social costs are included then Q1 is the optimal amount. If nothing is done the farmer will produce Q2, a socially inefficient high amount. The breeding has to be cut to Q1 either by a judicial decision or by a regulatory or fiscal measure.

From this perspective the decision of the judge is wrong because it fails to internalize a proven externality.

**D2 Coasean economics.** From a Coasean viewpoint Geurs and Laporte are reciprocally involved in a competition for the use of resources. The damage is caused as well by Laporte by his breeding activities as by Geurs who came to live there nearby. The existence of the externalizing activities by Laporte is only an efficiency problem when they are due to prohibitive transaction costs in the relationship between Geurs and Laporte.

Suppose that these transaction costs were so trivial that they do not prevent a deal between the two parties.

Suppose also that the costs imposed to Geurs amount up to 100, while the benefits for Laporte of his breeding activities amount up to 80. In this case Geurs would have offered Laporte an amount of at least eighty and at maximum 100 to stop the breeding activity, an offer Laporte would have accepted because it improved his situation anyway.

However no deal was made, even not after the conciliatory proposal by Laporte. For a Coasean judge this could point to two different situations.

Either there is no deal because the situation is efficient because the benefits from the externalizing activities are higher than the costs to the victim. Suppose we have now the inverse situation, that is, 100 benefits for Laporte and 80 costs for Geurs. In this case the judge should not change the allocation and further allow the rooster-chicken-breeding. She can eventually award damages to the neighbour for reasons of justice.

Or there is no deal because transaction costs are prohibitive. Because there are only two involved parties the prohibitive level of transaction costs is not due to external circumstances (number of parties, information problems, problems of enforcing a deal) but rather to the attitude of the parties. The parties may have developed strategic behaviour. Suppose that the costs for Geurs were higher than the benefits of Laporte and that the 'bribing' by Geurs of Laporte would have been the efficient exchange. It could be however that Laporte exploits his position in this bilateral monopolistic setting and asks extortion prices to Geurs by which Geurs refuses a deal. In his case the judge should replace 'the market' and reallocate herself the involved rights by awarding injunctive relief to Geurs.

In the decision of the judge the relevant question about transaction costs is not raised so that this decision should be qualified, from a Coasean perspective, as a wet finger-one.

**D3 Neighbourhood-principle and coming to the nuisance.** Both courts (the justice of the peace and the civil court, sentencing in appeal) consider the dominant use of the area, i.e. a rural one, as crucial for the excessive character of the imposed harm. Because the area is rural and because the noise of the roosters is normal for rural areas, all claims of the neighbour should be dismissed. From an economic point of view this consideration can be sustained. When the land uses in an area are more or less homogeneous, most inhabitants are at the same time perpetrators and victims of harmful activities. Farmers raise roosters and hear their and neighbours 'roosters. As a result the subjective harm, created by activities typical for the area, is very probably substantially less than in areas with heterogeneous uses. By not awarding claims from non-typical, here non-rural, inhabitants against homogeneous uses courts are stimulating the further homogenization of areas. Potential non-typical movers-in are discouraged by the signal, sent by the courts, that they have to endure the disturbances, proper to the homogeneous use, because no claim against these disturbances will be upheld. By this courts also stimulate efficient ex ante strategies among potential movers-in to avoid possible harmful impacts. By taking of the dominant use of the area as a yardstick for excessiveness of the harm, the courts, one could say, adopt the defence of coming to the nuisance. The farmers 'uses are historically established first and the non-rural movers-in came later. As mentioned before the adoption of the coming to the nuisance-defence could lead to inefficient racing (see earlier in this chapter, the section on "Coming to the nuisance"). This type of criticism to the coming to the nuisance defence is however only valid when it concerns a sequence of a first user towards a second user in an area without a dominant use. Suppose an unsettled area in which a farmer comes first followed by a residential settler. When courts would endorse here the coming to the nuisance defence they would give a signal to potential farmers to move in and receive freely a right to externalize which will lead to inefficient racing and premature establishment. However when there is already a dominant use established by many settlers such inefficient racing is impossible, while on the other hand there is a strong efficiency argument to uphold the dominant use as a yardstick for excessiveness of the harm imposed and the decision to sustain or not claims for injunctive relief. From this economic perspective the discussed decisions should be endorsed.

## 3. Marcic v. Thames Water Utilities Ltd; *Decision of Judge Richard Havery QC[2001] 3 All ER 698; Court of Appeal Civil Division[2002] EWCA Civ 64; House of Lords [2003] UKHL 66*

**A Facts and legal sources.** The plaintiff, Mr. Marcic, lives in a house in Middlesex, in the greater London area. Since years he suffers from repeated flooding in his property. At heavy rainfall or long time drizzle the foul water of the sewers overflows. The foul water mixes with surface water which cannot be absorbed by the over flooding sewers. The problem is aggravated by the neighbouring householder lifting the covers of the inspection chambers of the sewers on their property in order to relieve them from surface water, thereby allowing accumulated surface water to enter the foul sewer. The mix of foul water and surface water enters the front garden of the plaintiff. In order to prevent the water entering his house the plaintiff has to open his side gate and garage door to allow the water streaming in his back garden. Most often the water subsides only after some days, leaving deposits of sludge and debris in the back garden. The plaintiff constructed a manhole connected to pipes so that some flood water is carried back from his front garden underneath his garage and to the bottom of his back garden. The construction of this all has cost the plaintiff £16,000. The flooding occurred twice in 1992, once in 1993, 1994, 1995, 1996, twice in 1997, four times in 1999 and four or five times in 2000. The plaintiff complained already in 1992 to the local authority. They referred his complaint to the defendant upon which they sent him a cheque of £40. The plaintiff however returned the cheque.

Thames Water Utilities Ltd. is a statutory sewerage undertaker, providing sewers for the removal of surface and foul water. It is responsible for 80000 km of public sewers in size ranging from 100 mm to 6 m and connecting 5.4 million properties in the area. The company operates under the Water Industry Act of 1991 and under the regulatory supervision of the Director General of Water Services. It generates its revenue from charges to the connected households, fixed by the DG of Water Services. The company receives also special allowances for properties at risk for internal flooding of foul or surface water. The properties at risk are put in categories A, B and X. In a strategic business plan, to be submitted to the DG Water Service the company has to indicate which properties can be removed from which risk category following appropriate improvement works to the sewerage. The property of Marcic is however not included in the risk category because it does not suffer from internal flooding. In total about 18,000 properties are at risk of overflows. If all properties, like the one of Marcic, had to be remedied it would cost Thames about £1000 million while the profits of the company are only at £344 million. In the absence of an increase of charges it would take many years to alleviate the problems of all the customers at risk.

The legal rules relevant for this case derive from two different legal sources. First the common law on liability for nuisance, more specifically the *Ryland's v. Fletcher* liability which implies a strict liability for acts of a landowner imposing harm on neighbouring landowners. Second, the 1998 Act bringing the UK under full application of the European Convention for the Protection of Human Rights and Fundamental Freedoms. In this latter Convention art. 8 on the respect for a person's home and art. 1 of the first Protocol on the right to peaceful enjoyment of possessions are relevant for this case.

B **Claims and defences.** The plaintiff claims damages from Thames as being liable under *Ryland's v. Fletcher*-nuisance. The defendant was negligent as he breached a statutory duty which is causal to the harm suffered by the plaintiff. The defendant denies this liability invoking the precedent Glossop (1879), stating that there can be no liability for breach of statutory duty when the breach would consist merely of absence of action by the defendant. Only when an explicit order to perform a statutory duty is enacted by a higher authority and this order has been disregarded, the Glossop precedent does not apply. Such an enforcement order, however, was not made to Thames. The plaintiff, followed in this by the court of appeal, challenges this approach, based on the Glossop precedent. An occupier is liable when he allows a harm to be continued with knowledge and without taking reasonably prompt measures to abate it. By this nuisance and negligence assimilate. It has to be checked whether it was reasonably foreseeable whether the acts or the non-acting of the occupier would cause harm. When a statutory duty is involved it is clear that the statutory body is not liable when the harm is the inevitable result of the exercise of that statutory duty. This is however not the case here. The court of appeal also considers that it is to the defendant to prove that he took all reasonable steps to prevent the harm. It is not to the plaintiff to prove that the defendants omitted to take such steps. Thames did not prove that they have done all that was reasonable, neither did they prove that their scheme of priorities was fair. Moreover Thames had enough possibilities to avoid the nuisance.

Concerning the claim under the 1998 Act the plaintiff, again followed by the Court of Appeal, argued that Thames failed to show the fairness of its priority policy. As a result there is no fair balance between the protection of the private interest and the necessities of public interest.

The Court of Appeal also remarks that the necessity to make a disproportionate expenditure to prevent the nuisance is no reason to deny the liability, but it may be a reason for the court to award damages in respect of the nuisance rather than a mandatory injunction to abate it.

C **Sentence and considerations.** The case was first brought before Judge Havery QC in 2001. The claim of the plaintiff, as far as based on nuisance and negligence, was dismissed because there was no breach of a statutory duty by Thames. The judge did however accept the claim under the 1998 Act considering that Thames had infringed art. 8 ECHR by interfering in persons' home and family life and the First Protocol by interfering in the peaceful enjoyment of possession. Because both provisions only apply since 1998 the judge did not award damages for the flooding before 1998. Thames appealed against its liability under the 1998 Act and Marcic cross-appealed against the dismissal of his claim under nuisance and negligence.

The Court of Appeal dismissed the appeal of Thames because it did not show that the judge has been wrong. It allowed the cross-appeal of Marcic on the liability of Thames under nuisance and negligence for the reasons mentioned earlier under B.

The House of Lords decided on the case in 2003. The House of Lords reversed the decision of the Court of Appeal by stating that a sewerage undertaker like Thames does not operate as a normal land owner, but under a statutory scheme. This scheme struck a reasonable balance between the users of the sewers and between the plaintiff and the public authorities. As a result the statutory remedies, provided by the legislation, exclude the common law remedies. Also the claim based on the infringement of the 1998 Act did not find any mercy in the eyes of the Law Lords. Also this claim fails because of the presence of a statutory remedy.

**D** **Economic analysis.** This case is more complex than the previous one, dealing with a conflict in which the two parties were acting under the rights and the duties embedded in the civil law. In this case however one of the parties, Thames Water Utilities Ltd, is a provider of a public service, operating within a statutory framework, following rules and targets, determined by statutes and under the supervision of a public authority, the Director General of Water Services. Consequently the question rises whether this special position of the defendant affects its liability for the harmful impact on the plaintiff.

**D1** **A service relationship.** Other than in the previous case, the plaintiff and the defendant are ex ante connected by a service relationship. Thames Water Utilities Ltd has to provide a sewerage service, that is, draining away foul and surface water from Marcic's property, and while Marcic has to pay the fixed fees. In general the level of the service provided and the price for it is efficient when they correspond with the intersection of the demand and supply curve (see Figure 3.2).

Suppose Marcic and Thames could freely bargain about the sewerage service level and the price, and suppose both parties are fully informed, then Marcic would take a q-level of services at price p. At this price-level the demand-curve of Marcic and the supply curve of Thames match. In case of harm infliction due to the bad functioning of the sewerage the judge should investigate whether Thames provided indeed the service level q and whether an eventual under provision was causal to the harm.

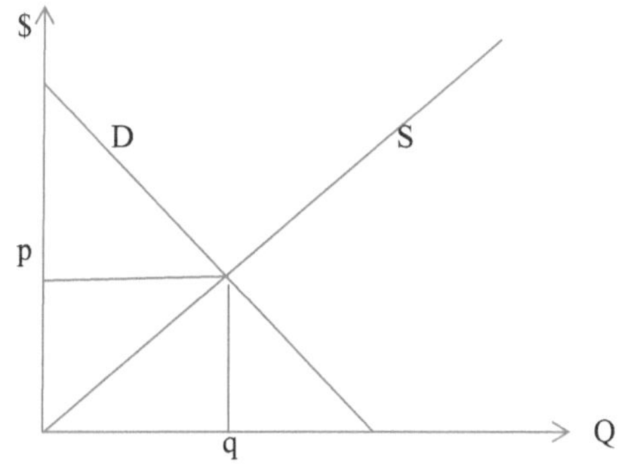


*Figure 3.2* Demand-supply services

**D2 Sewerage as a club good.** Sewerage is however not a private good in the economic sense, but rather a club good or collective good. First the consumption of it is to a large extent non-rival. Once a collective sewerage infra-structure, that is, all sewerage infra-structure except the sewers 'connection of the users' property and the sewer system, is constructed, the number of users do not influence the provision cost level, at least to a certain level. If too many users are admitted to use the system, crowding-out may occur and the service-quality declines. Second, the consumption of sewerage services is excludable. It is possible not to connect or to disconnect inhabitants in the sewers 'area. Consequently the providers can charge the users. Sewerage is a club good but not a public good in the economic sense.

Efficient price- and service level in sewerage provision are illustrated in Figure 3.3.

Suppose that with spending $TC^{cs}$ a given area can be serviced with sewerage in a satisfactory way (no internal or external flooding under normal weather conditions). The more users are connected the more the total costs of the collective infra-structure can be shared, so the fee will decline. This is shown by curve $IC^{cs.}$ At a certain number of users the system becomes overused (too much foul water, too much surface water due

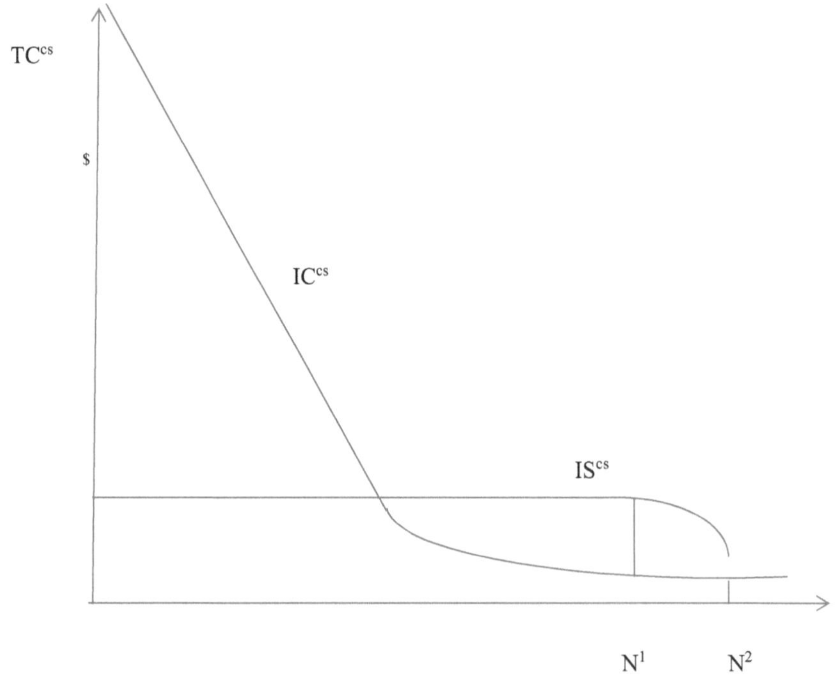


*Figure 3.3* Efficient price and service level in sewerage provision

to concrete terraces, etc.). From $N^1$ the service quality (IC CS) starts to decline. At $N^2$ the service quality dips below the fee charged at that number. From that number on the users pay inefficiently too much. Efficient provision of collective sewerage infra-structure should allow $N^2$ users at a price $TC^{cs}/N^2$.

**D3 Monopoly and information asymmetry.** The planning and the construction of collective sewerage infra-structure and the fees charged to the users are not freely determined by the provider. The provider retains from the public authority a territorial monopoly in a given area to provide sewerage. Such a monopoly is unavoidable in order to avoid waste due to duplication of collective sewerage infra-structure. In return, in order to avoid monopoly abuses (too high fees, too low service levels) the government negotiates with the provider the planning of the sewerage infra-structure (priority schemes, risk reduction) and the fees to be charged. Between provider and public authority information asymmetries may prevail by which the provider is able to extract monopoly rents from his position (fees above $TC^{cs}/N^2$ and more users than $N^2$ leading to suboptimal quality).

**D4 Liability of the parties.** From the analysis in D2 it follows that the agents, responsible for sewerage provision should be held liable for the infliction of harm to a user like Marcic when there is a causal link between the harm and the underperformance by the provider, i.e. performance below the $IS^{cs}$-level at $N^2$. The liability should concern all parties who are able to influence by their decisions the service-level of the sewerage. By holding these parties liable for harm due to underperformance, courts provide incentives for future providers to perform efficiently. This is the *ex ante* perspective of tort law. In this case it is clear that the concerned agents, to be held eventually liable are the Director General of Water Services and Thames Water Utilities Ltd. Both agents have an impact on sewerage provision. However, due to the likelihood of information asymmetries and the possibility of monopoly rents for the provider it seems to be recommendable to hold the provider in first instance liable, but allowing him to prove that the under provision was the necessary result of statutory restrictions, imposed by the Director General of Water Services.

**E Economic evaluation of the court decisions.** Both Judge Havery QC and the House of Lords in the final decision discarded a liability for Thames Water Utilities Ltd under nuisance and *Ryland's v. Fletcher* liability because the provision of statutory remedies excludes any common law remedy. The House of Lords took the same position concerning the alleged infringement of the Human Rights Act of 1998. By cutting off the users of sewerage from any common law remedy and forcing them to rely exclusively on statutory remedies the mentioned courts took a dangerous path. In public choice literature ample attention is spent to the possibility of regulatory capture, that is, political collusion between public authorities and private companies in order to provide privileges to the latter at the expense of the interests of consumers and taxpayers. By allowing a residual control by the judiciary, based on the general rules and remedies of the common law, such a regulatory capture can be limited and corrected. Judge Havery partially and the House of Lords in general, exclude this residual control by which in the future sewerage providers are able to make deals with political instances on the statutory provisions and remedies, generating different forms of regulatory capture. From this regard the mentioned decisions should be qualified as judicial failures from an economic point of view. Although we miss in the decisions of the Court of Appeal any firm economic analysis on the due level of care of sewerage provision, its decision at least maintains this residual common law-control by which regulatory capture could be avoided or at least limited.

Nevertheless, even when the general opinion of the House of Lords that the presence of statutory remedies excludes common law-ones can be seriously challenged, the House of Lords may be right in its decision to dismiss the claim of Marcic because he did not exhaust all his legal remedies of the statutory kind. Section 94(3) of the 1991 Water Industry Act provides that a sewerage undertaker's duty to provide an adequate system of public sewers under section 94(1) is enforceable by the Director under section 18. The Director has not made an enforcement order with regard to the drainage of Mr. Marcic's property but Mr. Marcic has not advanced a complaint that by not making such an order the Director is in dereliction of his duty under section 18, although his opportunities in this regard were drawn to his solicitors' attention early in 1998. Mr. Marcic still had the possibility to pursue judicial review proceedings against the Director or Secretary of state for an alleged failure to make the enforcement order as required by section 18. Due to Mr. Marcic's failure to use his last remedy the courts had no possibility to investigate whether the public authorities upheld a due care level in their supervision of the sewerage provider. By doing this and eventually sanctioning them, the courts would have had the occasion to provide appropriate incentives to public authorities to enforce the due level of care. Judicial systems however most often rely on the legal principle of '*dominus litis*', that is, the litigating parties remain in control of the actions to be taken. Also this is a principle which can be sustained from an economic point of view. First, this principle leaves it to the subjective valuation of the interested parties to take legal action. This is in line with the economic principle of consumers' sovereignty. Second, the application of this principle provides incentives to the concerned parties to optimize their information about their chances to prevail in legal action. As a consequence, the courts in this case could not apply the statutory remedies, provided in the 1991 Water Industry Act and judicial review when the concerned party, Mr. Marcic, did not ask for it. Because the remedies of the common law should be considered as residual, i.e. applicable only when the statutory remedies fail, the failure to exhaust all statutory remedies bar also the possibility to invoke the general common law remedies. As a consequence, the end result of the case, that is, the dismissal of the claim of Mr. Marcic, can be sustained. The general position that the availability of statutory remedies excludes per se the use of general common law remedies however not.

### *4.* Frustzwerge in Nachbars Garten *(Gnomes of Frustration), AG Grünstadt,* Urt.v.11.2.1994–2aC 334/93; *NJW 1995, Heft 13, 889*

A **Facts and legal sources.** The relationship between two neighbours, living in adjacent houses, is profoundly broiled. One of the reasons is that the plaintiff filed some months before a suit against the defendant for music noise nuisance and this claim is pending before the *LG Frankenthal*. To retaliate against this suit the defendant placed several gnomes in his garden. The gnomes are very visible to the plaintiff because the plaintiff has to pass this garden daily to commute to his job. The type of the gnomes placed shows clearly the intention to irritate and to insult the defendant. One of them shows his middle finger, another one his tongue, a third hangs on a tree like a dead body, a fourth holds a shield with the slogan '*Pfälzer in die Pfalz, Wuppertaler in die Wupper*' (the plaintiff is originally from Wuppertal).

The German Constitution (*Grundgesetz*) protects the human dignity (art.1, I), the free development of personality (art. 2, I) as well as free speech and artistic freedom (art5, I and III). In the civil code (*Burgerliches Gesetzbuch*) art. 1004, I, provides the remedy of injunction for nuisance while art. 823, I, provides the remedy of damages for damage inflicted by intention or negligence.

B **Claims and defences.** The plaintiff asks the removal of the gnomes by mandatory injunction of the court because of the violation of his human dignity by the offending gnomes. According to the defendant however the placement of gnomes should be considered as an exercise of artistic freedom, protected by the German Constitution.

C **Sentence and considerations.** The Court considers that artistic freedom, guaranteed by the Constitution, finds its limits in 'personality rights', also protected by the Constitution. The gnomes are considered as insults violating the personality rights of the plaintiff. Consequently the court awards injunctive relief to the plaintiff in order to remove the insulting gnomes.

D **Economic analysis.**

**D1 A Coasean approach.** As already mentioned in the theoretical part, there are differences in the economic approach to nuisance. In this case these differences really matter for the end result. From a Coasean viewpoint the conflict has to be framed in a reciprocal way: the defendant imposes costs on the plaintiff by placing the gnomes in his sight, but the plaintiff imposes costs on the defendant by his sensitivity for insult. If transaction costs would have been non-prohibitive, plaintiff and defendant would have made a deal yet. Either the plaintiff had bribed away the gnomes because his valuation of being non-insulted is higher than the valuation of the defendant to insult, or the plaintiff had consented in the placement of the gnomes because his valuation of not being insulted was lower than the insult pleasure of the defendant. Apparently the transaction costs are prohibitive because one of the parties makes an appeal to the judge. This may due to strategic behaviour of one of the parties, both caught into a bilateral monopoly situation. As a consequence it is up to the judge to balance the revenge pleasure of the defendant against the anger of the plaintiff for the gnomes. For both elements the judge has to develop measurement proxies to make them comparable. The result of this comparison will be decisive for the awarding of remedies. If the revenge pleasure-value of the defendant is higher than the insult anger-value of the plaintiff then the judge has to allow the gnomes and eventually award some damages to the plaintiff. In the opposite case the judge has to grant injunctive relief to the plaintiff in order to remove the gnomes. As a result a judge, following a Coasean approach, may reach the same decision as the *AG Grünstadt*, but based however on very different grounds.

**D2 A Smithian Approach.** According to Smith (see earlier in this chapter, the section on "Smith: exclusion and governance regimes") courts are rather reluctant to award relief for non-tangible aesthetic nuisances because this does not fit with the dominant exclusion logic in which locational variables remain crucial. Non-tangible effects cannot be perceived as a physical intrusion into the column of space around the resource (Smith 2004: 998). The development of measurement proxies for non-tangible impacts such as being insulted of revenge pleasure is very difficult and would require high information costs. As a consequence, 'visual' pollution such as is the case with the gnomes of frustration would be denied relief in this logic.

E **Economic evaluation of the court decision.** Consenting with Smith, it has to be recognized that a balancing of the competing resource-uses in this case would be very difficult, not to say impossible due to the absence of credible measurement proxies. There are no market prices for the revenge of the defendant and the protection from insult for the plaintiff because both are caught in a non-market setting, that is, a bilateral monopoly. As a result, an exclusion regime, rather than a governance regime should prevail here. Moreover, individuals can anticipate to such visual and insulting exposure by ex ante strategies, for instance by moving into a house at more distance from neighbours, for instance by moving into a condominium in which such behaviour is banned by internal regulation, etc. Awarding the injunctive relief, such as the German court does, undermines the incentives for such ex ante strategies. Finally, the ruling of the court can be perceived in the wider society as a limitation of artistic freedom which may discourage artistic creativity. As a result, there are good economic reasons to reject the decision of the German court.

### *5.* **Watson and another v. Croft Promosport Ltd** ***[2009] EWCA Civ 15***

A **Facts and legal sources.** The Croft Motor Circuit covers 195 hectares and is built on a former aerodrome of World War II. It is situated in the rural area of Dalton-on-Tees. The plaintiffs, Mr. Watson and Mrs. Wilson are living in a family dwelling about 300 m north of the circuit. Between 1949 and 1957 the aerodrome was only intermittently used for motor races. In 1962 the owner of the airfield applied for a change of use so as to permit motor cycle races and other sporting events. The first application being refused for anticipated noise the applicant made a new amended one in which he promised to limit the use to not more than four motor races a year. Also this application was refused by the Croft Council but the applicant made appeal to the inspector who recommended a permission on the grounds that the area needed such a circuit and that due to the limitations, offered by the applicant, the noise was acceptable. The minister accepted this recommendation and granted in 1963 a planning permission in which the limitations, proposed by the applicant, were not mentioned. Between 1963 and 1979 the circuit was used for motor racing by no more than twenty races a year. Between 1979 and 1994 there were no races at all. In 1994 the defendant acquired a leasehold interest in a part of the airfield. He resurfaced the circuit and in 1997 the racing started again. In 1998, after a public inquiry on the conditions of the circuit, the defendant executed a unilateral undertaking made under Section 106 of the Town and Country Act 1990 for the regulation of the motor and motor cycle events. The schedule in Table 3.1 was proposed:

*Table 3.1* Use of motor circuit

| *Event* | *Noise level* | *Frequency* |
|---|---|---|
| N1 | under 95 dBa | no more than 10 days |
| N2 | 93 dBa | 40 |
| N3 | 85 dBa | 70 |
| N4 | 78 dBa | 110 |
| N5 | 70 dBa | unlimited |

In October 1998 the inspector agrees with the undertaking by the defendant and grants a planning permission on the agreement following Section 106 of the 1990 Act. Between 1998 and 2007 the activities of the circuit ranged from a low of 144 days in 2001 to 207 in 2000 all between N1 and N4 levels.

B **Claims and defences.** As victims of nuisance the claimants ask a mandatory injunction to limit the activities to twenty days within the N1 and N4 levels. In addition they ask damages (1) for the decline of the market value of their estate and (2) for the past damage. They deny that they came to the nuisance or that they acquiesced in the nuisance because there were long periods of non-activity. They also claim that the permission of the inspector in 1998 did not change the rural character of the area.

The defendants contend that the planning permission of 1963 and 1998, by which the level of activities were agreed under Section 106 of the 1990 Act changed indeed the rural character of the area. Consequently their activities were compatible with the character of the area. As a result there is no actionable nuisance. They contend further that the claimants did not act during a long time which implies acquiescence with the activities and the noise levels. Finally they point to the public interest aspect of their activities. They generate an economic surplus to the area.

C **Sentences and considerations.** In his decision, Judge Simon J, in Newcastle (January 2008, [2008] 3 All ER 1171) did not accept that the planning permission would have altered the rural character of the area. As a consequence the reasonable use level for the defendant should be fixed at forty days at N1-N4-levels and not at the levels agreed on Section 106. The judge neither accepted that the claimants had come to the nuisance or had acquiesced in the nuisance. Because the claimants have shown that they are prepared to be compensated for noise on N1-N4 days on more than twenty days, up to forty days, the judge did not grant an injunction, only damages. He granted £93,000 and £34,000 respectively to Mrs. Watson and Mrs. Wilson for the decline in market value of their estate and £2,000 per annum and £750 per annum to respectively Mrs. Watson and Mrs. Wilson for the past damage caused by the noise.

The Court of Appeal follows Simon J only partially. The Court agrees with him that the rural character of the area did not change by the planning permission. The Court relies on the principle, set forth in cited precedents, that the granting of a planning permission cannot affect the private rights of third parties, granted in the common law, unless such effect is specifically authorised by the parliament. As a result the level of reasonable use is up to forty days at N1-N4-level, which is covering the core-activities of the Croft Motor Circuit. Concerning the choice of the remedy the Court disagrees with Judge Simon J. that injunctive relief is the normal sanction for nuisance and only in exceptional circumstances it can be substituted by damages.

Similar circumstances do not appear in this case. The reason that the wrongdoer is considered a 'public benefactor' does not justify a denial of injunctive relief. The willingness to compromise on a certain level does not impair the right to claim injunctive relief. In exceptional cases damages can be awarded but this possibility cannot make of the court a tribunal for legalizing illegal acts upon payment. The high amount of damages granted by Judge Simon J proves the substantial character of the nuisance. This justifies largely the granting of an injunction.

D **Economic analysis.**

**D1 Analysis under a simplified institutional context: externalities and transaction costs.** If we make abstraction from the problem of the double-tiered rule level (common law nuisance rules and administrative planning permissions-see further D2) this case can be analysed either as a problem of externalities and market failure (Pigou) or as one of prohibitive transaction costs (Coase).

Croft Promosport Ltd externalizes costs to Watson/Wilson by producing noise (see Figure 3.4). The total marginal costs (TMC) are thus larger than the private marginal costs (PMC), namely, the costs incurred by the circuit manager himself. When allowed to externalize freely, the circuit manager would organize races at quantity $Q^1$, the level where his private marginal costs equal his marginal benefits. From a social point of view, i.e. taking into account all costs also the externalized ones, level $Q^2$ would be optimal. At this level the total marginal costs equal the marginal benefits. The reduction of $Q^1$ to $Q^2$ can be realized either by a general regulation of a command-and-control type, by taxing away the units between $Q^2$ and $Q^1$, by an individual regulation through injunctive relief, or by awarding damages covering the full damage to the victims. As there are apparently no general command-and-control- regulations neither special (Pigouvian) taxes for this type of externalities, nuisance is the remaining legal action either leading to either injunctive relief or to damages. From a Pigouvian point of view the choice of the remedy does not matter as long as the result, i.e. reduction from $Q^1$ to $Q^2$ is realized and the market failure is repaired.

A Coasean approach entails however a different analysis of the case. Suppose that the costs to make a deal between Croft Promosport Ltd

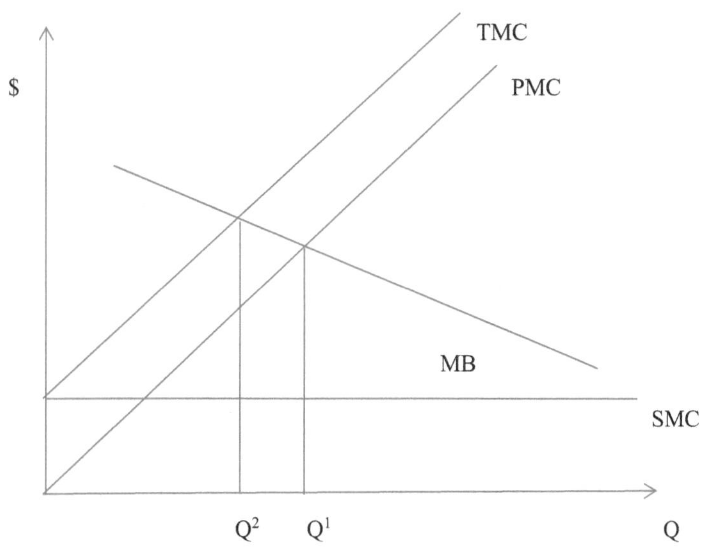


*Figure 3.4* Negative externalities motor circuit

and Mrs. Watson/Wilson are zero or at least very low, then the mere occurrence of externalities does not signal necessarily a market failure. When transaction costs are non-prohibitive and the damage to Mrs. Watson/Wilson is higher than the benefits Croft Promosport Ltd incurs from the externalizing activities, Mrs. Watson/Wilson would have made an offer to stop these activities and as their willingness to pay is higher than the willingness to sell on behalf of Promosport, a deal would have been struck. The fact that these activities continue would consequently mean, under the assumption of non-prohibitive transaction cost of course, that these activities are efficient, that is, the benefits are higher than the total costs, including the costs borne by Mrs. Watson/Wilson. It is however possible that the externalizing activities are inefficient indeed, that is, the benefits are lower than the costs, but that a deal between Promosport and Mrs. Watson/Wilson did not realize because either Promosport asked strategically too high a price or Mrs. Watson/Wilson offered strategically too low a price. In this case the judge has to intervene in order to mimic the non-operational market by eliminating the inefficient externalities either through injunctive relief or damages.

According to Smith the case should be dealt with either under an exclusion regime or under a governance regime. Under the first regime the noise emission of the motor races on the circuit should be considered as an invasion into the air pillar above the estate of Mrs. Watson/Wilson. Under the second regime the whole area of the circuit and the estate of Mrs. Watson/Wilson should be considered as one resource area about which the judge should decide who the most efficient user is and allocate the property rights accordingly. Under the first regime injunctive relief in favour of Mrs. Watson/Wilson is the exclusive remedy when the invasion is proven. Under the second regime the circuit may acquire the right to externalize when it is proven that it is the most efficient user within the area eventually under the condition to pay damages to the claimants. The choice between the two regimes depends on several variables: information costs to sort out the most efficient use of the resources concerned, the transaction costs of an eventual reallocation due to an inefficient allocation by the court, the values at stake of the concerned activities. Concerning the first variable it seems plausible that the information costs to decide about the most efficient user are not prohibitive at all. The market value of the activities of the circuit can be calculated while also the losses in market value of the estate of Mrs. Watson/Wilson can be reasonably assessed. Before the claimants went to court they made an offer to be compensated for some noise levels (see before A. Facts and legal sources). This self-assessment implies that a monetary valuation of the noise disturbance is possible. The transaction costs of an eventual reallocation of property rights may be prohibitive due to the bilateral monopoly situation. Suppose that the judge grants an injunction to Mrs. Watson/Wilson- this is what the Court of Appeal effectively decided- but that the surplus generated by the Croft Circuit largely surpasses the damages to Mrs. Watson/Wilson. In this case it would be efficient that Promosport buys back the right to go on with the races. It is however to fear that due to the broiled relationship between these parties such a deal never occurs. Finally, the values at stake seem to be high according to the decisions of the planning authorities. The activities on the circuit were considered as economically beneficial for the whole area. These three elements point to the application of a governance regime, the granting to Promosport of 'a right' to continue most of its activities upon payment of damages to Mrs. Watson/Wilson.

**D2 Analysis under a complex institutional context.** Such as is the case in *Canary Wharf v. Hunter and Marcic v. Thames Water Utilities Ltd* (see earlier) the case is made more complex due to a two-tiered rule system: on the one hand the common law rules on nuisance, on the other hand the administrative law rules and decisions devolving from the Town and Country Act of 1990. When a decision of the planning authorities allows an activity involving external effects, which should be qualified, according to common law rules as an actionable nuisance, both rules levels are in contradiction to each other. This can only be solved by establishing a clear hierarchy between both levels. If a statutory authorization provides immunity to the granted agent, the administrative level is considered hierarchically superior, and if not the common law rules are hierarchically superior. By stating that the private rights of third parties cannot be impaired by the permission of planning authorities, the Court of Appeal rejects clearly the idea of a general immunity by statutory immunity. Immunity seems to be only the case when the grant devolves from a parliamentary act. In this case immunity from nuisance is granted for all burdens, inevitable to operate the granted industry (see *Allen v. Gulf Oil Refinery* [1979] 3 All ER, 1008–1020).

From an economic point of view the two-tiered rule system is a source of institutional uncertainty for potential investors such as Croft Promosport Ltd. When investing according to the permissions of planning authorities, investors face, besides the endemic market uncertainty, three additional sources of uncertainty: (1) Whether courts will grant immunity from nuisance claims or not. It has to be remarked that the oldest precedents, quoted by the Court of Appeal, denying general immunity date from 1979, that is, years after the first planning permission was granted. At that moment it was impossible for the investor whether he would invest under the shadow of immunity from nuisance claims or not. (2) When not granted immunity the risk of nuisance claims to be filed. (3) The risk that these claims prevail and that an injunction or damages will follow and destroy or diminish the profit perspectives of the investment. Of course these uncertainties can be reduced by acquiring relevant information such as legal information on immunity and on nuisance case law and factual information about the inclination to go to court among neighbours. This information is costly too, but a rational actor will only acquire up to the level that the marginal information costs become equal to the marginal benefits of reduced uncertainty. In top of these costs the two-tiered rule systems also entail administrative costs, namely, the costs for the investor to get the necessary permissions and the costs for the public authorities to administer the planning permissions.

Suppose institutional reforms would be envisaged, which is of course beyond the scope of the judge, it would be recommendable to either attach immunity from nuisance claims to planning permission, or abolish the administrative permission system. In the first case the granting of permission should take into account the 'Pigouvian equation' (see D1). By this, the granting of planning permission would become more restrictive but the immunity following from it would reduce substantially the uncertainty of investors. By abolishing the planning permissions investors have only to watch the case law about nuisance in order to know how far their external impact may reach and what prevention devices they have to take. As mentioned also in our discussion of *Marcic v. Thames Water Utilities Ltd*, this second solution has the advantage to be less vulnerable to regulatory capture and lobbying from moneyed and powerful interest groups.

**D3 Damages or injunctive relief.** According to the Court of Appeal damages are not acceptable in this case because damages are only acceptable in exceptional circumstances and these are not present in this case. Further the Court of Appeal considers damages as a kind of paid license to commit illegal acts. From an economic point of view there are however two reasons to prefer the remedy of damages above injunctive relief.

First, as already mentioned when discussing the opinion of Smith, low information costs to assess the stakes involved (value of the activities, value of the damages), probably high transaction costs of eventual reallocation in case of inefficient allocation by the court through injunctive relief and the high economic value of the activity of the defendant point to applying a governance regime, and not an exclusion regime, in this case and consequently the awarding of damages.

Second, the institutional uncertainty, due to the two-tiered rule system which the investor had to face, seems to point to a second best solution of damages. In the seventies, when the initial investments were made, there was still a high uncertainty about the immunity devolving from statutory authorization. Only later case law endorsed the position that immunity can only follow from a parliamentary act. The defendant made his investments in the shadow of this uncertain institutional background. To treat the investor as if this non-immunity position has been always and clearly the case, would have a demoralizing impact on all investors in the future. On the other hand, neither the claimants should bear the full burden of this institutional uncertainty. As a consequence correctly assessed damages seem to be a fair treatment of their claims. The more because they had already before agreed in a monetary compensation of a part of their damage.

E **Economic evaluation of the decision.** From an economic point of view the decision of Judge Simon J to award damages has to be preferred on the decision of the Court of Appeal which awarded an injunction. This for two reasons. First because a governance regime fits better with the relevant variables of this case. Second because the institutional uncertainty of the two-tiered rule system, for which neither the defendant nor the claimant is to blame has to be taken into account. In the shadow of this uncertainty a damage remedy seems to be a judgment of Solomon, giving both claimants and defendant their due.

## *6.* Southwark London Borough v. Mills and others*;* Baxter v. Camden London Borough Council*; [1999] 4 All ER, HL, 449–470*

A **Facts and legal sources.** The claimants, Mrs. Tanner and Mrs. Baxter are respectively tenants from London Borough Southwark and Camden. Mrs. Tanner rents from LB Southwark an apartment in blocks built right after 1914–1918. Mrs. Baxter rents from LB Camden an apartment in a Victorian three-storey house. Before 1975 this house was divided into two apartments. After 1975 the house was converted into three apartments, one on each floor. By the conversion works the original isolation was substantially diminished. The claimants complain about the noise caused by their neighbours. They can hear not only the neighbours' televisions and their babies crying but also their coming and going, their cooking and cleaning, their quarrels and their lovemaking. The lack of privacy causes tension and distress. The terms of tenancy in standard form include a covenant in the following terms: 'The tenant's right to remain in and to enjoy the quiet occupation of the dwelled house shall not be interfered with by the Council' (LB Southwark) and 'The council shall not interfere with the tenant's rights to quiet enjoyment of the premises during the continuance of the tenancy. The council shall take such steps as are reasonably practicable to prevent the continuation of any nuisance caused to the tenant, having regard to all circumstances of the case' (LB Camden).

The discussion in this case concerns two legal questions: (1) whether the covenant of quiet enjoyment entails here the obligation for the landlord to provide sound insulation, or (2) whether the noise of the neighbours should be qualified as an actionable private nuisance.

B **Claims and defences.** The claimants ask the respective landlords to remedy the situation by installing sound insulation between the apartments. They ask from the court a mandatory injunction to order this to the landlords. According to the claimants the obligation to install sound insulation derives from the general common law obligation of the landlord to provide to his tenants a quiet enjoyment of the rented estate. They also claim that the neighbours cause nuisance which can only be stopped by sound insulation. The defendants deny the validity of both legal grounds in this case. The covenant to provide quiet enjoyment only protect the tenant against interference into his possession by the landlord and not against disturbances from third parties. The noise caused by the neighbours falls within the limits of normal neighbourhood charges and do not constitute a nuisance. If the neighbours do not commit a nuisance, the landlord cannot be held liable for nuisance.

**C Sentences and considerations.** Mrs. Tanner (and seven other tenants) initiated a procedure before the Arbitration Court and an order to install sound proofing was awarded by Judge Laddie. Upon appeal this decision was reversed and the order set aside. Mrs. Baxter filed a complaint before the Central London County Court, which dismissed her action. Also her appeal was dismissed by the Court of Appeal. Both cases are jointly dealt with by the House of Lords. Also the Lords dismiss the action from the claimants.

As far the covenant of quiet enjoyment, included in the tenancy terms, is concerned, the House of Lords considers that there is no implied warranty in the covenant that the real property is fit for the purpose for which it is let. The tenant takes the house in the state as it is and has eventually to negotiate such a warranty. Several regulations protect the tenants against this bleak state of laissez-faire. For instance, a regulation provides that low rent flats should be fit for habitation which includes lighting, heating and ventilation. This regulation does not provide for sound insulation. Local authorities have the power to close dwellings which are unfit for human habitation. The Building Act of 1985 aiming at preventing the creation of substandard housing provides the requirement that the walls and floors resist the transmission of airborne and impact sound. This regulation however applies to houses built after 1985, not for older buildings such as the ones concerned in this case. By lack of support in specific regulations the claimants fall back on the general common law obligation of quiet enjoyment. This rule however protects the tenant against interference by the landlord in his possession. In this case the interferences are caused by the neighbours. Furthermore, the interference must be substantial (e.g. a landlord flooding the land of his tenant), which is not the case here. Finally, the obligation of providing quiet enjoyment protects the tenant against interferences dating after the conclusion of the contract and not against situations which were already present at the moment of conclusion. *Caveat lessee.*

As far as nuisance is concerned the House of Lords considers first that the landlord is only liable for the nuisance committed by his neighbouring tenants when he has given consent to it. Moreover, the noise caused by the neighbouring tenants cannot be considered as nuisance. In neighbourhood relations the principle of good neighbourliness applies. This implies a 'give and take' and 'a live and let live' approach. The houses have to be used in their ordinary use involving reciprocal tolerance. The activities of the cotenants should therefore not be qualified as nuisance for they are a necessary by-product of ordinary occupation.

**D Economic analysis.**

**D1 Sound insulation: part of contractual obligation?** The claimants pretend that sound insulation is part of the contractual obligations of the landlord. Providing sound insulation devolves from the general common law obligation of the landlord to provide to the tenant a quiet enjoyment of the rented estate. From an economic perspective the problem in this case about the provision of sound insulation is related to the problem of information provision at the moment of the conclusion of the contract. A contract is a legally formalised exchange between two or more parties. In this case a right to inhabit an apartment is exchanged for a monthly payment. An exchange is efficient when it leads to a mutual benefit for the concerned parties. Applied to this case: when the willingness to pay of the tenant is larger than the willingness to sell (rent) there is a gain of exchange, which is, according to the negotiation skills of the parties, divided between these parties. An exchange may be not mutually beneficial when parties are not fully informed about the products, services or rights they acquire or sell. Suppose that a tenant signs a rental contract while badly informed about the conditions of the rented estate. Guided by this crippled information he assesses the value of a monthly habitation at £500 while the rent is only at £400. Consequently there is a consumers' surplus of a monthly £100 and he will sign the contract. After being better informed about the condition of the apartment his valuation declines to £300. In this case the exchange is not efficient at all. In cases of inefficient contracting due to under-information, the question is who should have provided the relevant information. Is it up to the tenant to scrutinize very accurately the rented estate before signing or is it up to the landlord to provide to his future tenant all information which could be eventually relevant for the habitation quality of the tenant. Applied to this case: was it up to the tenants Mrs. Tanner and Mrs. Baxter to control, before signing, whether the apartments were sound proof even against 'normal life disturbances 'by the neighbours, or was it up to LB Southwark and LB Camden to explain to the tenants that they should not expect from them a sound insulation against such disturbances. In the first case, the tenants don't have a claim, in the second case they can claim either the installation of sound insulation by the landlord or the resolving of the contract combined with damages. From an economic perspective it is efficient to place the burden of information provision to the 'better information gatherer', that is, the party which is able to acquire and provide the information in the cheapest way. In contractual relationships between an ordinary consumer and a professional seller, the professional is usually regarded as the 'better information gatherer', for the professional is specialised in this type of products' or service provision. Applied to this case it seems that both landlords, LB Southwark and LB Camden are the professional party, involved as they are in the renting of many apartments. At first sight it can be presumed they are the 'best information gatherers'. On the other hand the information costs for the tenants about sound insulation and the exposition to normal life disturbances of co-tenants, may be quite low too. It would have been economically correct if the court would have investigated this informational aspect from both sides. This informational aspect is only indirectly addressed in the dissenting opinion of Judge Peter Gibson of the Court of Appeal. Following his opinion the tenants do not have to tolerate the noise from the neighbour unless they had expressly or impliedly consented to the noise. Under such a condition the landlords are implicitly obliged to provide information about the lack of insulation, otherwise the tenants are not able to give their consent to it.

**D2 Private nuisance: locus standi?** Suppose that the disturbances by the neighbours should be qualified as actionable private nuisances (see D3), then the question arises which party is entitled to sue which other party. This case has a triangular structure: the landlord, the claiming tenants, the neighbouring tenants whose disturbances are the subject of the complaints.

A first question concerns the *locus standi* of tenants against other tenants. Is one tenant entitled to sue another tenant without the consent of the landlord or is the tenant obliged to involve the landlord in the case and when he refuses to sue him on contractual default? In the continental law of Europe tenants are granted a *locus standi* against neighbours (co-tenants or not) against all factual disturbances such as noise. This grant is considered by legal theorists as a 'reification' ('*Verdinglichung*') of the tenant's right. The tenant is granted a privilege which is normally only granted to the holder of an *'erga omnes'* real right, such as ownership or usufruct. As is stated in the discussion on 1. *Hunter and Others v. Canary Wharf Ltd.* the granting of such a *locus standi* is economically correct. One of the basic aims of a legal system concerns the effective internalization of external effects. Obliging the tenant to involve his landlord in his action against the interference in his rights would burden this internalization with additional transaction costs.

A second question concerns the *locus standi* of a tenant against his landlord for nuisance caused by his co-tenant. Granting such a *locus standi* would logically involve also the right of the landlord to sue afterwards the disturbing tenant for eventual damages he had to pay to the tenant-victim. In fact such a *locus standi* would establish a vicarious liability for the landlord. Unless such a *locus standi* is explicitly provided for in the rental contract, granting this *locus standi* is economically not advisable. First it would oblige the landlord to a costly scrutiny of his candidate tenants for each tenant involves then an additional risk because of the vicarious liability. Second, it would lead to additional costs of administration of justice because of the risk of doubling the number of suits, that is, those of the tenant-victims against the landlord and of the landlord against the disturbing tenant. In his opinion Lord Hoffman states that the landlord is only liable for the nuisance caused by his tenant when he has given consent to it. This opinion can be sustained also on economic grounds.

**D3 Normal life disturbance: private nuisance?** The disturbances by the neighbours in this case, which consist, according to the claimants, an actionable nuisance, are a normal by-product of modern life (television, radio, eating, lovemaking, children crying, etc.). They should be distinguished from disturbances to be qualified as excesses such as loud shouting by quarrelling (high dBa-music, fighting, etc.) or as professional disturbances (practising musical instruments, hammering, noise from machinery, etc.). Normal life disturbances have two typical characteristics: they are reciprocal and symmetric. What A does to B, B does to A more or less on a similar level. These characteristics are important for the choice of the legal regime. The main legal question about these normal life disturbances is whether they should fall below a nuisance-threshold, barring all possible nuisance claims.

To analyze this from an economic perspective we assume first that these normal life disturbances cannot be prevented. The only way to escape them is to move and go to live in a low-density neighbourhood. Suppose that normal life disturbances are actionable. As these disturbances are reciprocal and symmetric, a claim of A against neighbour B would soon be followed by a claim of B against A. The damages or injunctive relief, awarded by the judge to A for the disturbances by B would be followed by similar remedies awarded to B for disturbances by A. This would amount to a zero-operation for both parties. This zero-operation would involve however costs of administration of justice. As a consequence, none of the parties would incur any gain, but the legal system (the taxpayer) would lose. As a consequence, under the no-prevention-assumption, making normal life disturbances actionable would entail a waste for society. Under this assumption the nuisance threshold is efficient.

Under a second assumption, the more realistic one, also normal life disturbances can be prevented by technical isolation devices. Suppose the cost of prevention is P and that there is no continuum in prevention levels. The situation is binary, either full prevention at P or zero prevention. We also suppose that the prevention works in both directions. When A installs sound insulation A is protected against noise from B and vice versa.

Sound insulation is only efficient when ($P < D^a + D^b$). Both $D^a$ and $D^b$ express the willingness to pay by the parties for a total insulation from noise. Within the case of prevention-efficiency we have to distinguish two situations.

First $P < D^a$ and/or $P < D^b$. In this case prevention is already efficient for at least one of the parties separately. When normal life disturbances are not actionable in this case, the party, for which prevention is efficient also separately will likely install the sound insulation, may be after attempting the other party to contribute. But even when the other party refuses the insulation will be installed because it is beneficial, also for the installing party alone.

When normal life disturbances are actionable in this case both parties, even the party for which prevention is already efficient separately, will try to shift the costs to the other party through court action. Whatever the court decides, full costs for party A or for party B or splitting the costs between A and B, it will lead to additional costs of administration of justice compared to the situation without making these disturbances actionable.

Second, $P>D^a$ and $P>D^b$. In this case reaching efficiency requires collective action by both parties. Without coercive intervention by a third instance, such as the court, the parties might act like players in a prisoner's dilemma which results in a suboptimal equilibrium (see Figure 3.5).

Suppose that P = 20 and that both parties should contribute each 10. Suppose also that the gain is 15 for each party. If both contribute they spend together 20 but realize a gain of 15 for each party, a common gain of 30. This is the optimal outcome. If only one party contributes by putting insulation on her side, a gain of only 5 is realized for each party, a common gain of only 10. If none of both parties contributes the situation remains the same and nothing is gained for both parties. If one of the parties contributes and the other not, the contributing party loses 5 while the other party gains 5. The pay-off for both parties of the option 'contribute' is (5, −5) and of the option 'not contribute' is (5, 0). Individual

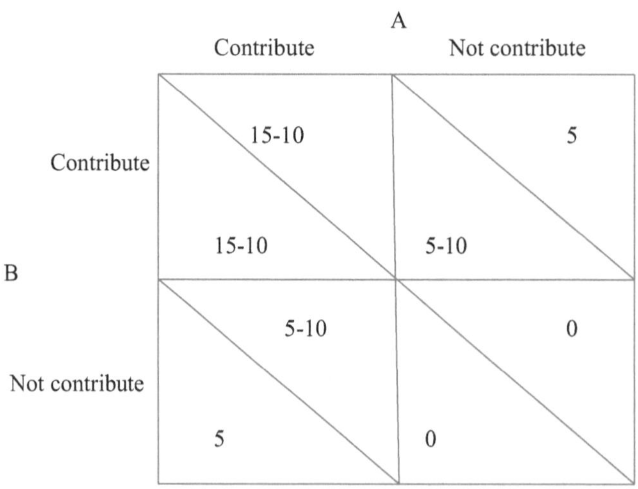


*Figure 3.5* Prisoner's dilemma: sound isolation

rationality leads both parties to option 'not contribute' while collective wealth would be enhanced by the option 'contribute'.

When the parties do not cooperate by both contributing, the optimal outcome can only be reached through a coercive imposition by the court. Consequently, making even normal life disturbances actionable would make efficient outcomes in this case more likely. Under a shadow of a legal regime which allows such actions, parties would be stimulated to make efficient cooperative deals.

When $P > D^a + D^b$ there is prevention inefficiency. It is cheaper for both parties not to insulate because the costs of it are larger than the gains of insulation. When normal life disturbances would be made actionable in this case the parties might be inclined to claim for insulation in order to shift the costs of insulation to the other party. If the court would decide in favour of such a claim it would impose to one of the parties the total burden of an inefficient level of prevention. Suppose the gain of each party is only 5 and the prevention costs are 30. By imposing prevention costs on one of the parties this party would lose 25 (30–5) while the other party would gain only 5. As a consequence, in case of prevention inefficiency it is better that normal life disturbances are not made actionable. It would likely lead to inefficient decisions and additional costs of administration of justice.

When all possible situations in the relationship between prevention costs and gains of insulation are aggregated it appears that in the majority of cases it is not advisable to allow nuisance actions for normal life disturbance. Only the case in which collective action of the parties involved is necessary to reach prevention efficiency ($P<D^a+D^b \wedge P>D^a \wedge P>D^b$) such action are advisable. The court is however not able to classify the concrete case, submitted to it, into one of the mentioned categories. The court may be able to assess the prevention costs, which is a technical given, but not the gains of insulation, which is a subjective value. When courts would ask parties about this variable, they might provide strategic answers. As a conclusion to the cases in which normal life disturbances can be prevented, it seems to be efficient not to allow actions for normal life disturbances because this would lead in the majority of cases to inefficient results.

E **Economic evaluation of the decisions.** The economic evaluation is different for the contractual aspect and for the nuisance aspect. In order to decide whether sound insulation should be included within the contractual obligation of the landlord the court should have investigated which party was the 'better information gatherer'. There is a strong presumption that the landlords, LB Southwark and LB Camden, had to be considered as such as being the professional party. This could have resulted in a court order to provide for sound insulation. The different courts, deciding in this case neglected to investigate this aspect.

As far as nuisance is concerned the decisions of the court can be sustained from an economic perspective. Granting *locus standi* to the tenants against their landlords for nuisance from their neighbours would lead to inefficient levels of costs of administration of justice. Considering normal life disturbances as actionable nuisances would lead under a majority of hypotheses to inefficient outcomes.

### 7. Öffentlicher Abwehranspruch gegen aufs Grundstück gelangende Füβballe *(Public law injunction against footballs getting into a neighbouring field);* Verwaltungsgerichtshof *(Administrative Court) Kassel; Decision 6 May 1993; NJW 1993, Heft 47, 3088–3090*

A **Facts and legal sources.** The plaintiff is a farmer whose land is adjacent to a soccer field. The soccer field is used by a soccer club but owned by the local municipality under conditions administratively determined by this municipality. One of these conditions is that the club is not allowed to make profits. The local municipality only charges the club for electricity, water, garbage cleaning and a sprinkler system. The relationship with the local municipality explains that the case is brought for an administrative court.

During the soccer matches balls get regularly into the field and players rush into the field to fetch them thereby destroying crops on the field. The damage to the crops is assessed by the plaintiff at 350 DM per year. A fence, to be erected to block the balls would cost about 24,000 DM while a net to stop the balls would cost at least 10,000 DM. These latter assessments are done by the court.

§1004 BGB provides that the land owner can ask an injunction against any disturbance of his property other than outright dispossession. When the owner has an obligation to tolerate such disturbances he has no action.

§906 BGB provides that the landowner cannot stop emission of gasses, vapours, noises, smoke, soot, heath, thrilling and other ethereal substances when the emission does not disturb the use of the land in a substantial way. When the emissions do not violate the regulations the disturbance is considered as not substantial. When the disturbance results from a land use which runs with the character of the area ('*ortsüblich*') and when a prevention measure is economically not bearable for the defendant, the plaintiff has to tolerate the emission but can be awarded damages when his land use is disturbed in a disproportionate way.

§ 242 BGB states that the promisor has to execute his obligation in good faith and following good mores.

B **Claims and defences.** The plaintiff asks an injunction from the court to order the installation of a fence with a length of 100 m and a height of 4 m. The cost of it is assessed at 24,000 DM. The plaintiff also points to the absence of a building permit on behalf of the soccer club.

The defendant claims that such a measure is too costly for them and that the soccer club operates under the authority of the local municipality.

**C Sentences and Considerations.** The court does not award the injunction but awards damages of 350 DM a year. These damages can be reassessed every year. The court considers first that §906 BGB is not applicable in this case for the incursions do not concern ethereal substances as mentioned in this article but a very tangible object, i.e. soccer balls and the rushing ins from the players. Because the first section of §906 is not applicable, also the second section of it, providing a damage remedy, is neither applicable. §1004 BGB however is applicable because the incursions of the balls and the rushing in by the players are a clear infringement of the property right of the plaintiff for which the remedy is in principle an injunction.

Although §242 BGB regards literally the relationship of a promisor and a promisee the rule of execution in good faith can be extended to a general principle of law. Consequently also the use of a legal remedy, such as an injunction, can sometimes constitute an abuse of a right.

The court considers the claim by the plaintiff as an abuse of right. The cost of the fence amounts up to 24,000 DM. Even if it would only cost half of it, it would be the equivalent of thirty-four years of paying damages. When only a net is installed, which costs are at least 10,000 DM, the equivalent would be twenty-eight years of paying damages. The court, comparing with other cases of disturbance by football playing, takes into account that the plaintiff does not live adjacent to the soccer play and that his field is not situated beyond the goals. An alternative to the installation of the fence or net is the reduction of the number of matches. According to the court this is not acceptable considering the investments in dressing rooms and the maintenance of the whole sport installation. The court also considers that the absence of a building license does not entail that injunctive relief should be awarded for the absence of a building license does not necessarily involve a violation of the substantial rules of zoning regulations.

**D Economic analysis.**

**D1 Externalities, transaction costs and prevention.** From a Pigouvian point of view the incursions of the balls and the players into the field of the farmer and the ensuing destructions of the crops are negative externalities and a potential source of allocative inefficiency. The soccer players and their supporters (and all who derive a certain value of the game) export a part of their costs to a third party (see Figure 3.6).

When we make abstraction from the possibility of prevention the only way to avoid or reduce the externalities is through stopping the game or reducing the frequency of it. When nothing is done to internalize the external costs the number of matches (N) will be at $Q^1$. This is inefficiently too high a number because at that point the marginal benefit (MB) is lower than the total marginal cost (TMC). By internalizing the

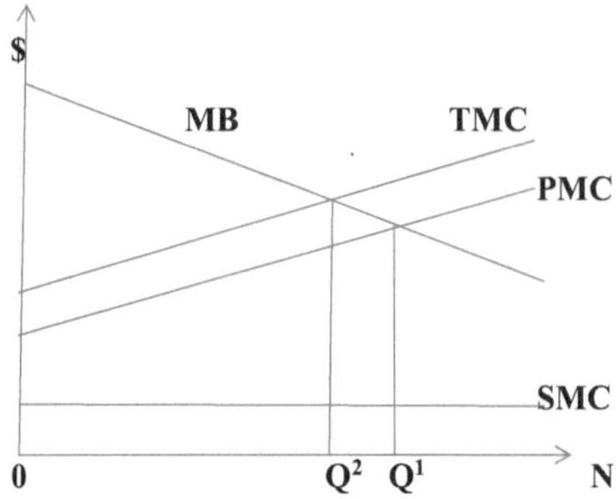


*Figure 3.6* Negative externalities of soccer play

social costs the number of matches will be reduced to $Q^2$, the efficient number.

By installing a fence or a net the social costs are reduced to zero but are replaced by the costs of prevention. Suppose that such a net or fence has to be replaced after a certain time and that during that time a certain number of matches ($Q^3$) will be played. Prevention will be efficient when $P < (Q^3 \times D^m)$, whereby P is the prevention cost and $D^m$ is the damage per one match. If the judge would be able to assess all these variables, it would be easy to take an efficient decision. This is the case for P, because the court is apparently able to assess this more or less accurately (24,000 DM for the fence and 10,000 DM for the net). This is also the case for a part of the damage. The damage on the crops is assessed at 350 DM per year by the victim himself. Another component of the damage, that is the incursions by the balls and the players, are however difficult to assess. The fact that your property is trespassed, even without any material damage is committed to it, may cause a subjective value reduction, which is difficult to assess.

The existence of this difficult to assess component of the damage would, according to Smith, imply that this case should be brought under an exclusion regime and that this case should be dealt with as trespass. As ruled in *Jacque v. Steenberg Homes Inc.* (see before this chapter, 4. Smith: exclusion and governance regimes) the defendant would be enjoined whatever the cost implications for him. Afterwards the parties can renegotiate and eventual strike a deal by which a more efficient result is reached. Suppose the court awards an injunction and orders the soccer club to put a net. To avoid the costs of the net the soccer club may offer the payment of annual damages of 350 DM plus a bonus for the subjective loss by the incursion. The total costs of this offer are however lower than 10,000 DM. If the plaintiff accepts this offer an efficient end result is reached. It is however not sure that the parties will strike such a deal. As they are caught into a bilateral monopoly situation, the parties may act strategically and inflate their prices, by which such a deal is never reached and an inefficient overinvestment in prevention is made.

As the subjective value reduction is only one component in the total damage, as the incursions do not affect the private life of the plaintiff and as there is a risk for inefficiency through over prevention, it seems more acceptable to not adopt a radical exclusion approach and consider, beside an injunction also other possibilities such as damages and no court intervention at all.

In order to decide between these three options we analyze the different possibilities:

1) Suppose $P > (Q^3 x\ D^m)$.

   a Injunction. When transaction costs are low and parties do not act strategically the soccer club will make an offer to pay damages. The parties will strike a mutual benefit deal for an amount which is lower than P but higher than $Q^3 x\ D^m$. When transaction costs are prohibitive however because parties act strategically, no deal will be struck and the soccer club will have to place an inefficient fence or net.

   b Damages. The judge grants damages, the material destruction plus a subjective value bonus, but still lower than P. In this case, whatever the transaction costs, the damages will be paid by the soccer club.

   c No remedy awarded. When transaction costs are low the farmer will offer a certain amount to reduce the number of matches from Q1 to Q2. Such a result is of course doubtful from a justice perspective. When transaction costs are prohibitive the inefficient situation will remain.

2) Suppose $P < (Q^3 x D^m)$.

   a Injunction. The net or fence will be placed. This is the cheapest solution for the soccer club and also the most efficient situation.

   b Damages. When transaction costs are low the soccer club and the farmer will make a deal. The soccer club will build the fence or net and pay to the farmer a bonus which is smaller than $(Q^3 x D^m) - P$. The farmer will be better off because relieved from the damage plus a bonus. The result is efficient. When transaction costs are prohibitive and no deal will be made the farmer will cash the damages and build with it a fence. The result is again efficient.

   c No remedy awarded. The farmer will erect and finance the net or fence because that is still cheaper than incurring the damage.

The result is efficient but of course doubtful from a justice perspective. It may lead to 'demoralization costs' in society.

When an injunction is granted there will be efficiency under supposition 2 while this is doubtful under supposition 1. When damages, such as stated, are granted there is efficiency under both suppositions. When no remedy is awarded the efficiency is doubtful under supposition 1 while under supposition 2 the result is efficient but unjust.

This comparison points out that damages, which include the compensation for the material damage plus a bonus for the loss in subjective value, generates the best guarantee for both efficiency and justice considerations. However, this solution always contains one element of uncertainty, that is, whether the bonus component in it covers more or less the subjective value loss.

E **Economic evaluation of the decision.** The decision of the court can be sustained from an economic point of view as far the choice of the remedy is involved. The choice for damages avoids the risk of inefficient over prevention. The decision can however be criticised from an economic perspective as it does not take into account an important component of damage, namely, the subjective value loss due to the incursions of the balls and the players.

### *8. Nuisance by scaffolding. Burgerlijke Rechtbank Gent (Civil Court Ghent), 21 February 1963; Rechtskundig Weekblad, 1963, 2060–2063*

A **Facts and legal sources.** The plaintiff, Mr. Detremerie, owns two small houses built against the walls of the Saint Nicholas' church, a gothic church built in the thirteenth and fourteenth centuries. With the belfry and the tower of the Saint Bavo cathedral, the tower of the Saint Nicholas' church is part of the most beautiful panorama of historic Ghent. Due to restoration works scaffolds have been placed on the sidewalks around the church and by this also hide the façade of the two houses owned by the plaintiff. The plaintiff ran a barbershop in one of the two houses. He stopped this business and gave his house for rent. The house does not get rented however. According to the plaintiff this is due to the scaffolds which make this house unattractive to let. The defendants are the Church Fabric of Saint Nicholas' church and the city of Ghent. The Church Fabric is an autonomous public body, financed by taxes and with the aim to care for the preservation of the church building as a place for worshipping and as a cultural monument.

According to Belgian law such a nuisance can be qualified in the first place as a negligence tort. When a causal link of such a tort with damage can be established, damages are owed by the tortfeasor to the victim (art. 1382 Belgian Civil Code).

The nuisance can also be qualified as a violation of the property right of the victim, as defined by art. 544 Belgian Civil Code. According to Belgian case law since 1960 (the 'Chimney case', *Cassation Court 6 April 1960, Pas. I, 915*) such a violation can involve a strict liability (see earlier in this chapter, the section on "Nuisance law: historical and comparative context").

**B** **Claims and defences.** The plaintiff asks a compensation for the rents he missed due to the scaffolds. The defendants deny any negligence from their part because the scaffolds are necessary for the restoration and because the restoration is urgent to avoid the collapse of the church. They also deny any causal link with the non-renting of the house.

**C** **Sentence and considerations.** The court considers the claim first under negligence liability and then under the strict liability of violation of a property right.

The court finds no evidence for negligence on behalf of the defendants and this based on four considerations.

First the scaffolds are placed following the state of the art, they do not lean on the houses of the plaintiff, and they do not penetrate into the walls of it.

Second, the restoration works and so the scaffolds are not the result of a negligence in the maintenance of the church but are necessary because of the erosion of the soft sandstones, used in the medieval building.

Third, there is no negligence by delaying the restoration because they were not necessary before and by carrying them out later, better and less burdening techniques can be used.

Fourth, some delay is due to the bankruptcy of the first contractor, for which the defendant cannot be blamed.

The court also dismisses the claim based on the violation of the property right of the plaintiff. According to the court every owner has the right to use his property and to enjoy it in a normal way, that is, according to the kind, the extension and the destination of the estate. The disturbances resulting from such a use have to be tolerated by neighbours. This latter implies that the disturbances the neighbours have to tolerate from each other can be very different because the kind, extension and destination of the estate can also be very different. The restoration works on the church are linked with the characteristics of the building. They are not carried out in order to change the nature of the building or to change its use, but just to maintain it. The restoration works and the disturbances following from them do not pass the level of bare necessity for the maintenance of the church. They have to be considered as a normal exercise of the property right of the owner. Moreover, the plaintiff knew, when he purchased the house, that is was adjacent to an old and decaying church and that, earlier or later, restoration works had to be carried out, including the need for scaffolding. The scaffolds are placed in such a way as to minimize the impact on the houses of the plaintiff. There is no physical intrusion, they do not bar the entries, they do not take away light. The only disturbance is of an aesthetic kind. Finally, the house of the plaintiff is old and decaying and is not situated in the main shopping passage of the city. Consequently, the link with the fact that the house does not get rented is very unlikely.

## D Economic evaluation.

**D1 Externalities for a public benefit. Analogy with takings.** As in the other cases of nuisance, discussed in this chapter, negative externalities are imposed to the plaintiff and as a consequence the question arises whether and how these externalities should be internalized by the parties who caused these externalities. There is however an important difference with former nuisance cases and this difference regards the economic character of the aim of the defendants. By restoring the Saint Nicholas' church the Church Factory and the city authorities of Ghent intend to produce a specific public good, i.e. the preservation of a cultural monument and by this enhancing the touristic attractiveness of the city. The public good-character is obvious as the view on the church, right within the centre of the town, is non-rival and non-excludable. Many private parties, such as culturally sensitive citizens, the touristic sector (hotels, restaurant, shop-keepers, etc.) and the tax collecting public authorities would profit from this restoration but none of them would be ready to finance it as they are not able to charge prices to other profiting parties. As a consequence, it makes economic sense that the defendants, both public authorities, have ordered this restoration and could finance it by taxation. This public good character of the restoration is completely overlooked by the court. The court considers the restoration of the church as a kind of natural necessity inherent to the character of the church building. Nevertheless other options than to restore are thinkable. For instance, the church could have been demolished in order to create a parking lot or establish a shopping mall. The mentioned authorities preferred restoration in order to produce the mentioned public good generating at its turn varied private benefits. Taking into regard this public good-aim, which is at the origin of the restoration, consequently of the scaffolding and consequently of the negative externalities imposed on the plaintiff, one cannot deny a strong parallel with a taking. Also in cases of taking we have to deal with a private interest which had to suffer in order to realize a public benefit. The difference however is that in a classical taking the victim suffers by a full loss of a property right or of a partial loss of it (regulatory taking). In this case the victim suffers by an imposed externality. Classical legal doctrine and case law consider this distinction as important. From a legal-economic viewpoint however it is not, for all reasons which can be advanced to compensate the victim of a full taking, are also valid in this case of quasi-taking by imposing a negative externality.

The first reason concerns the incentives of the public authorities. If these authorities would be not obliged to compensate for the external effects of their plans, they might be tempted to push through inefficient social projects. Because they are able to disregard parts of the costs of the project, as they do not have to compensate, they might push through projects the costs of which are larger than the public benefits. This latter constitutes a 'moral hazard'. The moral hazard-argument is applicable to all costs of public projects, not only to the full taking of an estate, not only to the diminution of value due to a regulation, but also to the diminution of value due to a negative externality.

The second reason concerns the spread of the cost of a public project. When the victim of a negative externality, imposed in order to realize a public benefit, is not compensated this victim is charged in a double way: first, by its contribution to taxation in order to finance the concerned social project, second by bearing the costs of the negative externality. In fact, the victim is burdened by a random extra-tax, which is in contradiction with the legality principle of taxation under the rule of law.

**D2 Negligence liability or strict liability**. The court considered whether negligence was involved by placing the scaffolds and whether this negligence was causal to some harm to the plaintiff. To decide on negligence the courts looked to the state of the art of the scaffolding, whether a lack of maintenance of the building was at the origin of the restoration and the scaffolding, whether the timing of the restoration was justified, whether the long duration of it could be blamed to the defendant. An analysis of negligence in this case from an economic point of view would have had another methodological structure. According to the so-called Justice Learned Hand-formula a party has acted negligently when the ex ante prevention costs were lower than the ex ante expected accident costs (N when P<EAC). When the ex ante prevention costs were higher than the ex ante expected accident costs the party is not negligent (nN when P > EAC). By expected accident costs are understood the costs of the accident multiplied by the probability of the accident. In this case the formula is even simpler. Because the probability of harm by the scaffolds is 100 percent the expected accident costs equal the accident costs. In this case the judge had to investigate whether the defendant (and his agent, the contractor) could have avoided the harm to the plaintiff at a minor cost than the cost of the harm. Suppose for instance that the scaffolds could have been placed in a less obstructing way and that this would have led to a surplus cost of X while the harm to the defendant was significantly higher than X, then the defendant should have been considered as negligent and eventually liable. In the opposite case however not. The judge did not investigate the negligence question in this way but decided on rather vague and superficial considerations.

Nevertheless a more substantial question concerning the liability of the defendant can be raised, i.e. whether negligence liability is the most efficient approach in this case and whether strict liability is not more appropriate. According to the legal-economic viewpoint strict liability is possible when the causation of the harm is unilateral. This is certainly the case here. The harm was unilaterally caused by the scaffolding. The position of the victim remained static during this process. Strict liability is moreover preferable when, for policy reasons, the level of the harmful activities should be influenced. Switching from negligence liability to strict liability does not affect the level of care adopted by the parties. Because the parties, developing harmful activities have to pay always under strict liability, even when P > EAC, the profitability of these activities becomes lower than under a regime of negligence liability. The policy reasons to adopt here a strict liability are already indicated in the former paragraph. Compensation for negative externalities which are a by-product of the realization of a social project should be compensated always in order to avoid a moral hazard among the public authorities, initiating the social project.

The court however dismisses also the strict liability of the defendant, based on the violation of the property right of the defendant (art. 544 CC). The four reasons the court invokes for this dismissal are however also very challengeable from an economic point of view.

First, according to the court, the external effect an agent is allowed to produce depends in the kind, the extension and the use of the property of that agent. If this is accepted as a general rule owners may act strategically and select these types of use for which external effects will be allowed. In fact, this type of reasoning announces a hidden way of subsidization of some uses.

Second, according to the court, the plaintiff knew that the church had to be restored when he purchased the houses. The court adopts here the 'coming to the nuisance'-argument. As mentioned in the theoretical part (see earlier in this chapter, the section on "Coming to the nuisance") this argument is economically deficient because, when it is adopted as a general rule, a race will develop in order to 'homestead' rights to externalize.

Third, according to the court, the houses of the plaintiff are old and decaying and outside shopping passage. This fact may be relevant for the level of damages, not for the liability itself.

Fourth, according to the court the causal link between the scaffolding and the fact the house was not rented is doubtful. The court should have made here a risk-assessment. One cannot deny that a house without scaffolds is more attractive than one with scaffolds. To assess damages the court should have assessed in how far the scaffolds affected the probability of renting.

E **Economic evaluation of the decision.** The decision and the considerations of the court cannot be sustained from an economic point of view and this for several reasons. First the court overlooked the fact that the harm was committed within the context of public works and that it could be treated as a quasi-taking and that this justifies strict liability and compensation. Second, the analysis of negligence does not reflect any efficiency concern and neglects the Justice Hand formula. Third, the reasons to dismiss the strict liability, based on a property violation, are either challengeable or regard the level of the damage.

### *9.* Empress Car Co. (Abertillery) Ltd v. National Rivers Authority, *House of Lords, [1998] 1 All ER HL, 481–494*

A **Facts and legal sources.** The defendant, the Empress Car Company is located in Abertillery (South Wales) close to the river Ebbw Fach. It maintained a diesel tank in a yard draining directly into the river. The tank was surrounded by a bund, to contain spillage but the company had overridden this protection pipe on the outlet of the tank so as to connect it to a drum standing outside the bund, because it was easier to draw oil from the drum than directly from the tank. On the outlet from the tank there was a tap without a lock. On 20 March 1995 the tap was opened by an unknown person and the entire contents of the tank ran into the drum, overflowed into the yard and passed down the drain into the river. There was a history of local opposition to the company's business. The incident coincided with a public inquiry on a disputed footpath to be held on the following day. There was no finding on the identity of the person who turned on the tap.

Section 85(1) of the Water Resources Act 1991 states: 'A person contravenes this section if he causes or knowingly permits any poisonous, noxious or polluting matter or any solid waste matter to enter any controlled waters'. The river Ebbw Fach, close to the premises of the defendant, is included in the category of 'controlled waters'

B **Claims and defences.** The National Rivers Authority claims damages from the defendant for the pollution of the river. The defendant is liable under the mentioned section of the Water Resources Act 1991 because he neglected to take appropriate measures to prevent the spilling, more precisely by not putting a lock on the tap and by this facilitating the spilling of the oil in the river.

The defendant denies any responsibility in the spilling of the oil. The responsibility lies entirely with the person who opened the tap. In order to be liable for such damage the law requires a positive act causing it, which is not the case regarding the defendant.

C **Considerations and sentences.** The case has been discussed before three jurisdictions, i.e. the Tredegar Justices sitting at Gwent, Abertillery, the Crown Court of Newport Gwent, and the Queens' Bench Divisional Court. All three courts sentenced that the defendant was responsible for the spilling of the oil by failing to take appropriate prevention and consequently liable under the Water Resources Act 1991. The defendant appealed to the House of Lords contending that 'causing' for the purposes of Section 85(1) required some positive act and that the escape could not have been caused by any such act by the company.

In his opinion Lord Hoffmann agrees that in order to establish liability on behalf of the defendant a 'positive act' is required. Such a positive act does not have to be, however, the 'immediate cause' of the damage. The question is whether something the defendant has done that caused the pollution. Maintaining a diesel tank with a tab without a lock is 'doing something'. By this the requirement of a 'positive act' on behalf of the defendant is fulfilled in this case. Further Lord Hoffmann discusses the notion of 'causation' in this case. The relevant question here is not 'what caused the escape of oil' but whether the defendant did something that caused the pollution. It is possible that the pollution had many causes such as the intervention of a third party or natural forces. Whether the contribution of the defendant to the causation of the pollution implies his liability depends from the purpose and the scope of the rule. In this case it depends from a statutory construction of Section 85(1) of the Water Resources Act of 1991. According to the underlying policy purposes of this Act a strict liability was imposed to all agents who contributed to the causation of pollution. No 'mens rea' neither foreseeability in the strict sense is necessary. Whether causation by an intervention of a third party or an Act of God relieves the defendant from strict liability depends from the ordinary or extraordinary character of these facts. If they are a normal fact of life the intervention into the causation does not relieve the defendant from his strict liability. If they are not, the defendant should be acquitted. Concerning this case, the intervention by an unknown third person, who opened the tap of the tank, should not be considered as something extraordinary, especially because the establishment of the company caused some animosity in the neighbourhood. Consequently the appeal was dismissed.

## D Economic analysis

### D1 A problem of externalities. Strict liability. Exclusion or governance.

As in many countries water pollution is governed in the UK by a '*lex specialis*', the Water Resources Act 1991, which imposes a strict criminal liability to the offenders. In terms of the distinction made by Smith (see before this chapter, 4. Smith: exclusion or governance regimes) the WRA reflects rather an exclusion approach. When enforcing the WRA judges are not supposed to balance the efficiency of water polluting activities against other conflicting uses and award an entitlement to the most efficient activity. They are expected to punish the polluters with rather heavy punishments. Section 85(6) provides when on summary conviction an imprisonment maximum of three years is possible eventually combined with a fine of maximum £20,000 and when on conviction by indictment an imprisonment maximum of two years, eventually combined with a fine is possible. Because this criminal liability is strict the judge does not have to consider whether there was negligence, 'mens rea' or not. Simple causation is sufficient for conviction. It is clear that an exclusion logic prevails here, or to put it in Calabresian terms, a mere property rule to protect the controlled waters. The option of the legislator of the WRA in favour of mere exclusion is certainly sustainable from an economic viewpoint. In case a governance regime was adopted the judge was required to balance the efficiency of water polluting activities with alternative competing uses of the water (fishing, swimming, regatta sports, hiking and biking along the river, other industrial uses of the river, etc.), situated downstream the river. A governance approach would require huge information costs because a multitude of affected downstream uses of the river had to be balanced against the polluting activity. The criminal liability imposed by the WRA implies in fact that the use of the water is controlled ex ante by awarding licenses of water use and by the rights of riparian owners who are entitled to make a correlative and reasonable use of the water.

**D2 External intervention. Liability**. The defendant in the case was found liable even when the pollution had been caused also by an external intervention. The court held that when the causation chain was broken by an ordinary event, the defendant should be found liable, but not in case of extraordinary events. From an economic point of view the choice of the liability rule has an impact on prevention levels among the riparian owners and their activity levels along the river.

Suppose that the riparian owners attach a negative value to the sanctions of the WRA of S, disregarding hereby, for simplicity, the variety of sanctions provided in the WRA. The real costs of a WRA-offence is determined by the apprehension rate and this apprehension-rate is also influenced by the choice of the liability regime. Within the discussion about this case we can distinguish three possible liability regimes:

1) An agent who caused the pollution is always liable even when the chain of causation was broken by extraordinary events (e.g. exceptional weather, terrorist attacks). The probability of being convicted then is $P^1$
2) An agent who caused the pollution is liable even when the chain of causation was broken by an external event but this event has to be of an ordinary kind. This position is adopted by the House of Lords in this case. The probability of being convicted then is $P^2$
3) An agent who caused the pollution is never liable when the chain of causation has been broken by an external event. This was the defendants' position and this regime prevailed also in the case *Impress (Worcester) Ltd v. Rees* [1971] 2 All ER 357. The probability of being convicted then is $P^3$

Of course: $P^1 > P^2 > P^3$.

The costs of crime, either $P^1S$, $P^2S$ or $P^3S$, influence the prevention levels among the riparian owners. Acting economically rational they will spend on prevention up to the equimarginal level, that is, up to the level where marginal reduction of crime costs is equal to the marginal prevention cost. As crime costs are smaller under $P^3$ than under $P^2$ and under $P^2$ smaller than under $P^1$ the according prevention levels (PR) will also reflect this order, as shown in Figure 3.7.

The question however is which of the three prevention levels is socially the most efficient. This question can only be answered by the relationship of prevention costs and damage costs. The socially optimal level of prevention is again at an equimarginal level, but now at the level where the marginal reduction of damage costs (dDC) equals the marginal prevention costs. Suppose this level is $PR^{max}$. Because the court in this case has only the choice between $PR^1$, $PR^2$ and $PR^3$ it has to find out which one of the three levels is the closest to $PR^{max}$. For instance on the graph $PR^{max}$ is the closest to $PR^2$, so then the court should select the second liability. In the real world courts are

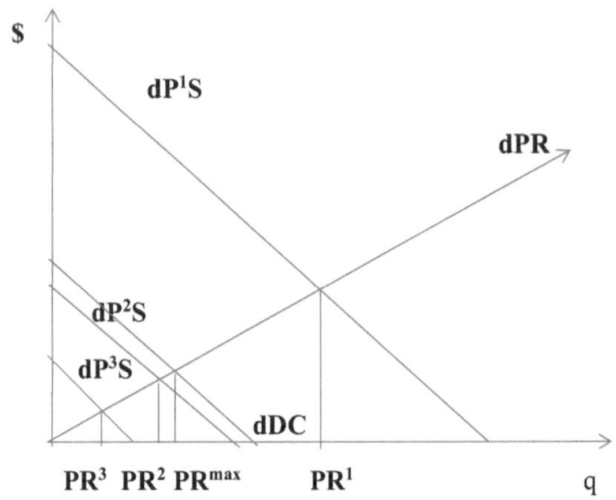


*Figure 3.7* Prevention level: theft of diesel

not able to assess this in a more or less accurate way. The numbers of data which have to be made available to make these calculations are immense and courts do not dispose over enough time or means to do this. The only way to minimize error in such cases is to rely on broad economic intuitions which indicate rather which option not to take than which option to take.

If we adopt the third liability regime, i.e. never liable when an external cause (see *Impress Ltd v. Rees*), economic intuition indicates that such a regime will lead to under prevention ($PR^3$). Riparian owners know that any external intervention in the causation leading to the water pollution will make them immune for legal sanctions. As a consequence they will not take appropriate measures to protect their installations against third intruders or against recurrent weather conditions. The level of prevention will be only determined by the probability of their own damage costs, such as in this case the spilling of the oil by which there is no alignment with the socially optimal prevention level.

If we adopt the first liability regime, i.e. always liable when an external cause, riparian owners would be pushed to adopt very high levels of prevention in their activities. In this case they are obliged to anticipate to even extraordinary events such as abnormal weather conditions and terrorists attacks. This would involve very high information costs. In order to avoid sanctions as provided in the WRA (imprisonment, fines) riparian owners have to study for instance the evolution of the weather or the international situation concerning terrorism. Such high prevention cost levels would erode profit levels of many riparian activities by which many useful activities would have to be stopped. Adoption of this liability regime also runs against economic intuition.

If we adopt the second liability regime, the one chosen in this case, riparian owners have to anticipate to external interventions of an ordinary kind.

The information costs for this anticipation are usually very low as knowledge on recurrent events is often present through general life experience. Often it does not involve much additional cost. Nevertheless the riparian owners will be pushed to take prevention measures to cope with ordinary external events, as they can be held liable even when the eventual third intruders remain unknown.

E **Economic evaluation of the decision.** In this case of water pollution, that is, a case of external costs, the court could rely on a specific legal rule, the Water Resources Act 1991, endorsing rather an exclusion regime than a governance regime. This choice of the legislator can be endorsed economically as a governance regime would imply very high information costs due to the multiple uses of rivers. In its application of this legislation the court opted for a rather severe but not unreasonable liability regime, that is, liability also in case of an external event at the condition that this event is not extraordinary. The economic intuition indicates that this regime seems to be the best choice as it avoids on one side under prevention and while it does not, on the other side, render many businesses by riparian owners unprofitable due to excessive prevention requirements.

## Cases

*Boomer v. Atlantic Cement Co.*, 257 N.E.2d 870(N.Y. 1970)

*Bove v. Donner-Hanna Coke Co.*, (1932) 236 A.D. 37; 258 N.Y.S. 229

*Burgerlijke Rechtbank Gent (Civil Court Ghent), 21 February 1963; Rechtskundig Weekblad, 1963, 2060–2063*

*Empress Car Co. (Abertillery) Ltd v. National Rivers Authority, House of Lords, [1998] 1 All ER HL, 481–494*

*Frustzwerge in Nachbars Garten (Gnomes of Frustration), AG Grünstadt, Urt.v.11.2.1994–2aC 334/93; NJW 1995, Heft 13, 889*

*Glossop v Heston and Isleworth Local Board ([1879] 12 CH.D,102–109)*

*Hunter and others v. Canary Wharf Ltd; Hunter and others v. London Docklands Development Corp*

*Jacque v. Steenberg Homes Inc. {563 N.W.2d 154(Wis.1997)}*

*Marcic v. Thames Water Utilities Ltd; Decision of Judge Richard Havery QC[2001] 3 All ER 698; Court of Appeal Civil Division[2002] EWCA Civ 64; House of Lords [2003] UKHL 66*

*Sturges v. Bridgman* (1879) LR 11 Ch. D 852

*Tribunal Civil de Nivelles (Belgium), 31 Mars 1982, Revue Générale des Assurances et des Responsabilités, 1984, 10828*

*Watson and another v. Croft Promosport Ltd [2009] EWCA Civ 15*

## Bibliography

Bouckaert, Boudewijn and Gerrit De Geest (1998) 'The Complexity of Belgian Nuisance Law: An Economic Analysis', in Robert Cooter and Edgardo Buscaglia, eds. *Law, Economics and Development*, MAKLU, Antwerp

Calabresi, Guido and Douglas A. Melamed (1972) 'Property Rules, Liability Rules and Inalienability: One View of the Cathedral', *Harvard Law Review*, Vol. 85, 1089–1128

Coase, Ronald H. (1960) 'The Problem of Social Cost', *Journal of Law and Economics*, Vol. 3, 1–44

Cordato, Roy E. (1998) 'Time Passage and the Economics of Coming to the Nuisance: Reassessing the Coasean Perspective', *Campbell Law Review*, Vol. 20, 273

Davids, W.J.M. (1999) *Burenrecht*, Deventer

Lueck, Dean (1995) 'The Rule of First Possession and the Design of the Law', *Journal of Law and Economics*, Vol. 38, 393–436

Merrill, Thomas W. and Henry E. Smith (2001) 'What Happened to Property in Law and Economics', *The Yale Law Journal*, Vol. 111, 357–398

Ott, Claus and Hans-Bernd Schäfer (2008) 'The Dichotomy Between Property Rules and Liability Rules: Experiences from Germany', *Erasmus Law Review*, Vol. 1, no. 4, 41–58

Parchomovsky, Gideon and Alex Stein (2009) 'Reconceptualizing Trespass', *New York University Law Review*, Vol. 103, 1–53

Polinsky, Mitchell A. (1979) 'Resolving Nuisance Disputes. The Simple Economics of Injunctive and Damage Remedies', *Stanford Law Review*, 1075–1113

Sagaert, Vincent (2014) *Beginselen van Belgisch Privaatrecht V. Goederenrecht*, Wolters-Kluwer, Mechelen

Singer, Joseph William (2001) *Introduction to Property*, Gaithersburg, Aspen Publishers, New York

Smith, II George P. (1995) 'Nuisance Law: The Morphogenesis of an Historical Revisionist Theory of Contemporary Economic Jurisprudence', *Nebraska Law Review*, Vol. 74, no. 4

Smith, Henry E. (2004) 'Exclusion and Property Rules in the Law of Nuisance', *Virginia Law Review*, Vol. 90, no. 4, 965–1049

Swanson, Timothy and Andreas Kontoleon (2010) 'Nuisance', in Boudewijn Bouckaert, ed. *Property Law and Economics*, 2nd Edition, Encyclopedia of Law and Economics, Edward Elgar, Cheltenham, Vol. 5

Van Es, P.C. (2005) *De Actio Negatoria, Een studie naar de rechtsvorderlijke zijde van het eigendomsrecht*, Wolf Legal Publishers, Rotterdam

Wittman, Donald (1980) 'First Come First Serve: An Economic Analysis of Coming to the Nuisance', *Journal of Legal Studies*, Vol. 9, 557–568

# 4 Fragmentation of property rights

## Easements

### 4.1 Fragmentation of property rights and easements in the economic theory of law

1 **Fragmentation of property rights. Types.** Property, understood in its Bartolian-Blackstonian sense consists of a bundle of rights, which can be fragmented by the owner both in real as in personal rights (see Chapter 1) As remarked by Stake (Stake 2010: 127) fragmentation of rights may occur in three ways.

First, rights can be fragmented through the physical division of their object. Land can be divided spatially and the parts assigned to different owners. In addition, mobile goods, especially amounts of money can be divided physically. Through spatial division of land, sub-dividers are able to plan the use of space such as habitation quarters or industrial zones and business areas. Often the law provides procedures to convert physically indivisible goods into divisible goods in order to solve potential conflicts between co-owners or the co-heirs of an inheritance. When co-owners or co-heirs do not agree about the assignment of an indivisible good such as a house, a jewel, a painting, the law provides a procedure to convert these goods into an amount of money through a public auction.

Second, rights can be fragmented in a temporal way. Some rights have a perpetual character (e.g. fee simple, civil law property), while some have a temporal character. In both cases, the law often allows the holder of those rights to make temporal subdivisions. The most prominent examples in common, respectively civil law are life estate and usufruct. In both cases, the owner grants to another very wide use rights on the assets for his/her whole lifetime. A temporal division may cause a problem of efficiency as the temporal right holder will not make long term investments in the assets because that would create positive externalities for the subsequent rights holders (Stake 2010: 134). This efficiency problem will be alleviated when the temporal division is based on a mutual transfer. This will allow the grantor to compensate the risk of underinvestment by charging a higher price or diminishing this risk by negotiating side agreements obliging the grantee to make the necessary investments. The efficiency problem is however difficult to correct when a temporal division occurs outside a mutual agreement, as for example as the result of a bequeath in a will. In addition, temporal divisions within a public policy context may be problematic. Governments awarding short-term concessions to private firms on natural resources may provide incentives to overexploit the natural resources.

Third, the fragmentation can relate to the bundle of rights itself. As mentioned in Chapter 1, full ownership or fee simple consists often of several, more limited rights. In civil and common law, these rights are standardized and fixed in number when they have a 'real' character (see Chapter 1). When they have only a personal character such rights are in principle open for contractual creativity. However, also for personal rights certain standardization is often the case through default law and statutory regulation of contracts (e.g. regulatory law and default law concerning tenancy). In difference with real rights, however standardization through default law does not limit the possibility of creating new personal rights.

The fixed number of real rights, which can be fragmented from full ownership, the so-called '*numerus clausus*' (see also Chapter 1) implies a limitation of the freedom of contract. As freedom of contract carries a prima facie preference in economic theory because it enhances mutual benefit transactions, such a limitation seems to be at odds with economic efficiency. As argued by Merrill and Smith (2000) and Hansmann and Kraakman (2002) some good economic reasons may justify the '*numerus clausus*'. Because real rights are '*erga omnes*' and bestow legal obligations on a class of parties, extending far beyond the two contracting parties, these latter parties would in fact impose significant information costs on third parties. Free proliferation of real rights would mean that third parties could be obliged to screen a multitude of different obligations, implied by the varied fauna of specific real rights generated by contractual interaction. By limiting and standardizing the real rights, information costs are minimized. The simple mention that A is the usufructor signals for instance to potential buyers of the asset the bundle of rights and obligations in A's legal relationship with the asset. Free proliferation would mean that they have to scrutinize each contract separately on its specific content.

The distinction between real and personal rights is however not always straight. In civil law, for instance it is accepted that the right of a tenant, although categorized as personal, has an '*erga omnes*' character as far as nuisances are concerned. Consequently, the tenant has a right of standing against nuisances and does not have to involve his/her landlord in his/her claim. In case however when a third party claims a right on the rented estate the tenant has to involve his/her landlord as a defendant (Sagaert 2014).

2 **Easements/servitudes in civil and common law.** Servitudes in civil law find their historic origin in Roman law. The *servitudo* in Roman law was considered a 'real right' on the property (*dominium*) of somebody else ('ius *in re aliena*'). A *servitudo* was considered to establish a relationship between a dominant estate enjoying an interest in another estate, the servient estate. As a

relationship between estates makes only sense as a metaphor, this expression means in fact that the *servitudo* sticks with the land and can be claimed by the succeeding owners of the dominant estate and has to be tolerated by the succeeding owners of the servient estate. In Roman law a *servitudo* could only relate to an obligation of tolerance (*tolerare*) and not of acting (*facere*). The most common servitudes in Roman law were: right of way (*'iter, actus, via'*), right of water conduct ('*aquaductum*'), right of pasture ('*ius pascendi*'), right to support an overhanging construction ('*servitus onus ferendi*'), right to prevent the neighbour to build higher ('*servitus altius non tollendi*'), right to light ('*servitus ne luminibus officiatur*') (Van Oven 1948: 148–153).

During the French revolution the notion of 'servitudes' received a negative connotation as it was associated with feudalism. Servitudes were nevertheless allowed in the Civil Code but art. 638 of this code stated clearly that the servitudes, as provided by the Civil Code, could not establish any hierarchy between estates. By this the drafters of the code wanted to distance their code from any systems of land tenures (Fenet 1827: 318; Laurent 1878: 145). The non-feudal character of the law of servitudes in the civil code is embedded in art. 686, stating that servitudes cannot have a personal character but have to be to the benefit of the (use of) the dominant estate. A servitude, imposing for instance to the owner of the servient estate to bring flowers every Sunday morning to the owner of the dominant estate is consequently void. Servitudes such as a right of way, water conduct, limitation of building altitude, etc. are allowed because technically linked with the use of the dominant estate. In civil law this requirement is called *prediality*.

In common law rather the term 'easement' is used. While the civil law tradition views these rights from the standpoint of the servient estate-owner, the common law tradition looks to them from the dominant estate-owner's standpoint (Pollock and Maitland 1968: 145). Compared to civil law the English common law is, concerning the establishment of easements, much less flexible. While according to the civil code owners can establish freely the servitudes they consider useful, at the condition of 'prediality' however, only easements of the accepted list by the courts are allowed in English common law (Harwood 1982: 358). As in the civil law also the English common law requires that 'the right (i.e. the easement) must accommodate (i.e. be for the benefit of) the dominant property, and not merely a personal benefit for the dominant owner' (Harwood 1982: 361). As the civil law the American common law is flexible concerning the establishment of easement by consent between the owner of a dominant estate and of a servient estate at the condition however that the easement is not personal but linked with the use of the dominant estate. This condition is called 'touch and concern'. According to Stake (Stake 2010: 144) courts find that the condition of 'touch and concern' is satisfied when the successor-owner of the dominant estate enjoys the benefit more than the original promisee.

## 3 Economic theory on fragmentation of property rights and easements.

Fragmentation of property rights, either in personal or real rights, allows a more efficient allocation of property rights and use of resources. Through the flexibility, allowed by fragmentation, property rights 'allocation can be tailored to a more varied set of preferences of the users of assets. For instance, suppose on one side an owner of a mansion who is not interested to live in it, but would like to bequeath it to his children; suppose on the other side an older childless couple who is interested to live in the mansion and would like to have certainty of habitation until the end of their life. The owner can offer a usufruct (in common law: a life estate) on the house. By this, the couple has certainty of habitation while the owner is able to retain the mansion for his siblings.

As mentioned before (see before this chapter, 1. Fragmentation of property rights. Types), fragmentation, especially temporal division, may create problems of efficient use. Moreover, fragmentation involves additional costs in the operation of the property system. Agents operating within the property system are faced with higher information costs as the fragmentation involves a higher complexity of the legal situation vis-à-vis the resources. With complex fragmentation it is for instance impossible to rely exclusively on possession as a check on property rights so that more sophisticated systems such as a registration system, in which the fragmented rights are documented and made public (see also Chapter 5), are necessary for the smooth working of markets.

Easements or servitudes are probably the most popular type of fragmentation and contribute a lot to a more efficient use of land and buildings. According to the English Law Commission at least 65 percent of freehold titles are subject to one or more easements and 79 percent are subject to one or more restrictive covenants. On the utility of easements and restrictive covenants the Law Commission adds:

> Without the vital role that easements and covenants play in the regulation of the use of land in England and Wales, the full extent to which land can be enjoyed could not be realised. Many properties would be unable to exist fruitfully without rights over neighbouring land. Neighbours' co-operation is, to an extent, based on social convention, but is supported in the majority of cases by enforceable rights and obligations.
>
> (Law Commission 2008: 39)

The right of way illustrates for instance the efficiency of easements. Without this easement enclaved parcels would have a very low value on the market. In order to get access to the public road the owner of it has then to buy all the parcels situated between the enclaved parcel and the road. This could be a very costly solution to the problem. By providing an easement of a right of way the owner of the enclaved parcel can solve his problem at a much lower cost. Suppose the value of an enclaved land for A is only €20,000. By getting access to the public road the value doubles to €40,000. Suppose the price of the intermittent parcel is €40,000 but A is not interested at all in this parcel and is not willing to pay this price. As a result, the enclaved parcel remains underused. Suppose A can purchase a right of way for €5,000. By paying €5,000 the value of his enclaved parcel increases by €20,000, a net gain of €15,000. The example shows that a more efficient use of land is made possible merely by allowing the fragmentation of rights on the intermittent parcel.

As mentioned earlier (see before this chapter, 2. Easements/servitudes in civil and common law) easements are considered as real rights in the civil law terminology, or '*run with the land*', in common law terms. The real character of easements saves certainly in transaction costs. Suppose easements would be merely personal rights, the easement has to be renegotiated at each transfer either of the dominant or servient estate. A possible perverse effect of this could be that the owner of the servient estate puts his estate for sale only for getting rid of the easement. By awarding to easements a real character, such inefficient sales are prevented. The real character of easements creates however other problems such as problems of bilateral monopoly and anti-commons.

4 **Economic theory on easements. Bilateral monopoly and anti-commons.** A market setting with only one seller and only one buyer is called a bilateral monopoly. In this setting either supply and demand are respectively controlled by only one agent. When both parties are exploiting their monopoly position by adopting strategic behaviour, this could lead to high negotiation costs and a possible breakdown of the negotiations and the missing of a mutual benefit opportunity. Concerning easements, bilateral monopoly settings are possible either in situations where the establishment of an easement would be efficient or in situations where the extinction of an easement would be efficient.

Take the already mentioned example of the enclaved parcel, the value of it can be raised from €20,000 to €40,000 by establishing a right of way to the public road. The owner of the intermittent parcel may be aware of this substantial value increase and tries to exploit this by an exorbitant inflation of his price for the easement. The owner of the enclaved parcel does not accept this and breaks off the negotiation by which a Pareto-efficient transaction fails to happen. Such efficiency problems in the establishment of monopolies are remedied in the civil law by providing easements, which can be established beyond mutual consent. Such easements are called either easements originating from the location of parcels (art. 640–648 Civil Code) or legal easements (art. 649–685 Civil Code). In common law similar easements are provided, i.e. the easements by necessity.

Examples of the civil law:

- The owner of a parcel without any access to the public road can claim an easement of right of way from the owner of the intermittent parcel. The latter owner can charge for the costs of it, but he has to allow the easement (art. 682 Civil Code; art. 917 and 918 BGB; Louisiana Civil Code 1870, art. 609–701). The establishment of such an easement can be qualified as a private taking. The taking is not initiated by a public authority but by a private person. As with takings, also here compensation to the servient estate-owner is due.

- The owner of land on a slope to receive the water from higher land. The owner of the lower land is not allowed to build for instance a dam to keep the water up and transform neighbours' land into marshland (art. 640 Civil Code).
- An owner can ask the owner of adjacent land to build a fence between the two parcels on common costs (art. 646 Civil Code). This easement, established through private taking, is a remedy for free ridership. The owner, who is building first a fence on the border of his land, provides a positive externality to his neighbour. This could lead to a suboptimal Nash-equilibrium in which each party waits for the other one to build first.

Civil law also distinguishes so-called public servitudes. This category involves all kind of limited charges public authorities can impose on private land, without any compensation. Examples are the charge to attach city lights on the facades of private houses, the charge to tolerate a telephone cabin on his land and the charge to tolerate military signalling installations on his land. These easements differ from the others by the fact there is no dominant estate, only a servient one. From an economic point of view public easements should be considered as takings, which are so trivial that the transaction costs of a compensation arrangement are too high compared with the sum of compensation.

In common law jurisdictions without statutory provisions on easements beyond mutual consent the problem of landlocked land is dealt with by the doctrine of right of way by necessity. Often the landlocked character of a parcel finds its origin in a grant in which a parcel is subdivided. Although in most of such grants a provision is made to grant access to the parcel, sometimes such a provision is omitted. The grantee may have accepted such landlocked land for several reasons such as betting on the possibility to get a right of way on the other adjacent parcels. Courts will most often award a right of way to the landlocked grantee under the supposition that the right of way was implicitly intended in the grant. The courts in fact construe transactions in the grant in such a way as to avoid making the use of land impossible by depriving it of a means of access (Bradbrook 1983: 43; *Nickerson v. Barraclough* 1982). This doctrine leaves however the awarding of the right of way largely to the discretion of the court. In several common law countries statutory acts provide a right of way and other necessary easements with a legal base. The Property Law Act 1974–1978, Section 180 of Queensland Australia provides for instance that the court may impose on a servient land an obligation that is necessary in the interest of effective use of the dominant land. For such an imposition, the owner of the servient land has to be adequately compensated. By this provision, the artificial construction of an implied grant has been made redundant.

Beside bilateral monopoly problems, the accumulation of easements on one estate may create the even harder problem of the anti-commons (Heller 1998: 621; Depoorter and Parisi 2003; Bouckaert 2001: 949). Because most of the easements have a perpetual character, many easements may burden an estate during many years. For a buyer-developer these easements may be annoying obstacles and in order to carry out his plan he may need the consent of all the easement holders. Their consent to abolish the easement is complementary, so that every easement holder is in the position to bar the project. This is a typical anti-commons setting, in which every 'anti-commons' agent has a right to exclude from the use of the resource. It is the mirror concept of a commons (better: an open-access good; see Chapter 2) in which no commoner has the right to exclude others from the use of the resource. Compared with a simple bilateral monopoly situation an anti-commons setting involves additional problems:

1 The sheer number of anti-commoners multiplies the transaction costs.
2 As it may be strategically good to be the last to give the needed consent, such strategic behaviour may lead to a 'dragging with the feet' strategy and result in long, even endless negotiations.
3 As suppliers of a complementary good the anti-commoners are in the position of a Cournot-duopoly. This may lead to prices, even higher than monopoly prices. When a monopolist increases his price beyond the monopolistic equilibrium-price, this will backfire on him due to a decrease in demand. When a complementary duopolist increases his price, he externalizes the cost of it on the other duopolist, because also he suffers from the decrease in demand. The latter may adopt a similar strategy leading to spiralling higher than monopoly prices (Buchanan and Yoon Yong 2000).

Owners, when establishing an easement may not be aware of this possible problem in the future. The establishment of an easement has a 'one sided stickiness': it is easier to establish one than to abolish it in the future. The civil law doctrine of *prediality* (see before, this chapter, 2. Easements/servitudes in civil/common law), or in common law the requirement of 'touch and concern' (see par. 2) can be explained as a remedy to limit this problem of the anti-commons. Suppose that any easement, even a service with no link with the use of the land, would be possible. The danger could become real that many estates become useless in fact due to the hopeless negotiation burden with the numerous easement-holders. This anti-commons problem may also explain why for instance in the Belgian civil code the court can abolish any easement which has lost its usefulness for the land (art. 710 bis Civil Code). The only impact of such useless easements is redistributive. The holders of it may cash a rent with the abolishment. Finally, this operation is a negative sum one, as this merely redistributive operation involves transaction costs.

## 4.2 Case analyses

### *1. Britel Developments (Thatcham) Ltd v. Nightfreight (Great Britain) Ltd; [1998] 4 All ER, Ch D, 432–438*

1 **Facts and legal sources.** The conflict between the mentioned parties finds its origin in the ambiguity of the wording of two deeds concerning land use.

In 1985 a deed was made between on one side the companies Tozer Kemsley and Millbourn Estates plc (further referred to as 'Penta') and Florco plc. In the deed, a right of way on a road (further 'Florco road') was agreed to Penta and the subsequent owners of the land of Penta. The deed states that the use of the Florco road is for

the present and future use of the Property (i.e. Penta land) to go pass and repass over the Florco Road subject to the Transferee paying to the Transferor promptly on demand one half of the costs of maintaining and repairing the Florco Road. The wording for the present and future use of the Property' seems to indicate that the right of way has the legal character of an easement and not of a personal right and applies consequently also to the future owners of the Penta land, the dominant estate.

In 1992 another deed was made between Penta and Britel Developments Ltd (the plaintiff), owner of neighbouring land. This deed is less clear concerning the character of the rights transferred. The clauses in this deed are related to the problem of run-offs of water from the land of Penta to the land of Britel. In order to manage this problem efficiently Britel has to lay drainage pipes before his land on the land of Penta. The problem however is that the legal characteristics of the clauses, awarding these rights to Britel are not identical. The right of drainage, awarded in clause 1(3), seems to have the character of an easement as this clause states that the right is awarded 'for the benefit of Britel's land and every part of it'. Clauses 1(1) and (2) however, related to the installation of pipes and the right to enter the land do not include such terms and seem to suggest that the rights are only personal and would end when either the dominant estate (Britel's land) or the servient estate (Penta's land) would change hands.

Later on, the lands of Penta had passed to other hands. The drains proposed by Britel have to be constructed on Penta land, now owned by Hewden Properties Ltd and Alltruck plc. Nevertheless, in order to construct the drain on these parts, Britel needs to access that part of Penta land, now owned by Nightfreight Ltd, the defendant.

The conflict relates to the question on the extent of easements. Is it possible to use an easement such as a right of way for the benefit of land other than that which is intended according to the deed the dominant estate? In the case *Harris v. Flower & Sons* (1905) it was decided that an easement of a right of way granted to the benefit of a certain parcel, cannot be used for the benefit of another parcel, of which the owner of the dominant estate has become the owner too. Easements have to be given a strict interpretation. The question in this case is whether the right of way on Florco Road, granted for the benefit of Penta land, may be used for works on Penta land (i.e. drains), to the benefit of the land of Britel. Does the restriction, stated in the Harris case also applies to the easement of the right of way on the Florco Road.

B **Claims and defences.** The plaintiff Britel wishes as a matter of urgency to exercise the rights granted by the deed of 1992, that is, to drains on Penta land and thereby giving access to the private Florco road. The plaintiff claims that these rights are running with the land and can be exercised also against the new owner, namely, Nightfreight, the defendant. The latter party opposes the exercise of this right by arguing that the rights in the deed are personal, as the running with the land is not repeated in each clause. Further, the defendant argues that the right of way on Florco road is exclusively to the benefit of Penta land and not to the benefit of other land such as the land of the plaintiff.

C **Sentence and considerations.** The court decides in favour of the plaintiff and orders that the defendant allows the plaintiff the exercise of his rights, i.e. the drains on Penta land and the use of the private Florco road. The court construes the meaning of the grant as having awarded all rights with the same extent, namely as rights running with the land and not as personal rights. The fact this mention is omitted in some clauses does not suggest that the rights awarded in these clauses should be given a different legal characteristic. The court construes the meaning of the deed in a homogeneous sense. All awarded rights are running with the land and not personal. As concerning the right of way on the Florco road, the court considers that the right of way on Florco road in favour of Britel is clearly within the meaning of the deed of 1985 because Britel has to execute drainage works on Penta land to the benefit of its land. Because Britel's right falls within the meaning of the deed of 1985 this case is different from *Harris v. Flower*. The court also decides that the fact that the Penta land has now three different owners (Nightfreight, Hewden, Alltruck) does not affect the rights of Britel on the use of Florco roads.

D **Economic analysis.** The first question in this case is whether the rights, transferred in the 1992 deed from Penta to Britel, are transferable to the subsequent owners of Penta. The courts 'answer to this question is based on the construction of the implicit meaning of the deed. From a legal economic point of view the construction of the meaning of a legal document (a deed, a will, a contract) which is ambiguous, unclear, contradictory or incomplete, should be based on the choice an economic rational agent would have made. When transferability is agreed, the cost structures of both parties are similar. Britel incurs a sunk cost for the construction of a factory whose income-stream depends positively on the execution of the deed. The drainage with pipes on Penta land are necessary to build the factory. Penta incurs the sunk cost of the easement that will affect the price of the land in a future sale. When the rights would not have been transferable only Britel would be faced with a sunk cost.

Penta, knowing that the profitability of Britel's sunk investments are depending of the renewal of the rights at the occasion of a sale, could exploit this position towards Britel. By accepting transferability, Penta signals to Britel that it abandons any opportunity to engage in long-run exploitation. The ex post construction of the agreement by the court reflects consequently a solution which is ex ante credible for the parties.

The second question in this claim is whether the easement of right of way on the Florco road agreed in the 1985 deed to the benefit of Penta land should extend to Britel because they need to access on this road in order to use the easement on the Penta land. It has to be considered that there is a chain of necessities between the different concerned use rights. Should Britel be awarded a use right on the Florco Road because it needs this in order to use its easement on the Penta land? Or, in other words does an easement on a servient estate A awards you also the right to make use of another easement, of which estate A is the dominant estate and which you need to use the first easement? If Britel cannot use the Florco road, it cannot use its right on Penta land to lay the drainage pipes and without draining it cannot finish the investments to be made on its land. If the right of way, originally agreed for in favour of Penta, would be denied to Britel, the subsequent owner of Penta land, as for instance Nightfreight, may also engage in long-run exploitation of Britel. From an ex ante perspective it seems economically rational to infer that Penta, the owner of the dominant estate in the relationship with Florco, had the intention to extend the use of the right of way also to the party that needed access to its land (i.e. Britel) in order to improve the use quality of its own land. Britel is in fact enjoying an implicit licence from Penta, to use its right of way vis-à-vis Florco.

Although Britel's right is based on an implicit licence from Penta, its right should be protected by a property rule. Florco (and subsequent owners) has a monopoly position on road access to the property of Penta (and subsequent owners). If the right of way of Britel is only protected by a liability rule Florco can exploit its monopoly position by denying the access and bet on the high litigation costs for the other party to get compensation. A protection of Britel's right as a property rule could involve for instance high punitive damages such as in the trespass case *Jacque v. Steenberg Homes Inc.* (see Chapter 3, 4. Smith: exclusion and governance regimes)

E **Economic Evaluation of the decision**. The decision of the court can be sustained from an economic point of view, both in case of the easement of laying drainage pipes on Penta land as in case of the use of Florco road. By these decisions the court avoids long run exploitation by one party through positions of bilateral monopoly and the eventual subsequent blocking of efficient economic activities. Obviously the court was inspired by economic intuition, as is often the case in private law adjudication (Ehrlich and Posner 1974; Posner 1994). The decisions of the court are however based on intellectually challengeable opinions such as the ex post construction of the intention behind a deed and run also against precedent (*Harris v. Flower & Sons, 1905*). The challengeable character of the opinions underpinning the decisions do not guarantee that in later similar cases courts will make economically justifiable decision. Economic intuition and artificial ex post construction of intentions are a weak base for decisions. Opinions, based on robust economic reasoning would provide more guarantee for efficient decision-making.

## 2. *Cargill v. Gotts, [1981] 1 All ER CA, 682–690*

A **Facts and legal sources.** The plaintiff, Cargill is in continuous occupation of the Grove farm since 1928. From already before that time the farm had drawn water from a pond (Mill Pond) in the river Mun, at Gimingham in Norfolk. Before 1927 a water cart, mainly for the purpose of watering horses and cattle, drew water. Such water carts carried a barrel between 50 and 100 gallons. In approximately 1942, Cargill began to use water from the Mill Pond to spray crops and the water was now drawn by a tank holding 250 to 300 gallons. In the late 1950s, the 250-gallon tank was replaced by a 900 gallons tank and this was later augmented by a second tank of 500 gallons. Between the middle of 1950s and 1977 the quantity of water abstracted increased tenfold. In 1977 the defendant, Gotts, became owner of the pond. In February 1977 the defendant forcibly prevented the plaintiff from drawing water from the pond.

The Prescription Act of 1832 Section 2 states that an easement of taking water can be acquired after an uninterrupted period of enjoyment of twenty years.

The Water Resources Act of 1963 Section 23(1) provides that the abstraction of water is made dependent from obtaining a licence. In Section 24 however an exception is made for abstractions less than 1,000 gallons, at the condition that 'it does not form part of a continuous operation, or of a series of operations, whereby in the aggregate more than one thousand gallons of water are abstracted.' Section 27 provides that the application for a licence is open for the occupier of land contiguous to the water supply or to anyone who has the right of access to the supply. Section 33 provides that anyone who abstracted water from a source of supply in the period of five years before 1 July 1965 is entitled to a licence under the Act.

B **Claims and Defences** The plaintiff claims by writ before court that he had an easement to draw water for the convenience of his Grove farm by virtue of the Prescription Act of 1832, or by common law or by the operation of the doctrine of the lost grant. He also claimed an injunction restraining the defendant to prevent the taking of water by force and asked damages incurred by this prevention.

The defendant claims that the plaintiff only established a right to take a limited amount of water, to the extent of 300 gallons a day only for the purpose of watering stock and operating steam machinery at the Grove farm. The taking of larger quantities are more recent and cannot be claimed on the base of the Prescription Act of 1832. Moreover, the plaintiff did not obtain a licence under the Water Resources Act, so any abstraction of water since 1965 is illegal. Therefore, he has the right to prevent the abstraction.

C **Sentence and considerations.** The High Court ruled on 26 October 1979 that the Water Resources Act did not confer any remedy to the defendant to prevent the abstraction of water. The plaintiff was allowed to take water by virtue of the exception in Section 24, because the water abstractions did not form a part of a continuous operation. Any abstraction below 1,000 gallons is consequently legal. As the forcible prevention by the defendant was not allowed, the judge awarded an injunction and damages to the plaintiff of £50.

With the opinion of Justice Templeman LJ the Court of Appeal agreed that the plaintiff has acquired an easement to abstract water from the pond. The court rejected the claim of the defendant concerning the increase of the water quantities abstracted. Referring to precedents (*Williams v. James 1867 LR 2 CP 577; British Railways Board v. Glass 1964 3 All ER 418; Woodhouse & Co. Ltd v. Kirkland Ltd 1970 All E R 587*) the court considers that the water was continuously used for operating the same farm and that the increase of quantities, due to changing circumstances in the operation of the farm, fall within the range of the easement, acquired by prescription. The court does not agree with the High Court on the application of the exception, provided by Section 24 of the Water Resources Act. According to the court the abstractions of water form definitely a series of operation, destined to run the farm. The total of the abstractions made exceeds clearly the 1,000-gallon limit. Therefore, all abstractions of water, made by the plaintiff since 30 June 1965 are illegal. The plaintiff could have obtained by declaration of his easement a licence for abstracting water, but he had failed to do so. Finally, the only remedy to act against illegal water abstractions resides with the relevant river authority or the Director of Public Prosecutions. However, because the plaintiff had no right to abstract water whatsoever, he did not suffer damage from the forcible prevention by the defendants and should be, consequently, denied any damages. On this latter point the other justices however disagreed and ruled in favour of awarding damages to the plaintiff on the base of the wording of Section 135 (8) of the Water Resources Act.

D **Economic analysis.**

D1 **On the acquisition of the easement by prescription.** In Chapter 5, the efficiency of prescription rules or limitation statutes are analyzed. Within a cost minimization model the optimal length of a prescription period is where the sum of uncertainty costs, investment costs, evidence costs and protection costs is the lowest. This is not only valid for a possessory title, but also for easements. When prescription periods are very long or even infinite (no prescription) the user of land, belonging to somebody else, such as in this case by abstracting water, remains during a long time in uncertainty, will refrain from making investments to improve the use, and discussions on the legitimate character and the scope of the easement will become more difficult because of possible decay of evidence.

When prescription periods are very short or even zero time, the owner of the land is barely protected against intrusions in his property and has to deploy costly monitoring and protection measures. The Prescription Act of 1832 specifies a period of twenty years for the acquisition of an easement. Very probably, this period is inefficiently too long. Since the enactment of the Act in 1832 monitoring and protection costs have become much lower due to higher mobility and all kind of devices of monitoring a property. Suppose an owner owning an estate on a distance of 100 miles from his home. In 1832 a check on his estate in order to control whether there was no intrusive use, which could lead in the end to an easement by prescription, required a long and costly travel. More than 100 years later such travel is rather easy and in present times, electronic devices such as Google Earth and Street View allow a very easy monitoring of even remote properties. A revision of the Act, providing a shortening of the prescription periods is consequently advisable. As long the Act is not revised it is, also from an economic point of view, advisable that courts stick with the even inefficiently long prescription period in the Act to avoid huge uncertainty throughout society about the validity of titles.

**D2 On the changes of the use of the easement.** The quantities of water that the owner of the dominant estate was abstracting increased very significantly over time. Both courts decided however that this increase was falling within the range of the easement. If the easement were limited to the initially taken quantity, the user would be obliged to renegotiate the easement with the owner of the servient estate each time circumstances impose a change in the quantities of abstracted water. Because easements are framed within a bilateral monopoly relationship, these renegotiations could lead to strategic behavior and extortion by the owner of the servient estate. This extortion position could be exacerbated when the farmer has made investments the use of which demands higher quantities of water. To avoid such possibility of long-run exploitation it is efficient to use a broad standard interpretation of the easement of water abstraction and to relate it with the evolving necessities of farming over time. The 'broadness' of the interpretation is of course not without limits. Suppose the user starts to abstract water to sell it on the market. In this case, his use cannot be linked anymore to the operation of his farm. If courts would allow such use, this would require future conveyancing parties, negotiating easements, to draft meticulously all details of the easement in order to avoid future overuse.

In this case, however the change of use occurred during the prescription period of the easement. One could argue, as the defendant in this case did, that the prescription period applies to the initial quantity of abstracted water and not to the accumulation of it during the prescription period. Suppose that the user abstracts during the first five years a quantity A, during the next five years a quantity A+B, during the next five years a quantity of A+B+C and during the last five years a quantity of

A+B+C+D. A restrictive application of the prescription rule would entail that abstraction of quantity A is prescribed after twenty years, of quantity A+B after twenty-five years – because B is then added during twenty years – quantity A+B+C after thirty years and quantity A+B+C+D after thirty-five years. If however the broad standard interpretation of an easement of abstracting water for farm use is applied, the acquisition through prescription of the full easement starts from the moment the farmer starts to abstract water, whatever the quantity. Suppose that a quantity of A+B+C+D falls within the limits of a standard easement of water use for farming, then the easement of abstraction of A+B+C+D is acquired even when the farmer-user did take far less quantities during the preceding years of the prescription period.

From an economic point of view, it is again more efficient to apply also for the prescription of easements the broad standard interpretation of the easement. A restrictive interpretation would involve very complicate measurements and huge problems of evidence production. The costs of administration of justice, often to a large extent externalized to the taxpayer, could be larger than the gains of efficiency connected with acquisition through prescription. By applying the broader standard interpretation such costly procedures are minimalized.

**D3 On the interpretation of the 1,000-gallons exception in the Water Resource Act.** The licences for water abstraction required by the Water Resource Act are introduced to cope with excessive water use and to avoid a 'tragedy of the commons' whereby individuals and companies use water without caring about the future water supply. The waiver of a licence for water abstractions of less than thousand gallons, provided by Section 24 of the Act, may be justified from an economic point of view, as the harm of abstracting such a small quantity may be less than the administrative cost of obtaining a licence. This cost consideration does not apply, however, when the water abstraction of less than thousand gallons has no single character but is part of a series of small water abstractions. In this case, the impact is the same as with abstractions of huge quantities. By allowing series of abstractions of small water quantities, the river authorities and the courts would undermine the general aim of the Water Resource Act and contribute to a tragedy of the commons the Act is aiming to prevent.

**D4 Licence as a regulatory taking.** Through the introduction of the licences, the government diminished the value of the easement of abstracting water. Suppose the farmer paid £1,000 for the easement because he valued the water abstraction facility at £1,200. By introducing licences the facility of water abstraction has become less certain because it is made dependent from administrative approval. If the administration denies a licence the easement is virtually without value. The farmer still can use the easement vis-à-vis the owner of the servient estate (Gotts in this case) and cross his land, but he is not allowed anymore to use this easement for its proper purpose, that is, abstracting water from the river. If a licence is denied, compensation should be paid to the farmer. If the government can take away rights without having to compensate, authorities will act under moral hazard and be tempted to develop socially inefficient public projects (see Chapter 5). Section 33 of the Act provides that any agent, abstracting water during a period of five years before the enactment of the Act is entitled to a licence. By this rule, administrative costs of paying compensations for regulatory taking can be avoided. This rule is of course only efficient when the incumbent water abstractions lasting longer than five years do not endanger the general aim of the Act, which is the protection of future water supply.

**D5 Injunction and damages.** The defendant claims that he was entitled to prevent the plaintiff forcibly from abstracting water for he had no right to do this by lack of a license. From an economic point of view this claim is not sustainable. First the absence of a licence does not render the easement legally invalid, so the plaintiff had at least the right to go to the pound over the land, owned by the defendant. Whether he was allowed to abstract water depended on the interpretation of Section 24 of the Water Resource Act, providing the thousand-gallon exception. By preventing the plaintiff to abstract water from the river the defendant, a private party arrogates itself the power to determinate the right meaning of the Act and to act accordingly. Such private interpretation and enforcement may be harmful for public peace as the other party might consider that the defendant is biased in his viewpoint and actions and might consequently retaliate (see also Chapter 6. Verification of Property Rights: Possession and Registration). The disturbance of public peace may result in harmful effects for third parties and is consequently inefficient. To award an injunction and damages for the use of force imposes a cost to such inefficient actions and should be sustained from an economic point of view.

**E Economic evaluation of the decision.** The different decisions by the court in this case are all sustainable from an economic point of view. However, the Prescription Act of 1832, on which one of the decisions is based, can be questioned in this respect. The awarding of the damages, however efficient, is not unanimous, and the justices sustaining this awarding did not advance a substantial argument but a rather sophisticated construction of the Water Resource Act. As in other cases, economic considerations would provide a firmer intellectual base for these decisions.

### *3. Attwood and others v. Bovis Homes Lt [2000] 4 All ELR Ch D 948–960*

**A Facts and legal sources.** The claimants, Stephen William, Lilian Joyce and Frank Dennis Attwood, are owners in possession of land known as Wall

End Farm. Their land is a servient tenement of an easement to the benefit of defendant's land, known as Thistle Hill, the dominant tenement. The easement concerns the drainage of water running off the lands of the defendants. On the land of the defendants, the water is received in a balancing pond and controlled by a V-shaped weir. From there the water runs off through a culvert under the public highway along a ditch through Wall End Farm. The claimants have owned Wall End Farm since 1989. The northern part of it is used for agricultural purposes. The southern part is subject to a management agreement with the Nature Conservancy Council, requiring specific water levels to be preserved in the ditches. The defendants acquired Thistle Field in 1998 in order to start a development project on the former agricultural land. This project involves the building of about thousand residential houses, a shopping centre, community facilities, a hospital, a school and the necessary infrastructure. The claimants brought proceedings against the developers contending that the radical change in the use of the dominant tenement precluded the exercise of the easement.

In several precedents, the question is discussed in how far an alteration of the use of an easement is permitted. Most of the precedents concern the use of a right of way. In most of the precedents neither an increase of the use of the right of way nor a radical change in the nature of the user leading to an increase of the burden for the servient tenement can be allowed (*Wimbledon and Putney Commons Conservators v. Dixon*, 1875 1 Ch D 362, [1874–80] All ER 1218; *British Rlys Board v. Glass* [1964 $ 3 All ER 418). If on the contrary, the alteration of the use or the mere increase of it does not impose an additional burden to the servient tenement, this alteration remains within the limits of the right of way (*Cargill v. Gotts* [1981] 1 All ER 682). The same principles find application concerning the right of support. The supported building or the use of it may be changed at the condition no significant additional burden is imposed on the supporting building or construction (*Lloyds Bank Ltd v. Dalton* [1942] 2 All ER 352).

B **Claims and defences.** The claimants ask a declaration that the defendants are not entitled to use a watercourse on the claimants land to drain surface water from the area of development. According to the claimants, the use of the dominant tenement was radically altered by turning agricultural land into a development area. Consequently, they are not entitled anymore to use the easement of drainage, which was acquired through prescription.

The defendants contend that the change of the use of the dominant tenement does not impose an additional burden to the owners of the servient tenement. Moreover, they are ready to adapt some installations in order to attenuate eventual burden for the claimants.

C **Sentence and considerations.** The court decides in favour of the defendants. In his analysis of precedent law Justice Neuberger distinguishes two different rules concerning the change in the use of an easement. A strict rule stating that a radical change in the use of the easement, due to a radical change on the dominant tenement, is not allowed as such. A more flexible stating that even a radical change in the use of the easement is allowed if the burden for the servient tenement is not significantly increased. The latter rule is more in line with common sense and a commercial approach of the matter. The former rule however provides more security in the relationship between the owners of the dominant and servient estate. An additional argument for the strict rule derives from the doctrine that an easement acquired by prescription is based on a fictional grant. This grant concerns the type of use and the level of use at the beginning of the prescription period. A later change is consequently not covered by the easement. The court, however, remarks that not all principles related to the easement of a right of way are applicable to all easements. The strict rule regarding the right of way could possibly involve the loss of this right following a radical change in the use of it. For other easements such as the right of support or eavesdropping, only the flexible rule applies, according also to precedent law. As the easement in this case, that is, the running off water through the servient tenement, is much more similar to the right of support or of eavesdropping, the flexible rule applies, which is in favour of the defendants.

**D** **Economic analysis.** The central question in this case is whether the defendants are still allowed to use the easement of drainage, originally acquired to the benefit of the exploitation of a farm, to the benefit of a radically different use of the dominant tenement, namely, a large residential project. As mentioned before, Justice Neuberger made in this respect a distinction between the strict and the flexible rule. From a legal-economic point of view, the flexible rule should be sustained in this case. A change of the use of the dominant tenement is allowed provided the burden for the servient tenement is not significantly altered. An easement such as the right of drainage in this case can be considered as a voluntarily accepted externality. The users of the dominant tenement shift a part of their costs – the running off water – to the owner of the servient tenement. According to Pigou, the founder of welfare economics, negative externalities may be at the source of inefficiencies within the economy. An agent externalizing part of his costs does not take these costs into account, which can lead to inefficiently high levels of activity, as illustrated in Table 4.1.

*Table 4.1* Internalization of costs

| *Activity Level* | *Marginal Benefit* | *Marginal Cost All Internalized* | *Marginal Cost Partially externalized* |
|---|---|---|---|
| 1 | 1000 | 700 | 500 |
| 2 | 800 | 700 | 500 |
| 3 | 600 | 700 | 500 |
| 4 | 400 | 700 | 500 |

When all costs are internalized, the activity level will be at 2 and when costs are partially externalized, the activity level will be at 3. From a social point of view this latter level is inefficient for the total costs of activity level 3 (500 + 200) exceed the marginal benefit (600). Level 3 will be reached however because the agent is able to export part of his costs (200). In the case of an easement, such as the drainage of water, the owner of the servient tenement accepts voluntarily some cost externalization by the user of the dominant tenement. To use the figures of the table, the cost of drainage amounts up to 200, so that the user of the dominant tenement will be at activity level 3, while, without easement he would be only at level 2. Does this imply that easements cause inefficient activity levels? Not necessarily so. The table suggests that the mentioned values of benefits and costs are objective givens, to be detected by an omniscient third observer. In reality, benefits and costs are the result of the subjective valuations of agents. When the easement of water drainage was vested through an agreement, the owner of the dominant tenement paid a price for it. This may have been a monetary price (explicit market) or a non-monetary price (a benefit, a service, i.e. implicit market). The price paid for the establishment of the easement was the result of the valuation by the owner of the dominant tenement (willingness to pay) and the valuation by the owner of the servient tenement (willingness to sell). The price paid for the easement is the result from the negotiation between the two owners but will be situated between the willingness to pay and the willingness to sell. So for instance, the owner of the dominant tenement's willingness to pay for each unit could have been 220 and the owner of the servient tenement's willingness to sell could have been 180, resulting in a negotiated price of 200 per unit. From the perspective of the mutual valuations by the two parties, the establishment of the easement is to their mutual benefit, thus wealth maximizing, thus efficient. According to the subjective valuation by the owner of the dominant tenement, the easement abated his costs per unit by 220, while according to the subjective valuation by the owner of the servient tenement, the costs imposed on his property amount to 180 per unit while he received a price of 200 for it. Therefore, if we take the subjective valuations by the involved parties as a yardstick, the establishment of the easement allowed for an efficiency enhancing internalization.

The question arises, however, whether this is also valid for easements acquired through prescription. In this case, the owner of the dominant tenement did not pay any price. By tolerating however the externalization during the whole prescription period (twenty years) the owner of the servient tenement has signalled implicitly that he/she attaches only a very low value to the costs imposed on their property. The prescription period can be stopped by legal action such as writing a summons to stop the externalizing activity or to start an action for injunctive relief. Apparently, the imposed costs are implicitly assessed by the owner of the servient tenement as being lower than the costs of such legal actions. Consequently, it seems very likely that the amount of cost-abatement, realized through the easement, is significantly higher than the valuation by the owner of the servient tenement of the imposed costs. So even without a price being paid, there is a high probability that the establishment of the easement through prescription is efficiency enhancing.

These considerations remain of course valid only when the owner of the dominant tenement does not inflate the cost-externalization beyond the original level. If this happens, it is possible that the cost-imposition becomes higher than the willingness to sell of the easement by the owner of the servient estate and which generates an inefficient level of activity. The same applies for an easement vested by prescription. However, here the yardstick is not the willingness to sell of the owner of the servient estate but his valuation of the costs to stop the prescription. From an economic viewpoint, it is efficient that the court focusses on the impact on the burden for the servient tenement to decide whether the change on the side of the dominant tenement is compatible with the easement.

A last question concerns the distinction made by Justice Neuberger between easements such as water drainage, support and eavesdropping on one hand and the right of way on the other hand. The Justice perceives in precedent law a difference in approach. For the former easements, the flexible rule applies without any proviso. For the right of way, also the strict rule often finds application. Is this difference in treatment also viable from an economic point of view? Concerning easements such as water drainage and eavesdropping the only relevant variable concerning cost-imposition is the quantity. Water is water and drops are drops. Whether the variation in quantity is caused by a qualitative change in use on the dominant tenement is irrelevant for the burden for the servient tenement. The only relevant question consequently is whether the changes in quantities increase the burden for the servient tenement or not. This consideration is even the more evident for the easement of support. Changes in the use of the supported construction do not matter as long as the burden on the supporting construction does not increase significantly. This may be different with the right of way. Not only may the frequency of passage on the way be relevant but also the type of passage. It makes a difference when the passage concerns tractors of farmers or lorries of a factory, even when the frequency might be the same. Consequently, it makes sense to adopt the mere change of the activity on the dominant tenement as a criterion rather than the mere quantum, for a radical change in the activity in the dominant tenement might have an evident impact on the burden for the servient tenement. In the case of easements such as drainage, eavesdropping and support using quantities as the sole criterion is the cheapest approach with respect to costs of administration of justice. In the case of a right of way checking the type of use of the way may be relevant because the type as such and not merely the quantity can involve a higher cost-imposition for the servient tenement.

E **Economic evaluation of the decision.** On the base of the economic theory of externalities, the decision of the judge is certainly sustainable. Again, as in the previous case, the argument would, especially the one regarding the distinction between and eventual different treatment of the easements, be more convincing by referring to economic common sense and not only to the authority of precedents.

### *4. Patel and others v. WH Smith (Eziot) Ltd and another, Court of Appeal 28 January 1987, Ius Commune Casebooks for the Common Law of Europe, Property Law, Chapter 2 The Protection of Property Rights*

A **Facts and legal sources.** The plaintiffs own a property at 34 Mansfield Street, Leicester. The western side of their property is a yard, bounded by the property of the defendants at number 32 of the same street. Both properties were originally one ownership but were separated in 1948. In the conveyance of 1948 a right of way was conceded in favour of the defendants including the right to park cars for the purposes of loading and unloading for the business of the defendants. However, since 1948 the defendants made a wider use of the yard at number 34 by parking eight vehicles in a single line along the outside wall of the yard and also placing a dustbin over there. In a letter of 19 May 1978, the defendants admit that they do not have a right to park their cars. In 1986 the plaintiffs sent letters to the defendants giving notice to each of the defendants that the licence to park cars, granted to them when they acquired the property, was terminated and required them to stop parking cars.

The plaintiffs claimed an injunction at the county court of Leicester restraining the defendants from parking in the yard, but the court dismissed the claim because there was a defence to be reckoned with and that there was a serious issue – a right of way through prescription – to be tried. The effect of the injunction would be difficult to quantify and the parking of the cars is already lasting since long. Consequently, the balance of convenience is against an injunction.

Some precedents sustain that an injunction should be granted also in cases where there is no harm done at the trespassed property. If infliction of harm would be a condition, the owner whose land is trespassed has no action anymore to stop the trespass (*Woollerton v. Wilson Ltd v. Richard Costain Ltd [1970]1 W.R.L. 411*). In other precedents it is argued that the judge may refuse granting an injunction if the landowner is not injured thereby (*Behrens v. Richards [1905] 2 Ch. 614*).

Precedent law indicates also that the acquisition of an easement by prescription ('as of right') must derive from a use against the will of the owner of the servient tenement. If the use is accepted or tolerated by the owner, the use is *precario* and not based on a right. In the latter case the use can be terminated by the owner, whose land is used (*Gardner v. Hodgson's Kingston*

*Brewery Co. Ltd [1903] A.C. 229; Thomas W. Ward Ltd. v. Alexander Bruce Ltd [1959] 2Lloyds Rep. 472*).

According to the Prescription Act of 1832, an easement can by acquired after a prescription period of twenty years.

B **Claims and defences.** The claimants ask an interlocutory injunction to stop all parking, going beyond the immediate need of loading and unloading and the removal of the dustbin. They deny that the defendants have acquired an easement for parking as such because the parking during the past years was based on a kind of licence from their side, which can be withdrawn at their will. The defendants claim that they have acquired an easement through prescription because the use as a parking lot lasted uninterruptedly for twenty years.

C **Sentence and considerations.** The court decides in favour of the claimants and grants an interlocutory injunction. Based on the evidence from the correspondence by the parties, the court considers that the use of the yard as a parking lot was based on a licence from the claimants and that consequently the defendants cannot invoke an easement for parking as such. It is for the court also impossible to say that there is no potential damage to be suffered by the plaintiffs if the injunction is not granted. Also, the argument by the claimants that by enforcing the injunction, no distinction can be made between parking as such and parking only for loading and unloading, is rejected by the court.

D **Economic analysis.** This case involves two issues, which can be discussed from an economic point of view. First, does it make sense to let the awarding of an easement depend on the distinction between a licence ('precario') and use against the will? Second, is the awarding of an interlocutory injunction sustainable from an economic viewpoint?

When either the use of someone's property devolves from an explicit licence by the owner or an implicit toleration this use cannot result in the establishment of an easement by prescription, even when the use has lasted during the length of the prescription period. This makes sense from an economic point of view. For in this case the owner either allowed the use in exchange for a monetary price (an explicit market transaction) or in exchange for some kind of a service to him/her or to people related to him/her (an implicit market transaction), or the owner just allowed it for charitable reasons without any award in return. In the last case, the owner linked in fact his/her utility function to the one of the user. The better the user is, the better I am. By commuting the explicitly or implicitly licenced use into a use 'of right' the court would award a legal benefit to the user which is stretching beyond the will of the of the owner-licensor. Such a decision would be tantamount to a kind of private taking. In contrast to an exchange or a voluntary gift, such a private taking does not guarantee that the shift from a licenced use to a right to use amounts to an increase of the common wealth of the owner and the user. It is possible that the loss for the owner exceeds the gain for the user. When however someone uses the property of someone else without explicit or implicit consent co the owner, but the owner does not oppose this during a very long period, the costs of uncertainty, investment and evidence (see Chapter 5) may justify a conversion of the adverse 'possession' of a use into a right to use, an easement in this case.

The second issue concerns the sustainability of the granting of an interlocutory injunction. A permanent injunction is granted as the final decision of the trial. In economic terms, such an injunction grants to the plaintiff a property-rule protection (Calabresi) or implies the application of an exclusion regime (Henry Smith) (see Chapter 3). Peculiar to an interlocutory injunction is its preliminary and provisional character. The injunction is awarded pending the trial. When the plaintiff does not prevail in the final trial, the interlocutory injunction receives an illegitimate character ex post. When the plaintiff claims such an injunction and when the court decides about it, they have to take into account this possible ex post illegitimacy. In legal economics an interlocutory injunction is only justified when it matches the so-called Leubsdorf-Posner formula (Posner 2007: 595–596; Grosskopf and Medina 2009: 923). An interlocutory injunction is economically justified only if $Ap>S(1-p)$, where A is the irreparable harm for the plaintiff if an interlocutory injunction is not granted and S is the irreparable harm for the defendant resulting from the granted injunction. (p) and (1−p) stand for respectively the rate of the claim prevailing and non-prevailing. A first condition put in this formula refers to the irreparable character of the harm. If the harm is reparable, the court can always compensate through awarding damages in its final decision. In this case there is no need to take the risk of an ex post illegitimate injunction for the harm can be perfectly redressed ex post. In this case, this condition is not matched. The harm the owner of 34 Mansfield Street is suffering by the parking of the cars and the placing of the dustbin by the defendant can be assessed in monetary terms and awarded ex post when the court would decide in favour of the plaintiffs. The awarding of such damages ex post can be combined with the issuing of a permanent injunction, for in cases of trespass the exclusion regime (Smith) or property rule (Calabresi) has to be preferred (see Chapter 3). From the evidence, mentioned in this case, it seems however that it is quite unlikely that the plaintiffs would not prevail in the final case, as all the evidence points to a licence of use and not to a use 'of right'. In terms of the mentioned formula, p is rather high while (1−p) is consequently low. The risk of an ex post illegitimate interlocutory injunction is consequently low. This however does not overrule the non-matching of the first condition of irreparability. By neglecting this condition, the court is sending a wrong signal into the legal world. It would stimulate other legal decision makers to take risks where such risk taking is not necessary. Often the plaintiff can be held liable for eventual damage resulting from the issuing of an interlocutory order. By this, the plaintiff internalizes the risk to a large extent. This possibility however does not undermine the argument against injunction in case of reparable harm. This liability of the plaintiff involves a difficult issue whether the responsibility for an ex post illegitimate injunction has to be shared with the issuer, the court, or not. When such damages are awarded this will entail another assessment of damages and additional costs of administration of justice. In cases of reparable harm, all this can be avoided by simply not granting an interlocutory injunction and rely exclusively on ex post compensation of the damage.

E **Economic evaluation of the decision.** The distinction made by the court hereby following the general legal doctrine between a use based on a licence and a use against the will of the owner, and the legal consequences of it, is certainly sustainable from an economic point of view. The decision to award an interlocutory injunction, however, is not. The first decision by the judge of the county court, who refused such a granting because the harm, inflicted by the parking of the cars, was obviously not very urgent because it was tolerated for so long, is much more sustainable from an economic point of view.

### 5. *Mulvaney v. Gough and others, Court of Appeal 24 July 2002, EWCA Civ 1078, 4 All ER [2002] 83–93*

A **Facts and legal sources.** The legal conflict concerns the rights of cottage owners on adjacent land, owned by another person. The cottages are located in Galgate, Lancashire, and are ranged in an L-shaped structure. Within the bend of the L-shape, there is a back yard (called 'blue land') and a strip of land adjacent to the cottages. After the death of the owner of the cottages in 1950, the trustees of the property sold off the cottages one by one. The conveyance of the purchase of the cottage by the claimant, Ms. Mulvaney, included: 'a right of way for all times and for all purposes in common with the vendors and all persons having a like right over and above the open yard adjoining the said premises and coloured blue on the said plan ("the blue land").'

Similar but not identical clauses were included in other conveyances concerning the sale of the other cottages. The conveyance of the purchase of cottage 1 East View stated 'a right of way and of use for drying purposes over and in the said yard . . . upon payment of a proportionate part of the expense of maintaining and repairing the same.' The conveyance of the sale of cottage Chapel Street 9 included 'The joint use of the yard or ground to the rear of the said property coloured blue on the said plan.'

Mr. Mulvaney tended a garden on the strip of land consisting of a grassed area and a flower-bed.

On 11 April 1996 the flower-bed and the grassed area were removed by the defendants by using a JCB and covered with gravel, in order to have – as the defendants contend – vehicular access to their land.

Ms. Mulvaney commenced proceedings by claiming a declaration that she was holding 'free hold' rights on the blue land for cultivating, mowing and hanging washing.

On 9 November 2000 the district judge declared that Mr. Mulvaney was entitled to an easement on the base of a long established use. On the base of many witnesses, the judge agreed that the rights of Ms. Mulvaney were established by prescription. The judge also observed that the many users of the back yard were able to develop over a long period rules on the use of the back yard and to avoid anarchy in the use thereof. The judge also awarded an amount of £200 to Mulvaney for the damages to the flower-bed and the grassed area. On appeal, the district court decided in the same way as the district judge.

As legal sources, the Property Act of 1925 section 62 was referred to by the claimant. This section states that when conveying a property all rights appurtenant to the property are also conveyed, except when expressly excluded by the parties.

The defendants and the judge also often refer to precedent law, stating that easements have their normal limits and cannot stretch so far that they preclude the possessory rights of the servient owner. In *Dyce v. Lady Hay (1852, Macq 105)* it is held that there cannot be prescriptive rights in the nature of a servitude or easement so large as to preclude the normal use of the property by the owner. *Copeland v. Greenhalf (All ER 809, [1952] Ch 488)* also states that a prescriptive right cannot go beyond the normal idea of an easement and cannot impair the right of possession by the servient owner.

Precedent law also accepts that a grant to enjoyment of a communal garden can be regarded as an easement (*Re: Ellenborough Park, Re: Davies, Powell v. Maddison [1955] 3 All ER 667 [1956] Ch 131*). In *London and Blenheim Estates Ltd v. Ladbroke Retail Parks Ltd (1993 All ER 307, 1 WLR 1278)* the right to park cars was not regarded as being in contradiction with the rights of the servient owners. In *Batchelor v. Marlow (2001, EWCA Civ 1051 [2003] 4 All ER 78)* however the court considered such a right as so extensive making the rights of the servient owner illusory.

B **Claims and defences.** The claimant, Ms. Mulvaney, claims an order to restore the flower-bed, the grassed area, and the reaffirmation of the £200 damages, as the district judge and court decided. On the base of the implied grant doctrine and the prescription through long established use, she claims the legal recognition of her rights to the communal garden.

The defendants (Goughs and others) refer to precedent law and contend that the rights claimed by Ms. Mulvaney stretch beyond the possessive rights always retained by the servient owners. As such they claim the right to access to their land and the maintaining of the gravel way.

C **Sentence and considerations.** The Court of Appeal considers that the district judge and court stretched out the rights of Ms. Mulvaney too far. The court recognizes the right of Mulvaney to use the communal garden but this use may not preclude the right of access of the servient owners. A further consideration of all the facts should point out in what way the rights of the servient owners and of the users of the back yard can be made compatible. Because the defendants destroyed the flower-bed and the grassed area without any notice to Ms. Mulvaney the payment due of £200 is maintained.

D **Economic analysis.** Two issues in this case deserve a closer analysis from an economic point of view: first, the problem of unclear and possibly conflictual property rights due to the different conveyances; second the question whether the rights transferred or acquired by prescription under the heading of 'easement' are naturally limited by the possessory rights of the servient owner.

The different cottage owners all enjoyed certain use rights on the back yard and the strip of land behind the cottages. As the cottages were sold off on different times, the wording of the conveyances, granting these use rights, are different and could eventually lead to conflicts between the cottage owners. Suppose for instance that the owner sells cottage 1 to purchaser A and grants a right to tend a garden on the back yard. Later the owner sells cottage 2 to purchaser B and grants a right to raise chickens in the back yard. Both grants are, literally taken, incompatible. From a legal logical point of view the first grant will supersede the second one, for the owner has already transferred the right to purchaser A. Consequently purchaser B can only raise chicken as far this is compatible with the rights of A, which is quite impossible. According to the Roman law tradition, '*Nemo plus iuris ad alium transferre potest quam ipse haberet*,' the owner has already transferred the use right to purchaser A and is consequently legally unable to transfer a right to somebody else, which could encroach upon the first right. Instead of applying this legal logic, the district judge followed a quite different path of reasoning. He remarked that despite the possible incompatibilities in the conveyances the cottage owners used the communal garden in a practical and non-conflictual way. The mutual relationships concerning the use of this communal garden were gradually developed over time leading to a harmonious cooperative situation among the cottage owners. The district judge considers this grown practice as a normative base to recognize prescribed rights on behalf of the cottage owners. From an economic point of view, this decision is certainly sustainable. In fact, the cottage owners were during all those years involved in what Axelrod qualifies as a repeated game (Axelrod and Hamilton 1981). The cottage owners know that they have to live together for the long run and are willing to adopt a cooperative attitude. Even when in a short-term 'game' it would be advantageous to be non-cooperative, the players are sensitive to the fact that this non-cooperative attitude can be punished by a non-cooperative attitude of the other players in a next game. In his analysis of the relationships between urban immigrants from the San Francisco-area and the original rural population of Shasta county Ellickson observes that such repeated game-situations are prone to develop sophisticated systems of rules, social controls and layered systems of non-legal social sanctions (Ellickson 1991). When groups abstain from exploiting unilaterally other, weaker groups, such as was the case with the Jim Crow-laws in Deep South US, social practice, based on repeated games will lead to a socially efficient relationship among the participants. By awarding legal recognition to the outcomes of social practice among the cottage owners, the district judge made an efficient decision. A different decision may be more based on mere legal logic, could have disrupted this micro-social equilibrium among the cottage owners.

The court of appeal followed a principle of precedent law by deciding that an easement finds its natural limits in the possessory rights of the servient owners. Applied to the case this entailed that the rights of the users of the communal garden were somewhat restricted to allow the owner of the land to exert his possessory rights such as his right of access to his land. One could take another position by contending that parties enjoy full contractual freedom and have the right to grant easement at their whim, even when this erodes completely the possessory rights of the servient owners. According to this position, an easement is what is called an easement in the conveyances granting such rights. Such a position of mere 'contractual nominalism' would however conflict with the 'numerus clausus' principle for real rights (see before Chapter 1, 2. Property within the civil law tradition). As we will further ague (see Chapter 5) the 'numerus clausus' principle, limiting in fact contractual freedom in the transfer of real rights, follows from the 'ergo omnes' character of real rights (see before Chapter 1, 2. Property within the civil law tradition). As real rights have to be respected, not only by the parties involved in the transfer but also 'by the whole world', the creation of a novel real right by contractual parties imposes additional informational costs to third parties (Hansmann and Kraakman 2002). To avoid possible inefficiencies caused by these informational externalities, it makes sense that the law-making authorities (legislator, judges developing precedents) put a limit on the number of allowed real rights. Such a 'numerus clausus' involves necessarily standardization of rights. Certain types of real rights are distinguished and the 'essence' of the definition of these rights is compelling to the contractual parties. Consequently, parties cannot call easements whatever they want to call them. When they use the term *easement* in their conveyances this term entails some essential characteristics of a right. One of the basic characteristics of an easement is its additional character. An easement is additional to the property right of the dominant owners. In this way an easement can never be a second, full property right. An easement is always complementary to another possessory property rights in order to make the use of this property right more efficient. If parties want to transfer also the possessory rights of the servient owner, they should use the legal term denominating such rights such as 'fee simple' or 'ownership'. By awarding 'fee simple' under the name of 'easement', the parties create confusion in the legal transactional world and externalize informational costs to third parties. By safeguarding the 'natural' limits of an easement and by protecting the basic possessory right of the servient owners, the court of appeal protected the essence of the easement and limited possible inefficient externalization of information costs. Consequently, also the decision of the court of appeal is sustainable from an economic point of view.

E **Economic evaluation of the decision.** Both decisions by the district judge and the court of appeal are sustainable from an economic point of view. The first, as it respects micro-social efficiency within the group of cottage owners, the second, as it protects society against inefficient informational externalities. The problem, however, is that the court of appeal remains quite vague about the way in which the two decisions have to be made compatible. On one hand, the spontaneous rules of the cottage owners about the use of the communal garden have to be respected, on the other hand, the possessory rights of the servient owners, which could be conflictual with the practices of the cottage owners, have to be respected too. It would be economically efficient if Kaldor-Hicks-efficiency could be reached in the relationship between these two categories of rights. This would mean that the servient owners are awarded possessory rights up to the point where the harm to the cottage owners becomes larger than the benefit to the servient owners. Based on this principle, a more concrete delineation of the respective rights should be elaborated.

## Cases


*Attwood and others v. Bovis Homes Lt [2000] 4 All ELR Ch D 948–960*

*Batchelor v. Marlow (2001, EWCA Civ 1051 [2003] 4 All ER 78)*

*Britel Developments (Thatcham) Ltd v. Nightfreight (Great Britain) Ltd; [1998] 4 All ER, Ch D, 432–438*

*British Railways Board v. Glass 1964 3 All ER 418*

*Cargill v. Gotts, [1981] 1 All ER CA, 682–690*

*Copeland v. Greenhalf (All ER 809, [1952] Ch 488*)

*Dyce v. Lady Hay (1852, Macq 105)*

*Gardner v. Hodgson's Kingston Brewery Co. Ltd [1903] A.C. 229*

*Harris v. Flowers & Sons 1905*

*Lloyds Bank Ltd v. Dalton [1942]* 2 All ER 352

*London and Blenheim Estates Ltd v. Ladbroke Retail Parks Ltd (1993 All ER 307, 1 WLR 1278*)

*Mulvaney v. Gough and others, Court of Appeal 24 July 2002, EWCA Civ 1078, 4 All ER [2002] 83–93*

*Nickerson v. Barraclough* (1982), 132 New L.J., 224

*Patel and others v. WH Smith (Eziot) Ltd and another, Court of Appeal 28 January 1987, Ius Commune Casebooks for the Common Law of Europe, Property Law, Chapter 2 The Protection of Property Rights*

*Re: Ellenborough Park, Re: Davies, Powell v. Maddison [1955] 3 All ER 667 [1956] Ch 131]*

*Thomas W. Ward Ltd. v. Alexander Bruce Ltd [1959] 2Lloyds Rep. 472*

*Williams v. James 1867 LR 2 CP 577*

*Wimbledon and Putney Commons Conservators v. Dixon*, 1875 1 Ch D 362, [1874–80] All ER 1218

*Woodhouse & Co. Ltd v. Kirkland Ltd 1970 All E R 587*

*Woollerton v. Wilson Ltd v. Richard Costain Ltd [1970]1 W.R.L. 411*

## Bibliography

Axelrod, Robert and William D. Hamilton (March 27, 1981) 'The Evolution of Cooperation', *Science*, New Series, Vol. 211, no. 4489, 1390–1396

Bouckaert, Boudewijn (2001) 'Een moderne zingeving voor juridische brocante. De "tragedy of the anti-commons" en de erfdienstbaarheden', in *Liber Amicorum Yvette Merchiers*, Die Keure, Brugge, 949–961

Bradbrook, A.J. (1983) 'Access to Landlocked Land: A Comparative Study of Legal Solutions', *Sidney Law Review*, 39–60

Buchanan, James M. and J. Yoon Yong (2000) 'Symmetric Tragedies, Commons and Anticommons', *Journal of Law and Economics*, Vol. 43, no. 1, 1–14

Depoorter, Ben W.F. and Francesco Parisi (2003) 'Fragmentation of Property Rights: A Functional Interpretation of the Law of Servitudes', *Global Jurist Frontiers*, Vol. 3, no. 1, Article 2

Ehrlich, Isaac and Richard A. Posner (1974) 'An Economic Analysis of Legal-rule Making', *Journal of Legal Studies*, 257–286

Ellickson, Robert C. (1991) *Order Without Law: How Neighbors Settle Disputes*, Harvard University Press, London, Cambridge, MA

Fenet, P.A. (1827) *Recueil complet des travaux préparatoires du Code Civil*, Imprimerie de Ducessois, Paris, XI

Grosskopf, Ofer and Barak Medina (2009) 'Remedies for Wrongfully Preliminary Injunctions: The Case for Disgorgement of Profits', *Seattle University Law Review*, Vol. 32, 903–941

Hansmann, H. and R. Kraakman (2002) 'Property, Contract, and Verification: The Numerus Clausus Problem and the Diversity of Rights', *Journal of Legal Studies*, 373–420

Harwood, Michael (1982) *Modern English Land Law*, Sweet and Maxwell, London

Heller, M.A. (1998) 'The Tragedy of the Anticommons: Property Rights in the Transition from Marx to Markets', *Harvard Law Review*, Vol. 111, 621

Kurz, Sheldon F. and Herbert Hovenkamp (2003) *American Property Law, Teacher's Manual to Accompany Cases and Materials*, 4th Edition, Thomson West, St.-Paul Minneapolis

Laurent, François (1878) *Principes de Droit Civil*, Bruylant-Pedone, Bruxelles, T. VII

Law Commission (2008) Annual report 2007–8

Merrill, Thomas W. and Henry E. Smith (2000) 'Optimal Standardization in the Law of Property: The *Numerus Clausus* Principle', *The Yale Law Journal*, Vol. 110, 1–70

Pollock sir Frederick and F.W. Maitland (1968) *The History of English Law Before the Time of Edward I*, Cambridge

Posner, Richard A. (1994) 'What do Judges and Justices Maximize?' *Supreme Court Review*, Vol. 3

Posner, Richard A. (2007) *Economic Analysis of the Law*, 7th Edition, Wolters Kluwer, Chicago

Sagaert, Vincent (2014) *Beginselen van Belgisch Privaatrecht*, V. Goederenrecht, Wolters-Kluwer, Mechelen

Stake, Jeffrey Evans (2010) 'Decomposition of Property Rights', in Boudewijn Bouckaert, ed. *Property Law and Economics*, Edward Elgar, Cheltenham, 126–160

Van Oven, J.C. (1948) *Leerboek van het Romeinsch Privaatrecht*, E.J. Brill, Leiden

# 5 Takings

## 5.1 The economic theory of takings

1 **Takings: legal-theoretical framework.** In its most general meaning, taking (or expropriation) concerns a legal but non-consensual transfer of an asset from an owning party to a non-owning party. In modern liberal-democratic legal systems three types of relationships between the government and its citizens concerning their property can be distinguished: (1) the nomocratic type: through private law the government develops and enforces a system of general rules, concerning the definition of property rights, the acquisition of property rights, the verification of property rights and the enforcement of property rights; (2) the regulatory type: through its police power the government can impose to owners specific rules concerning the use of their assets; (3) the expropriation type: deviating from the nomocratic rules, the government can appropriate unilaterally assets from its citizens for public use[1] and under the condition of full compensation.

Most often government bodies are the direct beneficiaries of a taking. When a private party is the beneficiary, there is a private taking. Three kinds of private takings can he distinguished: (1) by taking the government acts as a 'middle man': the government takes the land from a private party and transfers it again to another private party; (2) private taking by delegation: the government delegates a fragment of its taking power to a private party (e.g. a private railway company) (Bell 2009: 549); (3) in specific **circumstances,** defined by law, a private party is allowed to take property from another private

1 It has to be remarked that liberal democracies are reluctant to use the taking power for redistributive purposes. The huge levels of redistribution in modern welfare states are channelled through a system of taxation and welfare entitlements. Totalitarian and collectivistic systems however have made ample use of takings to destroy their political victims and to reward their political faithful. The national socialists in Germany first expelled and later exterminated their Jewish populations and redistributed their assets to the 'Arian' population (Götz 2007). The Czechoslovakian government in 1945 expelled its German population ('Sudetendeutsche') and redistributed their properties among communist supporters. In 1994, Rwandan Hutu militias mass slaughtered Tutsi farmers in order to appropriate their land.

party (e.g. making the party wall common; see before Chapter 2 and later in this chapter, 6. Economic theory: public use) (Bouckaert and De Geest 1995).

In most cases, the expropriated asset concerns land and constructions on it. When chattel is taken, other legal terms are common such as requisition or confiscation. This chapter concerns only the taking of land.

2 **Takings: legal historical and comparative context.** As early as in the Greek and Roman legal tradition, mentions can be found to takings by public authorities and compensations for them. The Athenian Constitution of Aristotle refers to a taking of houses by Athens in the city of Eleusis and the procedure of valuation and compensation (Mcnulty 1912: 556). As Roman public law was not compiled in a written '*Corpus*' as was the case with private law, there is no systematic record of the takings law in Ancient Rome. However, the Romans were very active builders of public infrastructure. For instance, they built 200,000 km of roads and aqueducts of more than 100 km long (Herber 2014: 7). It is hard to imagine that such public works could be effectuated without any legal taking procedure. Implicit mentions of such procedures can be found for instance in Frontinus, stating that strips of land adjacent to aqueducts can be taken from the owner (Herber 2014: 15–20; Mcnulty 1912: 556).

3 Within the context of feudal law, becoming predominant in medieval Europe, the legal meaning of taking underwent a drastic change. In Roman law, a taking implied a shift of land from a private domain to the public domain. The categories of public and private however do not apply to the feudal legal framework. As most land was legally enveloped into a pyramidal system of tenures, non-consensual transfers of land occurred most often within a relationship of lord and tenant. When a tenant committed a felony, by not complying with his feudal duties or by political rebellion, the fief, awarded in tenure, returned to the lord according to the doctrine of *escheat*. Properly speaking, takings do not exist within the logic of feudal law. One should rather speak of 'returnings'. The evolution of taking under feudal law depended largely on the power relationships between lord and tenant. The Magna Carta of 1215, resulting from a power shift from the Crown to the higher aristocracy ('the tenants in chief'), put several important restrictions to the doctrine of *escheat*. Chapter 39 provided that no freeman could be disseized of his freehold except by consent of his peers or by the laws of the land. Chapter 28 provided that expropriation of corn or other movable goods is only possible under the condition of due compensation. By the gradual shift of political power from the King to the parliament and economic power from the landed aristocracy to the merchants in the cities this feudal framework of *escheat* became gradually obsolete. Takings concerned more and more the transfer of land to public authorities for public purposes such as the construction of roads, mills, bridges, fortifications, waterways and so forth. The parliament and the cities became the most active agents in providing infrastructure and the subsequent necessary takings. From the sixteenth

century on, most authorizations from the parliament to condemn land for public purposes also provided for a compensation. As a common practice, the compensations amounted up to 110 percent of the value of the taken property. Benson explains this practice by the fact that landed owners had most voting rights in the parliament and served themselves with generous compensations (Benson 2008: 428). The English practice of condemnation and compensation followed the settlers in the American colonies. Benson remarks that the doctrine of 'eminent domain', the common term for takings in the United States, was often used also for mere private purposes such as the building of mills and dikes on private land. The doctrine of eminent domain finally found its way to the American Constitution in its famous Fifth Amendment. The author of the amendment, James Madison, followed the view of Thomas Jefferson that private property deserved the strongest possible protection and the use of eminent domain should remain the exception. Consequently, the Fifth Amendment submits taking to strict conditions such as compensation and the public use-requirement (Benson 2008: 430).

**4** On the European continent the medieval theory on the power to expropriate was often confused. Sometimes it was vested in the absolute power of the emperor or the king and based on Roman texts such as '*quod principi placet legis habet vigorem*'. The power to expropriate was consequently unlimited. Other legal theorists claimed that the ruler of the realm had no dominium on his whole realm but only *imperium* or *jurisdictio vel protectio*. According to this theory, the power to expropriate was only exceptional and required a special justification (Mcnulty 1912: 558). Very probably, the medieval practice of taking was framed as a forced sale '*justo praetio*', such as in the ordinance of Philip the Fair in 1303. From the sixteenth century on, the authors of the natural law school (*Vernunftrecht*) started to spend more systematically attention to the power of expropriation and the conditions for it. Hugo Grotius, Samuel Pufendorf, Jean Domat, Vattel (de) Emerich and Christian Wolf recognize a power to take on behalf of the sovereign when this is necessary for the public benefit but also require a refund of the value, lost by the private party. Montesquieu emphasizes the prevalence of the civil law 'which, with the eyes of a mother, regards every individual as the whole community.' (Mcnulty 1912: 561). Deviations from the civil law should be very exceptional and when necessary the owner must be fully indemnified.

The viewpoints of the natural law school were adopted by the French revolutionaries within the subsequent Constitutions and the Code Civil (art. 544). Through the Napoleonic conquests, these principles spread throughout the whole of Europe and were adopted in many constitutions and civil law codifications.

**5** **Regulatory taking.** Towards the end of the nineteenth century, governments in the industrialized world became more active on the regulatory level (rules on pollution, zoning law, industrial and trade policy, health regulations, etc.). The possible impact of such regulations on the value of property was not considered as a taking because no property right was really taken. The regulations only restricted the use of property. In the United States, this doctrine was sustained in the precedent *Mugler v. Kansas* (1887). The court did not consider the devaluation of investments by a brewer, caused by prohibition laws, as a taking. Consequently this did not qualify for compensation as it was considered as a mere use of the police power by the government. On this case a jurisprudential doctrine, the so-called 'noxious use' doctrine was built. As regulations were considered as tools to prohibit harmful behavior, one cannot claim compensation for the gains of his former 'noxious' behavior. Quite similar to this doctrine is the 'nuisance exception' (Epstein 1985: 1992). The prohibition of behavior, which would qualify in the common law as a nuisance, does not qualify either for compensation. As on the European continent courts relied on a mere formal criterion, namely, the completeness of the property right taken, to draw the borderline between the police power and the taking power of the government.

This changed with the landmark case *Pennsylvania Coal Co. v. Mahon* (1922). In this case the court ruled that the harm, the claimant suffered from a regulation that prohibited quasi entirely the use of its legally acquired mining rights, was so impactful that it was tantamount to a full expropriation. Justice Holmes, the author of the majority opinion in this case, admitted that the government could not compensate all harms, suffered by agents, submitted to regulations. 'The general rule at least is', Holmes stated, 'that while property may be regulated to a certain extent, if regulation goes too far it will be recognized as a taking' (*Pennsylvania Coal*, 415). Since this precedent, courts are willing to apply to regulatory harm cases a so-called 'diminution of value' test.

An additional condition for regulatory taking concerns the singling-out condition. In the case *Penn Central v. City of New York* (1978) Justice Rehnquist stated:

> Even where the government prohibits a non-injurious use, the court – quoting here from Pennsylvania Coal- has ruled that a taking does not take place if the prohibition applies over a broad cross section of land and thereby secures an average reciprocity of advantage.
>
> (*Penn Central v. City of News York*, 147)

Only when a party is disproportionally hit by a regulation, compensation can be awarded. In case where the benefits and the costs of the regulation are more or less spread among the concerned public, compensation is not justified because one may assume that the costs of the parties are compensated in kind by the benefits of the regulation.

Also on the European continent, the formal criterion of full expropriation was gradually abandoned. Often, specific regulations provide compensation for the impact of the regulation on the value of the estate. The Flemish zoning law for instance provides for compensation when an estate is substantially 'downzoned'.[2] A general doctrine of regulatory taking, mostly called 'quasi-expropriation', was, however, developed under the pressure of precedents by the European Court of Justice (Haeck 2007: 363–369). In the case *Papamichalopoulos and Others v. Greece* (1993), the Court ruled that the factual confiscation and use of a beach by the Greek Marine had to be qualified as a taking and that full compensation was due. This decision was based on art. 1 of the First Protocol of the European Convention of Human Rights, guaranteeing the protection of private property and the peaceful enjoyment of it. In a later case, the Court ruled that

> In the absence of a formal expropriation, that is to say a transfer of ownership, the Court considers that it must look behind the appearances and investigate the realities of the situation. . . . Since the Convention is intended to guarantee rights that are 'practical and effective'. . . . it has to be ascertained whether that situation amounted to a de facto expropriation, as was argued by the applicants.
>
> (*Sporrong and Lönnroth v. Sweden*, 1989, §63)

6 **Economic theory: public use.** In most legal systems, governmental bodies are only allowed to expropriate for 'public use'. During the nineteenth century, this notion was almost exclusively linked with the construction of public infrastructure such as roads, bridges, dikes, fortifications and so forth. This infrastructure was financed by general taxation and was open for free use by the public. As a corollary of the expansion of the interventionist state, the notion of 'public use' acquired gradually the wider meaning of 'public purpose'. As a result, all takings which could be in some way framed in one or another public policy strategy were considered as a lawful taking. A US-landmark case in this respect is *Berman v. Parker (348 US26 (1954))*. In this case the Supreme Court upheld the constitutionality of takings, made for urban renewal. The government expropriated houses to demolish them and make space for new houses. In the famous case *Kelo v. City of New London (545 US 469 (2005))* the Supreme Court went several steps further by upholding the constitutionality of the taking of houses to allow private company Pfizer to build new buildings for its business and the housing of its staff. While in *Berman v. Parker* the elimination of blight constituted the 'public purpose', the taking in *Kelo* was justified by the expectation of the city to increase its tax base. The *Kelo* decision triggered a fierce public debate on the scope of taking power of the government and led to several state referenda resulting in the passing of laws in thirty-one states, curbing down the scope of taking power by state governments.

In the economic theory on takings, the focus is not on the semantics of public use or the construction of the true will of the founding fathers of the

2 Vlaamse Codex Ruimtelijke Ordening, art. 2.6.1–2.6.3

constitution. The central question here is in which cases efficiency can be enhanced through non-consensual transfers. This discussion is in no way limited to relationships between governmental bodies and private parties. In addition, the possible efficiency of non-consensual transfers between private parties falls within the research scope of economic theory.

Consensual transfers enjoy in economic theory the presumption of efficiency, while non-consensual ones not. Consensual transfers, provided they occur between informed parties, shift assets from a lower valuing party to a higher valuing one. Markets are large networks of consensual transfers, channelling the assets to the highest bidders, that is, the agents expecting the highest return of the asset.

This guarantee of plausible efficiency of consensual transfer is lacking with non-consensual ones. This is utterly clear when the taking party has no duty to compensate. Also in case of a compensation duty, efficiency is not guaranteed. In case the expropriated party does not voluntarily accept the compensation offer by the taking party, the 'price' has to be determined by a third party, most often the court. There is no guarantee that the value, fixed by the assessing instance equals the willingness to sell of the expropriated party. In most liberal-democratic legal systems, compensations for takings should match the 'fair market' value of the taken asset. This does not necessarily account for the subjective value on behalf the expropriated party. A non-consensual transfer will be inefficient when $(V^s\text{-}V^{fm} > V^t\text{-}V^{fm})$ or when $(V^s > V^t)$ where $V^s$ is the subjective value, $V^{fm}$ the fair market value compensation and $V^t$ is the value for the taking party. Consequently, in order to justify a non-consensual transfer, it is necessary to show that the efficiency gains of it are larger than the risk of efficiency losses due to under-compensation of the subjective value of the asset taken.

Two sources of efficiency gains through non-consensual transfers may be distinguished. The first one is the occurrence of an anti-commons-setting (see also Chapter 4).

The candidate buyer/acquirer of an asset or combination of assets may be confronted with multiple rights holders, whose assent is complementary, to acquire the asset. The classical example is the situation of the government planning to build a road. In order to build it, it needs to assemble property of land of all owners whose land will be crossed by that road. Apart from the high transaction costs, this setting may involve, it allows the different rights holders (the 'anti-commoners') also to develop strategic behavior in order to maximize their gains. The anti-commoners may develop a feet-dragging strategy in order to be one of the last parties whose assent is needed. From this strong bargaining position out, they may try to capture the full profit of the project. Such strategic behavior can lead to the breakdown of the project, which may have been, making abstraction from the anti-commons-setting, a highly efficient one. When the candidate buyer/acquirer is a governmental body, the problem is even more stringent. Between governments and private parties, an information asymmetry may prevail (Bell 2009: 547). The government does not know per se the willingness to sell (reserve price) of the private party, while the private party does, due to the publicity of the procedure, the governmental body has to follow. When the candidate buyer/acquirer is a private party it can hide its reserve price, eventually send dummy buyers, pretending they are only interested in a part of the complementary set of assets, needed for the project, and later on transfer it to the real developer.

The second source of efficiency gains through non-consensual transfer is the situation of a bilateral monopoly. When a component of complementary assets, crucial for the success of the project, is monopolized by an agent, this agent can act strategically and attempt to capture the whole social profit of the project. This could lead to a breakdown of the negotiations and the abandonment of an efficient project. Suppose for instance a government instance is planning to build a road through a valley, surrounded by high and inaccessible mountains and land, necessary to cross with the road, is owned by a single person. This person is in a position of a bilateral monopoly. Without a possibility of taking, there is a risk for strategic behavior and a failure of the project.

When one compares these economic justifications for the taking power of governmental bodies with the jurisprudential doctrine of public use, the economic theory is in one respect more strict and in another respect broader than the classical jurisprudential doctrine.

In many cases, where the classical doctrine allows a taking under the heading of a wide reading of public use, takings cannot be justified according to the economic doctrine. Take for instance the case *Poletown Neighbourhood Council v. City of Detroit* (1981) in which the Michigan Supreme Court allowed a taking for the destruction of a whole neighbourhood (1,000 residences) in order to allow General Motors to build an auto plant. There might be problem of anti-commons with regard to this neighbourhood, but GM has many alternatives to invest somewhere else and to use this in the negotiations. It seems that this taking is rather related to corporate capitalist-interventionist policy and that a by-pass of the discipline of the market is not justified in this case.

The economic justification has on the other hand a wider scope than the classical jurisprudential doctrine in that it allows more takings in the context of private relationships. The economic theory encompasses several private law-situations under its takings theory, which are according to the classical theory foreign to takings and framed in other doctrines. To give some examples:

1) **The party wall**: the non-owner of the adjacent land can ask the party wall to be made common, in order to use it and so avoid a duplication of building (art. 661 Civil Code)
2) **Building across the border of your neighbour**: the property remedy should be demolition of the building. If the crossing is not substantial and the crossing occurred in good faith, courts will only award damages

(liability rule instead of property rule). In classical doctrine, this case is brought under the vague doctrine of 'abuse of a right' ('*abus du droit*') (*Cass. (B), 1971*). According to the economic theory, this is a case of a bilateral monopoly problem.

3) **Abolishment of servitude**: when a servitude (or easement) loses its use value for the dominant estate, courts can abolish it according to the Belgian Civil Code (art. 710 bis). The respective owners of the dominant and servient estate are in a bilateral monopoly situation. As the easement has become useless, the only impact of the easement would be redistributive. As redistribution is costly, this would be a negative sum game.
4) **Easements by necessity**: in cases of bilateral monopoly within relationships of landed owners, the law awards sometimes that one land owner can claim an easement on the land of his neighbour, even without his consent (Bell 2009: 550). This is the case with enclaved land for an easement of passage to the public road (art. 682–685 Civil Code), the easement of running off water towards lower land on a slope (art. 640 Civil Code) (see before Chapter 4, 4. Economic theory on easements. Bilateral monopoly and anti-commons).

7 **Compensation**: Most legal scholars agree that compensation for a taking is necessary for the sake of justice. According to Montesquieu, every individual, submitted to a taking has to be treated as if the whole community was involved and deserves consequently a due compensation (quoted by Mcnulty 1912: 561). The question here however is whether compensation is also efficient. If not, an embarrassing clash appears between concerns of justice and concerns of efficiency. Both questions are however not always strictly separated. Michelman, for instance, associates non-compensation with demoralization costs, that is, the costs to offset disutilities on behalf of losers and their sympathizers because no compensation was offered and future production (social unrest, impaired incentives) was lost due to demoralization of uncompensated losers and their sympathizers (Michelman 1967: 1214; Miceli and Segerson 2000: 335). Efficiency and justice concerns meet here to a certain extent because perceived injustice causes demoralization and unrest in society inevitably involving loss of wealth.

Economists are however far from unanimous about the efficiency of compensations. According to Blume, Rubinfeld and Shapiro compensation is inefficient because it bestows a moral hazard on landowners and investors. Because all the value of their land and investments, made on it, are compensated, landowners do not anticipate on potential takings. They will neglect to take optimal information on taking risks and invest on land with eventual high probability of a taking. This often leads to destruction of made investments in order to convert the land to the use, planned in the public project. This type of waste is the real cost of the inefficient compensation practice. With a no-compensation rule, or eventually less radical solutions such as a lump-sum-compensation of a less than 100 percent compensation, potential investors will have an incentive to take optimal levels of information in order to minimize the taking risk (Blume, Rubinfeld, and Shapiro 1984).

This rather non-conventional position has been countered in the literature by several arguments:

1 **Moral hazard by the government**: If governmental bodies would act like a private agent, they would only expropriate when the social profit of the project is larger than the cost of compensation. When these costs cover the full, subjective value of the taken asset there is a guarantee that taking will be always efficient because the cost of the taking is fully internalized. Of course, the government does not act like a private agent. As the link with the agency, deciding the taking, and the impact of the compensation on the budget is rather weak, taking decisions by the governmental bodies will be less efficient than when a private actor such as a company would be involved. Voters in a liberal democracy will barely establish the link between their increased tax bill and the compensations paid for takings. Information costs are prohibitively high in relationship with the futile influence an individual vote will have on the total vote. Nevertheless, even when the duty to compensate does not incentivize fully the taking decision makers, it is clear that a total of partial absence of a compensation duty would make things only worse. Absence of compensation duty would bestow a strong moral hazard on the taking decision makers because the impact of their decision will not appear at all on the budget and the tax bills of the citizens. It will only affect the patrimony of the non-compensated expropriated agent. Consequently, compensation is a necessary means to discipline governmental bodies and to push taking decisions to more efficiency.
2 **Genuine uncertainty**: the Rubinfeld-argument presupposes a continuous positive relationship between information costs and the predictability of taking decisions. The more you study government policy and plans, the more you will be able to predict which land will be taken. This is only true to a certain extent. The direction government decisions may take may become at a certain point completely unpredictable because dependent on political compromises, sudden exogenous accidents and circumstances.

   In so far this genuine uncertainty[3] is involved the incentive to search information on taking plans will not play.
3 **Inefficient investments:** According to Miceli (1991, 2000) a non-compensation rule will also stimulate inefficient investments. This argument however is only valid when the government does not operate under

3 Frank Knight (*Risk, Uncertainty and Profit*, 1921) developed the notion of genuine uncertainty. In cases of risk uncertainty, we know about the potential outcomes and the probability of their occurrence. Under genuine uncertainty, this knowledge is not available.

'fiscal illusion', that is, taking into account the budgetary impact of the compensation. Without compensation, the landowner will overinvest in order to reduce the probability of taking, because our rational 'Pigouvian' government wants to avoid social losses by destroying investments. In the reverse, when the government overcompensates, landowners may underinvest to attract a taking. In both cases, inefficient investments will be stimulated.

8 **Regulatory taking and economics**: the concept of regulatory taking does not fit quite well within the economic definition of property rights (see before Chapter 1, 5. Property in law and economics). The term suggests a binary distinction between on one hand a full taking of a property right and on the other hand a mere regulation of the use of a property right. When using the economic definition of property rights as a conceptual starting point, namely, an acting with scarce resources right (ASRR), a regulatory taking will also mostly consist of a taking of a property right. In the case of a classical 'full' taking, all property rights, enveloped by full ownership (access, withdrawal, use, manage, exclusion, destruction, alienation) are taken. In cases of regulatory taking only one or some of these property rights ('sticks of the basket') are taken. The difference between the classical legal and the economic approach is not merely conceptual. As the distinction between a full taking and a regulatory one is not binary and less absolute, the economic theory will be more inclined of considering a regulatory taking as a real taking, qualifying for compensation, not hindered herein by the formal hurdle of the classical legal approach.

Concerning the nature of government action as a criterion for a regulatory taking, the economic theory is grossly a sophistication of the classical jurisprudential doctrine. The 'noxious use' doctrine and the nuisance exception (see before this chapter, 5. Regulatory Taking) are converted in legal economic literature into the harm-benefit rule (Fishel 1995: 154–155). When a regulation aims at limiting harm caused by externalities, there is no taking and no compensation. If this were qualified as a taking, the legal system would provide incentives to potential polluters to externalize. Each polluter whose private gains are higher than his private costs will win in case of compensation. Normally the polluter will receive the difference between his private gains and private costs as a compensation. The polluter was however able to make his private gains thanks to his externalizing behavior.

When the regulation imposes a burden to an owner for the benefit of third parties, a regulatory taking can be envisaged if other conditions (see later) are matched. In case of non-compensation, the government would make an unintended and arbitrary redistribution from the victim of the regulation to the public, benefitting from the regulation, involving, as Michelman argued (1967), demoralization costs.

Also concerning the impact of the government action as a criterion for a regulatory taking, the economic theory is more or less in line with jurisprudential doctrine. According to Mercuro (1992: 4) the landmark case *Pennsylvania Coal v. Mahon* 'put the police power on a continuum with the power of eminent domain.' A no compensation rule for high impact regulation, matching the diminution of value test, would, as in the case of full taking, create a huge moral hazard on behalf of the government.

The criterion of diminution of value in the Pennsylvania case received a sharper content in the *Penn Central Transportation Co v. City of New York* (1978). In this case, frustrations of investment-backed expectations are considered as crucial for a taking. Miceli, however, argues again that such a rule could trigger overinvestment and stimulate inefficiency (Miceli and Segerson 1996).

Also the singling out condition of the jurisprudential doctrine (see before this chapter, 5. Regulatory taking) has a backing in economic theory. When the benefits and the costs of the regulation are more or less reciprocally spread among the concerned public, a compensation to the 'victims' and a taxation of the 'benefiters' would nearly not alter the distribution of wealth among the public but would involve huge transaction costs. When the regulation hits one party particularly, no compensation would entail non-intended and arbitrary redistribution and ensuing demoralization costs.

A last question concerns the capitalization of the threat of regulation. Some authors (Michelman 1967: 1238; Rose-Ackerman 1992) argue that an owner of regulated land is already compensated because the threat of regulation is already discounted ('capitalized') in the purchase price. Similar arguments are advanced in the discussion about 'coming to the nuisance' (see before Chapter 3, 5. Coming to the nuisance). Epstein, however, argues that this argument is flawed because in such cases in fact the seller would remain uncompensated because he receives a lower price. When the buyer will be compensated for the later regulation, his willingness to pay for the land will be higher and the seller will be indirectly compensated for the loss of value of the land (Epstein 1985: 151–158).

## 5.2 Case analyses

### *1. Hawaii Housing Authority v. Midkiff, U.S. Supreme Court, May 30, 1984; 467 U.S. 229*

#### A. Facts and legal sources

Until the nineteenth century, property rights on land in Hawaii were entirely submitted to tribal-feudal rules, according to the customs of the Polynesian inhabitants. The high chief of the island, the *'ali'i nui'* was considered as the ultimate owner of all land on the island. The high chief assigned tenures to sub chiefs in order to develop the land and these sub chiefs reassigned tenures to even lower ranked chiefs, who governed the farmers and tenants working on the land. Wholly confirming the feudal logic the '*ali'i nui'* could revoke the tenures by which the land returned to his trust. During the nineteenth century, Hawaiian leaders and American settlers attempted to reform the system and to divide land between the crown, the chiefs and the people but these attempts proved to be unsuccessful.

In 1960, after Hawaii acquired US statehood, the Hawaiian legislature conducted a research about the distribution of property on land on the islands. The findings of this research showed an extreme concentration of land ownership:

- 49 percent of the land was owned either by the state or by the federal government
- 47 percent of the land was owned by only 72 big land owners and 40 percent of it by only 18 land owners, owning estates of more than 21,000 acres.
- on Oahu, the most urbanized island, only 22 landowners owned 72.5 percent of the fee simple titles.

Consequently, the legislature decided to break up these large estates and to sell the land to the tenants. The legislature considered requiring the large landowners to sell the land to their tenants but the landowners resisted because of the high federal tax liabilities these transactions would involve. Therefore, the legislature decided to condemn residential tracts and then transfer the condemned fees simple to existing tenants. This method was adopted in the Land Reform Act of 1967. According to this act, tenants living on single-family residential lots in developmental tracts of at least five acres in size could ask to the Hawaiian Housing Authority (HHA) to condemn the property on which they live. When twenty-five eligible tenants filed the appropriate applications, hearings have to be organized to determine whether the takings matched with the public purpose requirement. If this was the case, the HHA could acquire the concerned tracts by prices decided either at a condemnation trial or by negotiation between lessors and lessees. Once compensation settled, the HHA could sell the land to the tenants who had applied for fee simple ownership. HHA is authorized to lend up to 90 percent of the purchase price to the tenants.

In April 1977 HHA conducted a public hearing concerning the land of the appellees. The public purpose requirement was considered to be matched. About the price, no agreement was reached and the fixing of it was submitted to compulsory arbitration. The appellees filed suit in February 1979 at the US States District Court asking that the state should be restrained to proceed against the appellees. This court declared the compulsory arbitration and the compensation formula unconstitutional but decided finally, in December 1979, that the remaining portion of the Act was constitutional under the Public Use requirement. The Act's goals were considered within the bounds of State's police powers and that the means chosen were not arbitrary, capricious or selected in bad faith.

The most important legal source for this case is the Fifth Amendment of the US Constitution ('Nor shall private property be taken for public use without just compensation') which has been made also applicable to the acts of the Hawaiian state.

Further, there is the Fourteenth Amendment forbidding states to 'deprive *citizens from their private property without due process of law.*'

In the case *Railroad Comm'n v. Pullman Co,312 U.S. 496,1941* it is held that federal courts should abstain from ruling when difficult and unsettled question on the state law, involved in the pending case, must be resolved.

In the case *Berman v. Parker, 348 U.S. 26, 1954* it is held that the state legislature is the main guardian of the public needs to be served by social legislation. When measures fall within the authority of Congress or state legislatures, these instances have also the right to realize their goals through eminent domain. The scope of the courts to review what constitutes public use is therefore extremely narrow.

## B. Claims and defences

The appellees claim that the Hawaiian Land Reform Act and the takings based on it are unconstitutional because they merely aim at the redistribution of land from private to private parties. Consequently, the public use requirement is not matched at all. The Court of the Ninth Circuit also adopted this point of view, to which the appellees appealed first. The Court concluded that the Act was simply 'a *naked attempt on the part of the state of Hawaii to take private property of A and transfer it to B solely for B's private use and benefit.*'

The HHA however maintains that this Act serves a public purpose as it attempts to break the oligopoly on land property and establish a properly functioning land market in Hawaii.

## C. Sentence and considerations

The Supreme Court upholds the Land Reform Act of Hawaii as constitutional. Referring to *Berman v. Parker*, the Court considers that the sovereign power to determine the extent of public use also applies to state legislature. Unless public authorities *'use (the taking power) palpably without reasonable foundation (United States v. Gettysburg Electric R. CO)'* the judge has to respect the extent of the public use requirement the public authorities are willing to give it. Although the application of the Hawaii Land Reform Act involves the transfer of private property from private parties to private parties, these transfers are subservient to a general public purpose, i.e. the abolishment of feudalism and land oligopoly. This policy is in line with the original intentions of the settlers of the first thirteen colonies. In the Act of May 1779, all the feudal incidents, large proprietors imposed on the lands of farmers, were eradicated. The Hawaiian land oligopoly remained an obstacle and an artificial deterrent for the smooth functioning of the residential market. It forced thousands of residents into the position of a lessee. As such, the Court considers the regulation of oligopoly as falling within the police power of the state, thereby referring to *Exxon Corp. v. Governor of Maryland.* The Court considers that the notion 'public purpose' should not be narrowed to its literal sense, i.e. that everybody enjoys or participates in the improvement, realized by the takings. It is sufficient that the takings serve a wider policy goal than the strict private interests of the parties, benefitted by the takings.

**D. Economic analysis**

This case on takings is rather atypical. As conceived by the US Constitution and the many liberal constitutions in Europe, takings are an exception to the liberal-nomocratic system of general rules, in which transfers of land property are primarily of a voluntary character. This voluntary character operates *inter vivos* through sales or donations and *post mortem* through wills or acquiescence to default inheritance rules. In this case, the takings procedure is used for a general redistribution of property rights on land.

Most often, such general redistributions of property on land occur during dramatic political episodes such as a revolution, after a war or during post-colonial reform. A major example of the first category is the French revolution. In the night of 4 August 1789, the *Assemblée Générale* abolished the feudal privileges of the nobility, without using the takings procedure and providing compensation only in some cases.[4] An example of the second category concerns the thoroughgoing reforms of land property in Japan in 1945–1948, by the American Military Authority, presided by General MacArthur.[5] The land reforms intended to break the power of the aristocratic class of big landowners, mostly living in the cities and constituting the backbone of the Japanese military. Another example of post-war general redistribution of property on land concerned the confiscation of agricultural property of Germans and Hungarians in former Czechoslovakia through the so-called Benesh decrees.[6] The confiscations were merely based on ethnic criteria and were executed without any compensation. Examples of the last category are the land reforms in South Africa and Zimbabwe. In Zimbabwe 110,000 $km^2$ of agricultural land was redistributed from Anglo-white farmers to black Zimbabweans, mostly followers of the government party. The so-called Fast Track Land Reforms often involved violence and the killing of the former owners.

As it appears from this overview, general land redistribution often occurred at the occasion of a constitutional discontinuity such as a revolution or military occupation after total defeat. To put it in terms of Hans Kelsen, general land

4 Impressed by the fall of the Bastille on 14 July 1789 and the waves of violence on the countryside, the *Assemblée Génerale* abolished with 19 Decrees – voted on from 4 to 11 August 1789 – nearly all rights and privileges associated with feudalism. The rights and dues originating from real or personal serfdom were abolished without any compensation. All other dues to the nobility were made redeemable. Further, the monopoly of hunting, the ban on killing pigeons by farmers, the tithes (church tax) and the manorial courts were abolished.

5 Imposed by the Supreme Command for Allied Powers (SCAP) the large absentee landowners were obliged to sell to the government at a price, fixed by the authorities, land, owned in excess of a certain quantity. Farmers, by preference the tenants working on the land, could buy this land at the same price. By this reform, about 30 million parcels, totalling about 2 million hectares, passed from big landowners to small farmers. The area, cultivated by tenants declined by 46 percent.

6 The Benesh decrees were issued during the war by the Czech government in exile and covered a variety of subjects. They were ratified retroactively by the National Assembly in 1946. Decree 12/1945 ordered the confiscation of all property owned by German and Hungarian persons, notwithstanding Czech citizenship. About three million German Czechs and 800,000 Hungarian Czechs were expelled, 2,400,499 hectares of agricultural land, 3,900 industrial firms and 34,400 commercial firms were expropriated without any compensation (Suppan 2006:34)

redistribution often goes hand in hand with the establishment of a new '*Grundnorm*' of the legal system (Kelsen 1960). It may be clear that the takings clause of the Fourteenth Amendment was not intended for such a general land redistribution. This amendment concerned an exception to the general principle of the common law that property passes from one party to another in a voluntary way. Only to avoid deadlocks in the execution of large public works by governmental bodies this exception was deemed to be necessary.

The situation in Hawaii concerning land reform differs substantially from the mentioned dramatic examples of constitutional discontinuity. The Hawaiian land reform was the result neither of a political revolution, nor of a post-war military occupation. The general land reform, introduced in 1967, had however become unavoidable because of the clash between on one hand the oligopolistic land distribution on the islands, which was the legacy of the precolonial and pre-US statehood tribal feudalism, and on the other hand the prevalence of the Jeffersonian yeoman-ideal, implying a thorough spread of land property, in the US federation, of which Hawaii had become a full member. In order to bring its land property situation more in line with the American-like Jeffersonian ideal the Hawaiian authorities used the takings procedure of the Fourteenth Amendment.

From an economic point of view, two questions can be raised concerning the Hawaiian land reform: (1) Is the policy reason, that is, breaking the oligopoly of land property economically justified? (2) Is it right to use the takings procedure for this policy purpose?

As is the case for markets in general, markets in land use rights will be more efficient when ownership of land is spread. On land markets, the agents aiming at acquiring rights on the use of land, belonging to others, constitute the demand on the land market, while the latter constitute the supply.

Suppose that ten agents are willing to buy one tract of land out of a total supply of ten (homogeneous) tracts. Suppose that the willingness to pay (WTP) among the buyers ranges from 11 to 1. Suppose finally that one landowner owns the ten tracts. As Table 5.1 indicates, the land monopolist will only sell five or six land tracts. When he lowers the price below 5, his total revenue is falling.

*Table 5.1* Impact of monopoly of land ownership

| *Price of one tract* | *Number of tracts sold* | *Total Return of Sales* | *Total Consumers' surplus* |
|---|---|---|---|
| 10 | 1 | 10 | 1 |
| 9 | 2 | 18 | 1+2=3 |
| 8 | 3 | 24 | 1+2+3 =6 |
| 7 | 4 | 28 | 1+2+3+4=10 |
| 6 | 5 | 30 | 1+2+3+4+5=15 |
| 5 | 6 | 30 | 1+2+3+4+5+6=21 |
| 4 | 7 | 28 | 1+2+3+4+5+6+7=28 |
| 3 | 8 | 24 | 1+2+3+4+5+6+7+8=36 |
| 2 | 9 | 18 | 1+2+3+4+5+6+7+8+9= 45 |
| 1 | 10 | 10 | 1+2+3+4+5+6+7+8+9+10= 55 |

When the tracts are however owned by several different owners, it is very likely that more tracts will be sold at lower prices. The different suppliers will compete with each other in order to sell their tracts. There is however no guarantee that all tracts will be sold, for the number of tracts sold depends on the willingness to sell (WTS) among the landowners. Suppose WTS is at 3, then the price will, due to competition, sink to 3 and 8 tracts will be sold. Suppose that the WTS of the land monopolist is also at 3, then still only 5 or 6 tracts will be sold, because at that number the total revenue of the monopolist is the highest. The higher the number of tracts sold, the higher the consumer surplus and the higher the wealth in society. A spread supply of land use rights on the land and the resulting competition on the land market consequently increases wealth in society.

The risk of monopolization of land markets depends of course largely on the geographic situation. If supply of land use rights is located in large contiguous areas (e.g. the big plains in Mid-West US) a land monopoly or oligopoly in a certain area can be avoided by searching for land in neighbouring areas. The costs of location may be somewhat higher for the land user, but he can avoid the monopoly-oligopoly prices of land in the better-located area. These alleviating geographic circumstances are however not present in the case of islands such as the Hawaiian Islands. In these cases, the supply of land is geographically fixed. To state it in economic terms, the costs of avoiding land monopoly or oligopoly by moving out of the area may be quasi infinite. A Hawaiian lessee could only avoid the monopolistic prices of land use on the islands by crossing the ocean.

The policy reason of the Hawaiian Land Reform Act, namely, breaking up oligopolistic land ownership structures and establishing a more open residential market, is consequently fully justified from an economic point of view.

Finally, one can ask whether the use of the takings procedure was appropriate in this case. As was already mentioned, the takings clause in the Fourteenth Amendment was not intended for overall land reforms changing thoroughly the property rights' system in a country but rather to facilitate the execution of public works and to avoid deadlocks or extortion prices.

If Hawaii would have been an independent state and adopted the same policy goal of large-scale redistribution of land holdings, the most plausible legal instrument would have been an encompassing land reform act, through which land titles would have been redefined and reshifted directly among owners, without relying on the takings procedure. Whether owners, losing titles, should have been compensated within such a context is a wider political question in which considerations of social justice and the historical background of the former property situation may be decisive. Often legislators, introducing such large scale land reforms strike a compromise between social justice considerations pointing to no-compensation and political appeasement pointing to a certain compensation. This was for instance the case with the already mentioned abolishment of feudal privileges during the French revolutions. For some privileges farmers had to pay compensations, for others not. Also for the abolishment of slavery in Russia in 1865, the freed farmers had to pay some compensation to their former masters.

Because Hawaii has acquired statehood in the US federation in 1959 such an all-encompassing redistribution of land with compensatory schemes *sui generis* would have been incompatible with the federal constitutional principles. Anti-feudal reforms in the rest of the US had been introduced at the occasion of the American Revolution. Hawaii had, concerning land reform, its American Revolution only in 1967 with its Land Reform Act. Because it had become a member of the US federation already, it had to respect the legal principles and tools of this federation, namely, the Fifth and Fourteenth Amendments of the US Constitution. The specific historical situation of Hawaii – a feudal country within a non-feudal federation – left the Hawaiian legislator no choice than to wrap the general land redistribution into the taking procedure, although this procedure was historically not intended for such a use.

### E. Economic evaluation

The pursued policy goal of the Hawaiian Land Reform Act, namely, breaking the land oligopoly on the Hawaiian Islands can be sustained from an economic point of view. As monopoly is detrimental for the functioning of markets in general, so is it also for land markets. Although it is clear that the takings clause in the US Constitution was not intended for such a large-scale land reform through which land property is reshuffled from private to private parties, the Hawaiian legislature had no other option to use this legal procedure because it had acquired statehood in 1959 and was consequently submitted to the US Constitution. Although its ruling upholding the constitutionality of the Hawaiian Land Reform Act can be supported, the Supreme Court should have made clear in more explicit terms that the use of takings in this case is linked with the exceptional historical situation of Hawaii, which had to make its American Revolution concerning land reform under the legal umbrella of the US constitution. By making this exceptional character of the use of the takings clause explicit, the Court would avoid the takings clause being used for redistributive purposes in situations where this historical exceptional situation does not prevail. By the lack of historical framing, this precedent risks being abused for justifying collective land redistribution which has nothing to do with the functioning of residential markets and everything to do with the favouring of particular or group interests.

## 2. *County of Wayne v. Hathcock, Supreme Court of Michigan, July 30, 2004; 471 Mich 445 (2004)*

### A. Facts and legal sources

In April 2001 the county of Wayne initiated actions to expropriate nineteen parcels of land immediately South of Detroit Metropolitan Airport. These expropriations were initiated because of a wider construction plan around this airport. The county invested $2 billion in the renovation of the airport. Due to raising concerns for noise from increased traffic to neighbouring landowners, the county started a program to purchase neighbouring land. This program was funded partially by the Federal Aviation Administration (FAA). The agreement of the county with FAA provided that the land acquired for noise abatement had to be put to economic productive use. The resulting Pinnacle project provided the outlay of a business and technology park. According to the county's plan, the project would generate thousands of jobs and tens of millions of dollars in tax revenue. Before the development of the project, the county had already purchased 500 acres. In a next round of voluntary sales, the county acquired another 500 acres. For the outlay of the park, more land was necessary and the already acquired land was distributed in a checkerboard fashion. In July 2001, the Wayne County adopted a Resolution of Necessity and Declaration of Taking, authorizing the taking of additional 300 acres, needed for the project. Twenty-seven owners accepted to sell, but for the last nineteen parcels, a taking procedure had to be initiated. In response, each owner filed a motion to review the necessity of the proposed takings. The Wayne Circuit Court and the Court of Appeals affirmed the county's determination of necessity.

As relevant legal source first article 10 §2 of the Michigan Constitution is involved: 'Private property shall not be taken for public use without just compensation therefore being made or secured in a manner prescribed by law'.

Second, article 213.23 of the Michigan Compiled Laws (MCL) states that any public corporation or state agency is authorized to take private property necessary 'for public purposes within the scope of powers for the use of the benefit of the public'.

The Michigan precedent *Poletown Neighborhood Council v. Detroit (1981)* allowed the City of Detroit to bulldoze an entire neighbourhood in order to give property to General Motors for an auto plant (see before this chapter, 6. Compensation). This was accepted because the takings served the public purpose of reducing unemployment.

In the precedent *Grand Rapids Board of Education v. Baczewski* (1954), the Michigan Court did not consider the taking of land around a school as necessary for public use because according to the plans of the school the land was only needed in a long term of thirty years. The acquisition of land was considered a speculative stockpiling.

In the precedent *City of Lansing v. Edward Rose Realty, Inc. (1993)* the Michigan Court balanced the public and the private benefits of a city ordinance allowing takings.

## B. Claims and defences

Wayne County, the appellee-plaintiff, argues that the takings in order to realize the Pinnacle Project are legal because they are enacted by a public corporation, acting within the scope of its powers and that the takings were necessary for realizing a project, serving the public benefit. The takings were constitutional because in the precedent *Poletown*, it suffices that the takings serve a public purpose even when also private parties benefit from the operation. What is considered as a public purpose falls within the scope of the sovereign power of the concerned legislator.

Hathcock and others, the defendants in appeal, argue that these takings violate article 213.23 of MCL and article 10 §2 of the Michigan Constitution because the takings cannot be considered as being necessary for public use because they serve mainly the private benefits of the future occupants of the business and technology park.

## C. Sentence and considerations

First, the court rules that the takings were not in violation of art. 213.23 of MCL, based on the following three considerations.

The public purpose of the project falls within the scope of powers, granted by Michigan law to Wayne County. This county has developed the project in order to create jobs, to stimulate investments, to stem the tide of disinvestments and population loss and to support opportunities, which would be lost otherwise.

The takings are necessary for the public purpose. The argument of the defendants that the county has not specified in detail the public benefit for each parcel is not valid. Contrary to the *Baczewski* case, where there was no immediate need for taking, the condemned parcels are necessary for the realization of the project. In addition, the fact that still some procedural hurdles (licenses, environmental concerns) have to be taken is not valid.

The fact that the county did not investigate whether the public benefits outweigh the private ones, does not invalidate the county's decision. The *Lansing* precedent, invoked by the defendants does not require such a balancing in order to match the condition of 'use or benefit of the public'.

Second, the Court rules that the takings do violate article 10 §2 of the Michigan Constitution.

The court refers first to Justice Cooley claiming that the Constitution is ratified by the people and should consequently be understood in the usual meaning of its terms. Only when complex legal terms are used, the terms should be given a meaning, which arises from scholarly use in legal precedents and jurisprudence.

In dissent with *Poletown* and following the considerations of Justice Ryan in his dissenting opinion in *Poletown* the requirement of public use is only met in one of the following situations: (1) when the assembly of parcels needed for the public project (e.g. building a railway line) is only possible through coordination by the government; (2) when the private entity, enjoying private benefits from the public project, remains in some way accountable to the public in its use of the condemned properties (public control, some use open for the general public); (3) when the selection of the condemned parcels itself is based on public concerns, such as for instance the demolishment of blighted houses for reasons of public safety and health.

None of the mentioned situations applies in this case. First, there is no unavoidable problem of assembly as it is not necessary for a business and technology park that all parcels are contingent. Second, the future occupants of the business and technology park will be in no way accountable to the public as only purely private business are involved. Third, the selection of the condemned parcels itself is not based on any public significance.

The Court considers that the reasoning in the *Poletown* precedent, allowing any public project for a public purpose as a valid base for takings, is a treat for private property and promotes only the benefit of powerful private interests.

The ruling of the court, overruling the opinion in *Poletown*, is given retroactive application to all pending cases concerning takings. The Court considers that its decision announces not a new law but rather a return to the pre-1963 case law in Michigan.

One of the justices dissents, not on the decision itself but for the reasons given for it. The Justice also dissents on the retroactivity of the ruling.

### D. Economic analysis

From an economic point of view, transfers of land property should be voluntary in principle. This allows land markets to function towards efficient allocation of land. The use of eminent domain is only justified in case of an anti-commons-setting or a bilateral monopoly (see before this chapter, 6. Economic theory: public use) The latter is obviously not the case here, as parcels of a plurality of owners could be used for the outlay of the business and technology park. This allowed Wayne County to profit eventually from price competition among the different owners.

In its considerations, the court refers explicitly to an anti-commons setting as a valid reason for the use of eminent domain. The court quotes Justice Ryan, a dissenter in the Poletown case:

> The exercise of eminent domain for private corporation has been limited to those enterprises generating public benefits whose very existence depends on the use of land that can be assembled only by the coordination central government is capable of achieving.

Further, Justice Ryan gives the example of the construction of a railroad from A to B. The owners between A and B are capable to blackmail the railroad company with extreme high prices, which could lead to a 'practical nightmare'. According to the Court, the facts of this case do not match with such an anti-commons-setting. The parcels, not acquired yet by the Wayne County, are located in a checkerboard structure in relationship with the already acquired parcels. This pattern does not prevent however to outlay the business and technology park. The court remarks that the outlay of this park does not require that all land, used for the park is perfectly contingent. The Court compares with the landscape of the county as a whole *'which is flecked with shopping centers, office parks, clusters of hotels and centers of entertainment and commerce'.*

This point of the view by the Court may have as impact that the area of the business and technology park is less well outlaid without the litigated takings than with them. The park may be *'flecked'* with spots still used for residential purposes or other purposes, alien to the businesses of the park. One could discuss whether, were the benefit of a likely better, more homogeneous outlay of the park not to prevail over the costs of taking (i.e. the difference between the subjective value of the parcels for the owners and their fair market value they would receive as compensation in case of taking ($V^s–V^{fm}$)).

Usually zoning regulations are introduced ex ante (i.e. before building occurred on the zoned areas). From an economic point of view zoning regulations can be efficient: (1) when they protect land uses with significant positive externalities (e.g. green areas, natural monuments) and (2) when they prevent activities which, when located in certain areas, would entail significant negative externalities and when these externalities neither can be bargained away due to prohibitive transaction costs nor can be internalized through the use of private law-remedies (tort, nuisance).

None of these reasons apply in this case in which zoning would imply an ex post-measure (i.e. the taking and eventual demolishment of already existing buildings and installations). First, because the parcels are already used, no areas which have to be protected because of positive externalities are involved. Second, the eventual negative externalities resulting from activities in the concerned parcels can be negotiated away with the agents operating in the park. Because they 'came to the nuisance' (see before Chapter 3, 5. Coming to the nuisance) through the outlay of the park, it is up to them to make an offer to buy away the eventual disturbing impact of such activities.

The court also mentions two other reasons for the use of eminent domain for private parties, given by Justice Ryan in the Poletown case.

A taking for the benefit of private parties is justified when some kind of public involvement can be continued in the condemned property (e.g. access by the public). This reason is close to the opinion of Richard Epstein, who proposes a two-pronged public use test in case of taking for the benefit of a private party. Besides the condition of a holdout problem (anti-commons, see before this chapter, 6. Economic theory: public use), the private party benefitting from the taking should not absorb all the gains of the taking but a substantial part of it should accrue widely to the public (Epstein 1985: ch. 12). In this case, however, the first condition, namely, the presence of a hold-out-problem, is not fulfilled. From an economic point of view, this second reason forwarded by Justice Ryan is not sufficient for a taking. The eventual benefit, deriving from some public use of the property, can be achieved by other, less drastic legal remedies, such as a covenant between the owner and the public authority or a regulation or a public easement, depending on the circumstances.

The selection of the condemned parcels itself can, according to Justice Ryan, be another reason for the use of eminent domain for the benefit of private parties. Justice Ryan refers here to the case *Berman v. Parker*, allowing takings of residential blighted houses for the removal of a slum quarter and the establishment of new comfortable dwellings. Also, this reason can be questioned from an economic point of view. Owners who neglect the maintenance of their properties and let their houses falling into decay are imposing negative externalities to their neighbourhood. Such negative externalities may be of a physical or mere economic kind. The decaying houses may collapse and create risks for neighbours and passers-by. Such houses also diminish the general image and climate of the neighbourhood and negatively affect the real estate value in the neighbourhood. The first task of the public authority is to stop such externalities and order, through either regulation or injunction, the redress of decaying property. In principle, it is up to the owners to cover the costs of this redress. Taking and compensation could imply that the taxpayer indirectly covers these costs, which could lead to a moral hazard on the side of the owners. Consequently, blight on itself is not a decisive reason for the use of eminent domain. Nevertheless, it is possible that a consistent plan of the renewal of a quarter is blocked due to an anti-commons setting. In this case, the use of eminent domain could be justified. The compensation paid to the owners of decaying houses should then of course reflect fully the decline of value of the houses, eventually diminished by a penalty for the negative value on the neighbourhood.

## E. Economic evaluation

The decision of the Michigan Supreme Court can be sustained from an economic point of view. The decision is a breakaway from the ever-widening meaning given to the constitutional term 'public use' in earlier precedents, such as the Poletown precedent. By substituting in fact the term 'public use' with public purpose the judicial control on the use of eminent domain is virtually abandoned. By giving political authorities free access to the use of eminent domain, the risk of inefficient use of eminent domain may increase dramatically. The ill-reflected use of eminent domain may lead to a complete neglect of the general superiority of allocation of land through markets. This precedent clearly signals an end to this tendency. The court decided correctly why one economically sustainable reason for eminent domain was not fulfilled. The two other reasons (valid in its eyes) for eminent domain also unfulfilled in this case are, however, mentioned in a too uncritical way. They deserve further discussion from an economic view, for they risk leading to other inefficient takings decisions.

## 3. *Die Dreizehnte Novelle des Atomgesetz zur Änderung des Atomgesetz vom 31. Juli 2011 (Thirteenth Act Amending the Atomic Energy Act of 31 July 2011); Urteil des Ersten Senats Bundesverfassungsgericht von 6. Dezember 2016 (Judgment of the First Senate of the German Constitutional Court of 6 December 2016); BVerfG, Urteil des Ersten Senats vom 06. Dezember 2016–1 BvR 2821/11 – Rn. (1–407), [BVerfG, Judgment of the First Senate of 06 December 2016–1 BvR 2821/11 – paras. (1–407)]*

## A. Facts and legal sources

Germany has developed peaceful use of atomic energy since 1959. The first act on atomic energy of 23 December 1959 regulated research and development of atomic energy and the protection against risk, and it made the operation of plants dependent on licenses, which could be withdrawn. During the 1970s and 1980s, the commercial exploitation of atomic energy developed and catered to 30–35 percent of total energy production. After the elections in 1998, the federal government negotiated with the operators of the plants a program of a gradual production exit. This led to the agreement of 11 June 2001 to submit the production of atomic energy to deadlines. The act of 22 April 2002 on the ordered phase-out of atomic energy did not fix clear deadlines for the phase-out. After the elections of 2009, with the 11th Act on Atomic Energy, the federal government awarded the producers the right to produce additional residual electricity volumes and pursued the aim of prolonging the operational lifetime of nuclear plants by eight years for plants built prior to 1980 and by fourteen years for plants built after 1980. These grants were awarded to the operators for the amortization of the investments made in the shadow of the preceding nuclear laws. In addition, a Klima fund was established in which the operators would invest a part of their profits. Residual electricity volumes were however awarded to the Mülheim-Kärlich nuclear power plant for a special reason. They were awarded in return for the cessation of public liability suits, initiated against the Land of Rhineland-Palatinate. On 11 March 2011, a nuclear catastrophe occurred in Fukushima, Japan, caused by a tsunami, caused in turn by a submarine earthquake that registered 9.0 on the Richter scale. The tsunami submerged the nuclear installations of Fukushima, spreading radioactive pollution widely throughout the region. In response to this catastrophe, the German government established an expert commission in order to check the safety of the German atomic power plants. The commission pointed out that the safety situation of the German plants was more robust than that of the Japanese and that the likelihood of disasters such as tsunamis was virtually non-existent. Another commission, the *Ethik-Commission*, advised, however, a total exit from nuclear energy not because of an objective increase in risk, but of an increase in perceived risk due to the Fukushima catastrophe.

On 31 July 2011, the Thirteenth Act amending the Atomic Energy Act was voted on. This act provided the total disconnection of all nuclear plants through a phase-out scheme from 6 August 2011 through 31 December 2022.

Three nuclear energy providers (E.ON Kernkraft GmbH, RWE Power AG and Kernkraftwerk Krümmel GmbH represented by the owning Swedish company Vattenfall Europe Nuclear Energy GmbH) filed suit before the German constitutional court claiming that the phase-out scheme of the Thirteenth Act violated their property rights protected by the Constitution.

The first concerned legal sources are all the Atomic Energy Acts of 2002, 2009 and 2011, first awarding the right to produce residual electricity volumes to the plaintiffs and then withdrawing these rights without any form of compensation.

The second legal source is art. 14 of the German Constitution providing that (1) property and inheritance rights are protected but that the content and the limits of these rights are to be determined by the legislator, (2) property implies obligation; the use of it should serve the general interest and (3) taking is only permitted in the general interest and can only follow from a legal decision that determines the way and the level of compensation; the compensation has to be fixed through balancing the general interest and the interest of the concerned party, and claims about the compensation have to be decided by the ordinary courts.

## B. Claims and defences

The plaintiffs argue that the withdrawal of the rights to produce the residual electricity volumes is a violation of property rights without compensation and consequently in conflict with art. 14 of the German Constitution. According to art. 87 of the Euratom Treaty the owners of a nuclear plant are entitled to unlimited use and consumption rights on their investments, but the German law submits the use of these rights to licenses. Because the ownership rights on the plants are complete without value when not linked to a right to produce the rights to produce are equal to full property rights and deserve the same protection. These rights to produce are similar to property rights as they are transferable. The revocation of the rights to produce the residual electricity volumes, granted in earlier legislation, constitutes consequently a taking in the sense of art. 14 of the German Constitution. To constitute a taking in this sense it is not necessary that a transfer of physical assets occurs. The contested law affects clearly the property position of the plaintiffs. Further, the contested law does not constitute a general reform of production rights but a focused and singling out revocation of specific production rights.

The taking measure, operated through the Thirteenth Act, has no legitimate aim because it does not react to a real increase of nuclear risk. In addition, the impact of a nuclear shutdown on the climate is not considered.

As the plant Krümmel is specifically concerned, the contested act has a retroactive character as it affects the legal consequences of an agreement with the government. Although this does not constitute a proper retroactivity because the legal consequences of the agreement are terminated yet, it constitutes certainly a non-permissible case of quasi-proper retroactivity.

The federal government, several state governments and environmental associations replied by stating that the utility of nuclear power is widely contested. Consequently, the public authorities have the right to limit the use of it. The assigned residual electricity volumes were large enough to recoup the made investments. Licenses do not equal property rights and do not deserve the constitutional protection of art.14 of the German Constitution.

## C. Sentence and considerations

The Court decides that the Thirteenth Act is constitutional and does not have to be avoided. In addition, the revocation without compensation of the prolongation of the operational lifetimes of the plants, granted in 2010, is constitutional in general. The Thirteenth Act contains however, an unconstitutional limiting of property rights insofar it prevents two plaintiffs (Krümmel/Vattenfall and RVE) to use up substantial parts of their residual electricity volumes, assigned to them in 2002. The court decides that the legislator has to revise the concerned parts of the Thirteenth Act in such way that it respects the rights of these two plaintiffs.

First, the court does not consider licenses to produce nuclear energy as stand-alone property rights, protected by art. 14 of the German Constitution. They constitute a permit by the state, not a full subjective right. The fact that heavy investments are made to use these licenses or that they raise expectations for profit, does not make property rights of them.

In addition, the residual electricity volumes, awarded in the course of the phase-out program should not be considered as property rights in the sense of art. 14. They are linked with the ordered extinction policy of nuclear energy. As their transferability is limited to other German nuclear plants, this characteristic does not make of them genuine property rights.

The Thirteenth Act does not involve a taking in the sense of art. 14, as it does not lead to a physical acquisition of assets.

Although the legislator is constitutionally competent for determining the content and the limitation of property rights, he has to respect also in this the principle of proportionality. The fact that the legislator can assign property rights does not mean that these property rights have to continue for the future. The reason to terminate property rights has to be important, otherwise, it would mean a breach of confidence towards the citizens.

Because the production of nuclear energy involves high public risks, the legislator has a wide margin to decide about the conditions of its production. Therefore, the Thirteenth Act is constitutional: it has a legitimate aim, its measures are proportional to reach the aim, it does not conflict in general with the confidence towards citizens and the equal treatment of them. Even when the objective risk of nuclear energy production has not increased after 2011, the legislator has the competence to evaluate the impact of nuclear accidents occurring abroad and to adapt its policy likewise. Most plants that were still operating in August 2011 will be able to exhaust their residual electricity volumes, assigned to them in 2002. For the plants operated by Vattenvall and RWE, this is, however, not the case. The charge on their property rights is disproportionally heavy as about 30 percent of their assigned production rights will no longer be usable. Such a strong breach of promises in the transition arrangement is not reparable by just referring to the high risks of nuclear energy production.

## D. Economic analysis

According the Bundesverfassungsgericht the revocation of the right to produce the residual electricity volumes by the Thirteenth Act does not constitute a taking in the sense of the Constitution because no acquisitions of physical assets are involved. The plaintiffs are still owners of their plants. The conceptual approach from an economic point of view would be quite different. The revocation of production rights by the Thirteenth Act definitely concerns a taking, not of full ownership, but certainly of some property rights, enveloped by full ownership ('sticks of the basket', see Chapter 1). Although the nuclear producers kept their rights to access and to exclusion, they lost their rights of withdrawal, use and, partially, alienation and destruction. The use of these latter rights is, for evident reasons, strictly regulated. By losing the right to withdraw and use, the value of the remaining rights drops in fact to zero and may even become negative due to the huge costs of dismantling the installations of the plants. From an economic point of view, the fact that the Thirteenth Act did not involve a taking of full ownership does not constitute a barrier to qualify it eventually as a taking and to link it with a right to compensation.

Nevertheless, the *Bundesverfassungsgericht* construed another legal base for the compensation of some producers. Article 14 §1 of the Constitution states that the legislator is allowed to change the content and the limits of property rights, established within the legal system. The *Bundesverfassungsgericht* qualifies the revocation of the nuclear production rights as such a change. This competence of the legislator is however not without limits. The legislator has to respect also here the principles of proportionality and public confidence. These are not respected in two cases, which necessitates a partial revision of the Thirteenth Act and an eventual compensation. By this legal construction, the *Bundesverfassungsgericht* probably reaches a result similar to what would have been reached by applying the economic theory on law. One can, however, question this legal construction. Changing the content and limits of property rights, as mentioned in art. 14§1 of the German Constitution, seems to refer rather to a general change in the property rights system, a change of the 'nomocratic' rules on property rights (see before this chapter, 1. Takings: legal-theoretical framework). Examples of such changes could be for instance: changes in the conditions and the length of terms for prescription, changes in the rules on nuisances, changes in the rules on transfer of property rights, changes in the rules of registration and so forth. Such changes affect the property system as a whole and are in principle applicable to all the 'players' in the property system. The revocation of the production rights, as foreseen by the Thirteenth Act, however, singles out a specific group of producers and submits them to an exceptional legal treatment. In this respect, a qualification as a taking, albeit not a full taking of ownership but of some more limited property rights, seems to be intellectually more correct. The very formal definition of taking, clearly still upheld by the *Bundesverfassungsgericht*, obliges this court to make this intellectual detour in order to reach a fair legal outcome.

Besides the question whether the revocation of production rights is a taking or not, the other question arises whether such a taking can be justified from an economic point of view. Instead of taking, the government could have bought off these production rights from the nuclear companies. To answer this, one has to analyze whether the relationship of the federal government with the incumbent nuclear producers can be qualified as a bilateral monopoly or as an anti-commons setting. If one of these is the case, a taking is justified. It is clear that an anti-commons setting is ruled out because none of the nuclear producers can veto the total shutdown. It is possible to buy off the production rights of one company without needing the consent of the other incumbent companies. A bilateral monopoly does not seem the case either because the federal government is faced with several partners in its relationship. Consequently, one is inclined to speak of an oligopolistic relationship. This is, however, not the case. As the government is aiming to reach a total shutdown of nuclear energy production, and as this aim is made widely public, one should rather speak of a collection of several bilateral monopolistic relationships. The federal government is placed with each of the incumbent producers in a bilateral monopolistic relationship. There is no market alternative for either the government or each incumbent nuclear producer. Consequently, given that the aim of a total shutdown is justified, the use of a taking procedure is justified. When the federal government would not have been allowed to unilaterally withdraw the concerned production rights, the companies could have strategically driven up their prices to the point where it became politically 'unsellable' for the federal government.

A third question concerns the right of compensation. According to the American case-law approach, compensations for regulatory harm are not due when the regulation bans a 'noxious use'. This is more or less endorsed by the economic approach according to which regulations banning harm should not lead to compensations while regulations imposing the provision of a benefit should (see before this chapter, 5. Regulatory taking and 8. Regulatory taking and economics). The 'noxious' character of nuclear energy production consists mainly of risk imposition (risk of nuclear accidents, risk of nuclear waste). According to the economic theory of risk management, risks should be reduced by preventive measures up to the point where the marginal benefit of risk reduction equals the marginal cost of risk prevention. In case of accident, the agents whose prevention level was below this point should be held liable for the damage, while agents whose prevention level was above this point should not.[7] The costs of risk are usually assessed as the product of the costs of the accident and the ex ante probability of the accident ('expected accident costs'). The application of this formula (the 'Justice Learned Hand' formula) should provide an incentive to nuclear producers to invest in prevention up to the point where the marginal prevention costs equal the marginal expected accident costs. The simple application of this theory to nuclear production, however, involves several problems. In the first place, the costs of an eventual nuclear accident (the destruction and contamination of a whole region and the loss of many lives such as in Chernobyl) are so huge that it is impossible to assess them and to calculate the expected accidents costs, which are one part of the equation. Secondly, the nature of nuclear accidents is often so destructive that most evidence about the level of preventive investments is destroyed so that is impossible to assess this also, the other part of the equation. This explains why specific legal regimes were developed for nuclear energy production. On one side, nuclear producers are submitted to a more than strict liability regime for they are also liable in case of natural disasters and terrorist attacks. On the other side, the amounts of damages, for which they can be held liable, are subject to a ceiling.

7 This is the famous Justice Learned Hand doctrine as espoused in the case *United States v. Caroll Towing Co.* For a synthesis and overview of the ample literature on this see Hans-Bernd Schäfer 2000:569; Hans-Bernd Schäfer and Andreas Schöenenberger 2000: 597.

This ceiling is necessary to make nuclear energy production insurable. This all is combined with severe command-and-control supervision on the safety of nuclear plants. By the elaboration of such a legal-regulatory regime the society, represented by its political authorities, is willing to accept a certain level of nuclear risk. The acceptance of this risk is balanced by the benefits of nuclear energy such as certainty in energy provision and low impact on climate change.

The nuclear accident in Japan did not affect the risk level accepted in Germany before the Fukushima accident. The commission of experts did not discover at this occasion new elements that could affect the risk level in the upward sense. What happened was a surge in public worry with a total shutdown as political response. The risks imposed by the nuclear producers were thus not more 'noxious' than before Fukushima. Therefore, the 'noxious use' doctrine (or the harm-benefit rule, or the nuisance exception) does not apply in this case and compensation for the revocation of the producers' rights is justified.

A last point of economic analysis concerns the investment-backed expectations argument. The nuclear producers invested huge amounts in their plants with the perspective of guaranteed profit streams. When in 2002 political authorities decided on a gradual shutdown, a long-term phase-out program was agreed to in order to allow the nuclear producers to recoup most of their investments. By the Thirteenth Act in 2011 these guarantees were partially frustrated, which placed some producers at risk of suffering huge financial losses.

As mentioned before (see before this chapter, 8. Regulatory taking and economics) the criterion of investment backed expectations should be amended by a good faith rule. Otherwise, it may trigger inefficient and riskless investments. In the considerations of the *Bundesverfassungsgericht* no mention is made on the good- or bad-faith character of the investments. Either the good-faith character is guaranteed through the strict ex ante control by the nuclear control agencies or this character is simple not checked at all, which would leave the door open for compensations of inefficient investments.

## E. Economic evaluation

The decision of the *Bundesverfassungsgericht* to revise the Thirteenth Act in order to eventually compensate two of the plaintiffs can be sustained also from an economic point of view.

The considerations leading to this decision are however open to economic criticism. The *Bundesgerichtshof* clings to a very formal definition of property rights and is intellectually obliged therefore to arrive at its decision through an intellectual detour, namely, the disproportionality and breach of public confidence when limiting the property rights of the plaintiffs. A more direct and convincing path to this decision would have been to accept that property rights were taken by which, other conditions fulfilled, compensation might be justified. Due to the path dependence imposed by the strict dogmatic character of German jurisprudence, such an approach seems to be impossible. Disproportionality and breach of public confidence as a base for compensation seem to be too abstract as convincing criteria for compensation. Such terms leave too much leeway for arbitrary decisions. The economic criteria, such as (1) bilateral monopoly as a justification for a taking, (2) absence of noxious use as a negative condition for compensation and (3) breach of investment-backed expectations as a positive condition for compensation, seem to be much sharper and more convincing for the decision reached by the court.

### 4. *Lorraine (Ville) v. 2646–8926 Québec Inc, 7 juillet 2018; 2018 CSC 35 (Cour Suprême du Canada*-Supreme Court of Canada)

#### A. Facts and legal sources

The plaintiff Québec Incorporation acquired on 7 July 1989 a large tract of land situated in the municipality of Lorraine, which is part of the regional municipality of Thérèse-de-Blainville in the region of Les Laurentides to the West of Montréal. The land is situated in a forested area. At the moment of the acquisition the existing zoning ordinances allowed the erection of residential units in the concerned tract. The plaintiff bought the tract with a plan to develop the area over a period of fifteen years. The aim was to build residential units and make this area contingent with the inhabited area of the centre of the town.

On 23 June 1991 the municipality adopted a zoning ordinance by which 60 percent of the concerned land was zoned as a wood conservation area, only open to recreation activities such as hiking, biking, horse riding and skiing.

Only in 2001 was the plaintiff was made aware of the ordinance and of the fact that the municipal authorities had installed infrastructure for hiking on the land such as hiking trails, bridges, steps, fences and public benches.

In 2003 the plaintiff asks the municipality to adapt the ordinance in such way that he is able to carry out his plans. The municipality refuses.

On 2 November 2007 the plaintiff files suit to the *Cour supérieure* of Québec asking for a voiding of the ordinance and the removal of all infrastructure, placed by the municipality.

In 2010 the regional municipal authority endorses the ordinance of the municipality of Lorraine.

In 2012 the plaintiff joins a claim for compensation to his pending claim. The plaintiff claims he is entitled to compensation for he is the victim of a 'hidden' taking.

The *Cour supérieure* of Québec rejects the claim for avoidance because the claim is filed beyond a reasonable delay. In fact, everybody is supposed to know the ordinance from its enactment and publication. The delay of sixteen years, from the enactment and of five years from effective knowledge of the ordinance is much too long. Also the fact that the plaintiff never visited the concerned area is considered as a burdening element by the court.

On 7 November 2016 the *Cour d'appel* of Québec agrees with the *Cour supérieure* in so far that it considers the claim for voiding beyond a reasonable delay. This court, however, erred by neglecting the fact that the municipality abused its regulatory power by imposing on the plaintiff a hidden taking. The court considers it is entitled to remedy this abuse by declaring the concerned ordinances as non-opposable to the victim.

Art. 952 of the Code Civil de Québec provides that no compelled transfers of ownership be allowed except when there is an expropriation for public utility and a just and prior compensation.

Further, several precedents concerning the reasonable delay for filing claims of avoidance are referred to, such as *Wendover-et-Simpson (Corp. Municipale) c. Filion [1992] R.D.I. 263*. In these cases the requirement to file within a reasonable delay is confirmed. In *Rimouski (Ville) v. Développements Vaillancourt inc., 2009 QCCA 1475, [2009] R.D.I. 457* it is stated that a taking under cover of a regulation constitutes an abuse of power. In the case *Benjamin v. Montréal (ville), 2003 CanLII 33374* it is stated that no such reasonable delay is required when the cause of avoidance concerns the lack of competence of the concerned public authority.

## B. Claims and defences

The plaintiff asks the voiding of the zoning ordinances because they constitute de facto a 'disguised' taking. For a taking, another procedure, as elaborated in art. 952 Civil Code of Québec and the *Loi sur l'expropriation* (RLQR, c. E-24) had to be followed. Because the municipal authorities acted *ultra vires* the reasonable delay requirement is not applicable in this case.

The municipal authority of Lorraine argues that the reasonable delay requirement is applicable in this case because the zoning ordinance falls within its competence and that only in cases of lack of competence this requirement does not apply.

## C. Sentence and considerations

The Court rejects the claim for voiding the zoning ordinance because the requirement of reasonable delay is applicable. This requirement is not only valid for voiding the ordinance but also for the non-opposability of the ordinance. Consequently, the Court reaffirms the decision of the *Cour d'appel*. The Court follows in this the precedent *Benjamin* according to which the requirement of a reasonable delay is only not applicable in case of lack of competence. This is here not the case for the municipal authority is competent for enacting zoning ordinances, even when they turn out to result in a disguised taking.

The court also states that the rejection of the claim for voiding and the revision of the decision on non-opposability does not affect the possibility of a claim for compensation for sake of a disguised taking.

The court considers that a regulation constitutes a disguised taking when its restricts the components of the right of ownership up to the point that the owner suffers a de facto expropriation. By this definition the court widens somewhat the definition of disguised taking, compared with the precedent *Chemin de fer Pacifique v. Vancouver (Ville de), 2006 R.C.S. 227* according to which a suppression of all reasonable utilizations of the estate was required.

The court confers the decision about the compensation for disguised taking to the *Cour Supérieure* of Québec.

### D. Economic analysis[8]

In Anglo-Saxon legal jargon the 'disguised' taking in this case would be called a regulatory taking, for the taking is an immediate result of a regulation. Nevertheless, the term may hide also a difference in content. 'The notion of 'disguised' taking refers to an intentional element. Public authorities may intentionally cover up a taking under the disguise of a regulation in order to avoid the compensation and the ensuing burdening of the public budget. In the economic theory, this intentional element is more or less reflected in the moral hazard problem created when no compensation is legally possible. In this case the government will act as if public projects involving takings are 'free' and will disregard its costs. When no compensation is possible in case of a regulatory taking it is of course very probable that the moral hazard problem will appear through such 'disguised' takings. In order to avoid compensation, public authorities will be tempted to 'take' through regulation instead of a regular taking.

The first question concerns the impact of the regulation. In American case law the impact of a regulation amounts up to a taking when it matches with the 'diminution of value test' (see before this chapter, 5. Regulatory taking and 8. Regulatory taking and economics). This rather vague criterion suggests that the impact may not be trivial and has to deeply affect the value of the regulated estate. Based on the economic definition of property rights a more detailed analysis is possible, however.

When considering the seven property rights composing the right of full ownership, it is clear that in this case the possibilities of the owner to act with his estate are seriously impaired:

1) Right to access: not impaired. The owner can still enter his estate
2) Right to use: serious impaired. By zoning his estate as a forested area, most possibilities to use are cut down
3) Right of withdrawal: because his use rights are seriously curtailed the owner is not able anymore to make profits from the exploitation of his estate
4) Right to manage: by the reduction of the uses few things are left to manage. Instead of a residential manager his role is reduced to a forester
5) Right to exclude: because he has to allow hikers, bikers and skiers, his exclusion rights are impaired too
6) Right to destroy: because the ordinance protects the wood on his estate also this right is reduced to zero
7) Right to alienate: this right is left to the owner

8 This analysis focusses only on the question about the disguised taking character of the regulation. For the question about the reasonable delay and the economic theory on it see Bouckaert (1993)

This analysis shows that most of the 'sticks' out of the basket of ownership are taken away by the regulation. Consequently this points to a matching of the 'diminution of value' test. An even more accurate measuring of the diminution of value could for instance follow from a market price. In this case the compensation would only become payable when the owner sells his property. His compensation would then amount to the difference between the assessed price before the regulation and the price he receives from the sale.

A second question concerns the harm/benefit rule (in classical legal terms: 'noxious use' or 'nuisance exception', see before this chapter, 5. Regulatory taking and 8. Regulatory taking and economics). When the ordinance aims at preventing harm no compensation is due. When it aims at providing a benefit to third parties, compensation is due. In this case, it is apparent that the latter is the case, for the ordinance restricts the land-use of the estate to nature conservation and nature exploration, open for the public.

A last question concerns the public use-requirement for this regulatory taking. As mentioned before, a taking is, from an economic point of view, only justified in cases of a bilateral monopoly or an anti-commons setting (see before this chapter, 6. Economic theory: public use). This applies of course also for a regulatory taking, for such a taking concerns also an imposed transfer of property rights in the economic meaning of the term (see before this chapter, 6. Economic theory: public use). To address this, a concrete analysis of the spatial environment of the estate is necessary. If the estate is the only spot left for the provision of the nature conservation and nature exploration in the area, a bilateral monopoly exists and taking is justified. If the acquirement of the estate is the last piece of a puzzle of land tracts, with which a larger nature area has to be composed and that without the estate no contiguous larger nature area can be established, an anti-commons setting prevails and taking is justified. If, to the contrary, the same level of nature conservancy and nature exploration can be attained through several alternative acquirements of forested areas in the neighbourhood, the municipal authorities could have bargained with several owners and have purchased the necessary land at the best price conditions. The considerations of the court do not provide, however, any data on the spatial context, which would allow us to answer these questions.

## E. Economic evaluation

When the court accepted that the concerned zoning ordinance is a taking, albeit it a disguised one, it should have investigated whether the taking was justified and whether buying on the land market was not the better alternative. This was not the case and constitutes, from an economic point of view, the major weakness of this decision.

When the taking would be justified, for the sake of a bilateral monopoly or an anti-commons setting, it would seem also justified to compensate the owner for his value loss because the diminution of value is not trivial and the taking aims at the provision of a benefit towards third parties. The decision of the Supreme Court of Canada to leave this possibility open and to leave the concrete determination of the compensation to a lower jurisdiction can be sustained from an economic point of view.

## Cases

*Benjamin v. Montréal (ville), 2003 CanLII 33374*

*Berman v. Parker (348 U.S. 26 (1954))*

*Cass (B), 10 september 1971, Arr. Cass., 1972, Pas. 1972, 28*

*Chemin de fer Pacifique v. Vancouver (Ville de), 2006 R.C.S. 227*

*City of Lansing v. Edward Rose Realty, Inc., 442 Mich 626,502, N.W. 2d 638 (1993)*

*Grand Rapids Bd. Of Ed. V. Baczewski, 340 Mich.265,272, 65 N.W. 2d 810 (1954)*

*Die Dreizehnte Novelle des Atomgesetz zur Änderung des Atomgesetz vom 31. Juli 2011; Urteil des Ersten Senats Bundesverfassungsgericht von 6. Dezember 2016; BVerfG, Urteil des Ersten Senats vom 06. Dezember 2016–1 BvR 2821/11 – Rn. (1–407)*

*Kelo v. City of New London (545 U.S. 469 (2005))*

*Papamichalopoulos and Others v. Greece, ECHR 24 June 1993 Publ. Court Series A, Vol. 260-B, §45*

*Mugler v. Kansas (123 U.S. 623 (1887))*

*Penn Central Transportation Co. v. City of New York (1978) 438 U.S. 104*

*Pennsylvania Coal Co. v. Mahon (260 U.S. 393(1922))*

*Poletown Neighbourhood Council v. City of Detroit (410 Mich. 616,304 N.W.2d 455, 1981).*

*Rimouski (Ville) c. Développements Vaillancourt Inc., 2009 QCCA 1475, [2009] R.D.I. 457*

*Sporrong and Lönroth v. Sweden, 23 September 1989 ECHR, Publ. Court Series A, Vol. 52 §63*

*Wendover-et-Simpson (Corp. Municipale) v. Filion [1992] R.D.I. 263*

## Bibliography


Aly, Götz (2007) *Hitler's Beneficiaries: Plunder, Racial War, and the Nazi Welfare State*, Metropolitan Books, New York

Bell, Abraham (2009) 'Private Takings', *The University of Chicago Review*, Vol. 76, no. 2, 517–584

Benson, Bruce (Winter 2008) 'The Evolution of Eminent Domain: A Remedy for Market Failure or an Effort to Limit Government Power and Government Failure', *The Independent Review*, Vol. XII, 423–432

Blume, L., Daniel L. Rubinfeld and P. Shapiro (1984) 'The Taking of Land: When Should Compensation Be Paid?' *Quarterly Journal of Economics*, Vol. 99, 71–92

Bouckaert, Boudewijn (1993) 'Verdwaald in de jungle van de wet. Biedt rechtsdwaling een uitkomst? Preadvies voor de Vereniging van de vergelijking van het recht in Nederland en in België', *Tijdschrift voor Privaatrecht*, Vol. 3, 29–81

Bouckaert, Boudewijn and Gerrit De Geest (December 1995) 'Private Takings, Private Taxes, Private Compulsory Services: The Economic Doctrine of Quasi-Contracts', *International Review of Law and Economics*, Vol. 15.

Epstein, Richard A. (1985) *Takings, Private Property and the Power of Eminent Domain*, Harvard University Press, Cambridge, MA, 362.

Fishel, William A. (1995) *Regulatory Takings: Law, Economics and Politics*, Harvard University Press, Cambridge, MA

Haeck, Yves (2007) 'Het eigendomsrecht als mensenrecht. Het Europees Verdrag voor de Rechten van de Mens als beschermer van het fundamenteel recht op eigendom in internationaal comparatief perspectief', Ghent 683, Ph-D-dissertation

Herber, Franz-Rudolf (2014) 'On the Importance of Expropriation in the Roman Empire and in Modern Europe', Lecture Conference Olszytn (available online)

Kelsen, Hans (1960) *Reine Rechtslehre*, Mohr Siebeck, Wien

Knight, Frank (1921) *Risk, Uncertainty and Profit*, Houghton Mifflin Co, Boston and New York

Mcnulty, William D. (1912) 'Eminent Domain in Continental Europe', *Yale Law Journal*, Vol. 21, no. 7, 555–570

Mercuro, Nicholas (1992) 'The Takings Issue: A Continuing Dilemma in Law and Economics', in Nicholas Mercuro, ed. *Taking Property and Just Compensation and Economic Perspectives of the Takings Issue*, Springer, Boston

Miceli, Thomas J. (1991) 'Compensation for the Taking of Land Under Eminent Domain', *Journal of Institutional and Theoretical Economics*, Vol. 147, 354–363

Miceli, Thomas J. and Kathleen Segerson (1996) *Compensation for Regulatory Takings: An Economic Analysis with Applications*, JAI Press, Greenwich

Miceli, Thomas J. and Kathleen Segerson (2000) 'Takings', in Boudewijn Bouckaert and Gerrit De Geest, eds. *Encyclopedia of Law and Economics, Vol. IV, The Economics of Public and Tax Law*, Cheltenham, 328–357

Michelman, Frank (1967) 'Property, Utility and Fairness: Comments on the Ethical Foundations of "Just Compensation" Law', *Harvard Law Review*, Vol. 80, 1165–1258

Rose-Ackerman, Susan (1992) 'Regulatory Takings: Policy Analysis and Democratic Principles', in Nicholas Mercuro, ed. *Taking Property and Just Compensation Law and Economic Perspectives of the Takings Issue*, Springer, Boston

Suppan, Arnold (October 2006) 'Austrians, Czechs, and Sudeten Germans as a Community of Conflict in the Twentieth Century', Working Paper 06–1, Center for Austrian Studies

# 6 Verification of property rights

## Possession and registration

### 6.1 The economic theory on verification of property rights

1 **Verification rules.** As mentioned in Chapter 5 (see before Chapter 5, 1. Takings: legal –theoretical framework) a developed system of property rights requires also a subsystem of verification. By this a check on the legal validity of a property right is made available to agents having one or another concern in it (e.g. the would-be purchaser, the would-be tenant, the heir, the tax agency). By such a verification subsystem, the concerned party is not confined exclusively to the assertion by the property holder him/herself, but has the possibility to check this assertion on information, independent from the one provided by the property right holder.

The rules and institutions of a verification subsystem aim at a reduction of the uncertainty in the transfer of property rights. By reducing the uncertainty about the legal validity of rights, voluntary transfers of rights are stimulated. This maximizes efficiency in society by channelling the rights to the highest bidders, that is, the agents expecting the highest utility from the transferred rights. Setting up and operating verification subsystems, however, involves costs. Hansmann and Kraakman (2002: 396) distinguish user, nonuser and system costs in a verification subsystem. The user costs are the costs for the party wishing to establish a right that can be verified in the subsystem (e.g. the owner of the dominant estate for an easement, banks for mortgages and an artist registering his painting). The nonuser costs are the costs imposed on parties wishing to check whether an asset offered in a sale is not encumbered by some rights or interests. In a certain way the user, for instance the establisher of the easement, externalizes costs on nonusers, for instance on the would-be buyer of the estate, burdened by the easement. The system costs involve general costs of operating the system such as the salaries of registrars, the costs of stockpiling the information and so on. These costs most often have a fixed character in relationship with the value of the vested or transferred rights, verified in the subsystem. In general, a verification subsystem is efficient when the rise in aggregate value resulting from the reduction of uncertainty is larger than the sum of user, nonuser and system costs. Investments in verification subsystems are efficient up to the point that the marginal reduction of uncertainty about rights is equal to the aggregate marginal user, nonuser and system costs.

2 **Possession and registration.** Throughout history a wide variety of verification rules and institutions has been developed. The Ancient Greeks, for instance, displayed the property situation of a parcel of land by putting a slab on the land (*horos*). On the slab people could read some basic legal data such as the identity of the owner and the eventual burdening by a mortgage (a *hypotec*) (Arruñada 2003: 6). The Romans for instance provided publicity to a land transfer by the '*in iure cessio*' (Van Oven 1948: 35). The purchaser filed a suit to claim the land against the owner-seller. By lack of opposition in court the seller acquired the land by decision of the court. The suit, in fact a simulated one, provided publicity for the deal. In medieval England the transfer of a freehold estate, called *feoffment*, involved the ceremony of *'livery of seisin'*. The transferor (*feoffor*) took the transferee (*feoffee*) to the concerned land and handed over a stick, a piece of turf or a handful of soil. Also here, the aim was to give wider publicity to the transfer (Garro 2004: 18).

In modern legal systems, however two types of verification subsystems seem to prevail: possession and registration.

Possession refers primarily to the physical control of an asset. It is '*potis sedere*', that is, to sit with might on a good. Possession functions in a legal system as a verification rule when the legal system awards to the possessor validity on his/her title after a certain period, specifically, the prescription period.[1] In this case third parties have to check (1) whether the other party is in physical control of the item and (2) whether the possession lasted long enough to meet the prescription requirement. Often the rule involves further complications such as a different prescription periods for good and bad faith possessors.

Registration implies that the vesting or the transfer of a property right has to be written down in a document and that this document (or data out of it) has to be entered into a systematized register, open for public consultation. In order to check the legal status of an item, the checking parties have merely to consult the register.

In most modern legal systems, the choice of the verification rule is largely determined by the classical subdivision of goods, namely, immobile goods (estates) vis-à-vis mobile goods (chattel).

In civil law, for instance, a vesting of a right on an immobile good (e.g. a mortgage) or a transfer of such a right requires a deed of the notary and a

1 Besides its verification function, possession may also have other legal consequences. First, peaceful possession as such is protected against violent and surreptitious dispossession, which means that in case of violent dispossession the possessor does not have to prove his legal title for being repossessed. This is the police function of possession (see the '*Friedenstheorie*' of von Savigny 1865). Second, possession may also have consequences for the burden of proof. In many legal systems, the burden of proof is on the non-possessor when mobile goods are concerned. The non-possessor has to prove he has a valid title in order to be repossessed. If he fails, the good remains with the possessor. The old precept 'Possession is nine-tenths of the law' expresses more or less this principle.

registration in the registers of 'hypotecs' (art. 1 Law on Hypotecs of 1851, integrated in the Belgian Civil Code as Title XVIII). The transfer of an immobile good is valid between parties through a simple contract. The transfer becomes however only valid towards third parties through the notaries' deed and registration. For mobile goods, possession is rather the verification rule. Art. 2279.1 of the Civil Code provides that for mobile goods possession as such implies a title. This means literally a zero time prescription. In art. 2279.2 important exceptions are however made on this zero-time prescription. For lost and stolen goods, a three years' prescription rule applies when the possessor is in good faith. When in bad faith, a thirty years' prescription period applies.

It has to be remarked that both verification rules can be combined. In civil law, for instance, possession also applies to immobile goods. The possessor in good faith acquires the estate after ten or twenty years, depending on the location of the estate, and the possessor in bad faith, after thirty years. Consequently, a party interested in the purchase of an estate under civil law, in order to be safe, has first to check the register and second to see whether the good was not possessed by an adverse possessor for ten, twenty or thirty years.

From an economic point of view, the question arises whether this mobile/immobile (estate/chattel) distinction is efficient as a criterion for the selection of a verification rule.

At first glance, a possession rule is very cheap for it does not require any further administrative cost. The possessor him/herself provides the verification by his/her physical control of the good. There is, however, a hidden cost in this type of verification. By accepting mere possession as verification, one awards at the same time the title to the possessor. Possession (during a certain time) means verification for third parties but by the same token acquisition for the possessor him/herself. By accepting mere possession as a title, the legal system provides incentives for acts of dispossession (theft, fraud) in order to acquire goods by remaining long enough in adverse possession in order to meet the prescription time. This impact on the level of dispossessing behavior may increase the costs of protection of property (Ellickson 1986; Baird and Jackson 1984) (see below this chapter, 3. The optimal length of prescription period).

As already mentioned, verification by registration involves costs for users and nonusers, and system costs. Most of these costs have a fixed character and are independent from the value of the items that are the object of the registered transfers.

Considering these general characteristics of costs, the following criteria may be important for the selection of the verification rule (Bouckaert and De Geest 1998):

1) **Transferred value**: as registration costs are fixed, high value transfers qualify more for registration, low value transfers rather for possession.
2) **Frequency of transfer**: again regarding the fixed cost character of registration high frequency transfers point rather to possession, low frequency rather to registration.

3) **Uniqueness of transferred goods**: unique goods are easier to register, while this is more difficult for goods in kind or serial goods. Serial goods can however be made artificially unique by tagging a specific sign to it. Cars for instance, which are serial, are made unique by engraving a frame number (VIN: Vehicle Identification Number) on it. This however also involves a cost.
4) **Durability of the good**: for durable goods rather registration applies, for ephemeral goods rather possession.
5) **Abstract character of transfer**: sometimes the transfer of a right on an asset does not involve a change in the physical possession of the asset. The transfer is abstract in this case. Consequently, possession disqualifies here as a verification rule. Examples include the sale of a rented house while the tenant remains in possession and the transfer of a share in a common property (Miceli and Turnbull 1997).

When applying these criteria, the distinction mobile/immobile (chattel/estate) may be questioned in terms of its relevance for the selection of the verification rule. Immobile goods (land, houses, and business buildings) certainly qualify for registering (rather high value, rather low frequency of transfer, unique by geographical location, durable), but also some mobile goods may qualify for registration according to these criteria. Cars have a high value, are not transferred too frequently, can be made unique artificially and are rather durable. Consequently, they should be put under a registration regime. This also applies for pieces of art such as paintings and sculptures (high value, no frequent transfer, unique 'par excellence', durable). For stolen and lost pieces of art for instance a very effective registration system, the *Art Loss Register* (ALR) has been developed by art brokers Sotheby's and Christie's, insurance companies and the International Foundation for Art Research. Besides this for many artists a detailed description of their works is listed in the so called '*catalogues raisonnés*'.

For most other mobile goods, possession is the more appropriate verification rule. Consumption goods such as foods and drinks are low value, not durable and not unique. The high frequency of transfer of money as a means of exchange puts also this kind of good under the possession rule.

3 **The optimal length of prescription period.** When possession qualifies as the best verification rule, the question arises about the length of the prescription period. Theoretically, this period can stretch from zero time to infinite. In the first case, the possessor obtains immediately title on the asset. In the second case, there is no prescription. Goods can be reclaimed from the adverse possessor for eternity, which also means that possession evaporates as a verification rule.

In a cost-minimization model in which the length of the prescription period is the independent variable, some costs are positively related to lengthening the prescription period and other costs are negatively related to it.

An important dependent cost variable, positively related to lengthening the prescription period, concerns the uncertainty costs. Although the certainty of the legal position of a possessor depends on multiple factors, such as the trustworthiness of the agents from whom the good was acquired, the integrity of the officers operating in the legal system (judges, police, etc.) and the level of public safety, as well as the length of the prescription period, are variables of this certainty. The longer the period, the longer the possessor can be bothered by claims of repossession by agents, claiming to have a better title. The increase of uncertainty for the possessor is however not the only impact of lengthening the prescription period. By this, the legal position of other agents, who are claiming that they are the true owners, is improved, for they get more time to sue in repossession. Consequently, the question arises as to whether the increased costs for the possessor are fully compensated by the increased benefits of the ones who claim to be the true owners and might claim repossession. If this were the case, the lengthening of the prescription period is a zero-sum-operation and has no impact on the overall efficiency in society.

This would be, however, only the case when agents are acting under risk-neutrality, which is an unrealistic assumption. Rather risk-aversion is the more realistic assumption.

Assuming risk-neutrality, the following equation prevails: $(V \times p^d) = (V \times p^r)$ where V is the value of the right, $p^d$ the probability of dispossession and $p^r$ the probability of repossession. An increase of $p^d$ by lengthening the prescription period also triggers an increase of $p^r$. On the level of society the equation $\sum (V^1 \ldots\ldots\ldots\ldots V^n)\, p^d = \sum (V^1 \ldots\ldots\ldots\ldots V^n)\, p^r$ prevails.

When assuming risk aversion these equations do not hold any more. A risk-averse agent values the cost of risk of dispossession as higher than the mere product of the value and the probability of being dispossessed. A risk-averse agent values the benefit of the probability of repossession as lower than the mere product of the value and the probability of being repossessed. When $a^{ri}$ is the rate of risk aversion and assuming this rate is equal among all agents, then the following relationships prevail:

$(V \times p^d/a^{ri} > v. \times p^d)$ and $(V \times p^r/a^{ri} < v. \times p^r)$ (1)

This means: $(V \times p^d/a^{ri}) > (V \times p^r/a^{ri})$ (2)

The real costs of uncertainty by increasing the prescription length are

$(V \times p^d/a^{ri}) - (V \times p^r/a^{ri})$ (3)

The uncertainty costs for the possessor are the lowest when the prescription period is zero time. Then $p^d = 0$ while also $p^r = 0$. By lengthening the prescription period, the costs for the (risk averse) possessor increase faster than the benefits for the (risk averse) potential claimant in repossession.

A second cost category positively related to lengthening the prescription period concerns the investment costs. As long as the prescription period has not elapsed, the possessor is not certain to keep the asset. As a consequence he/she will be reluctant to make long-term investments in it, while such investments might be the more efficient ones.

A third cost category positively related to lengthening the prescription period concerns the evidence costs. During the prescription period the possessor has to keep all evidence in his/her favor in order to defend his/her title against repossession claims. In addition, evidence tends to decay over time becoming always less trustworthy, by which administration costs of justice will increase (Epstein 1979)

As mentioned before (see before this chapter, 2. Possession and registration) there are also costs negatively related to the lengthening of the prescription period, or inversely, costs that increase by shortening the prescription periods. A shortening of the prescription period means in fact a shortening of the institutional protection of property rights through police and courts. A zero time prescription means in fact the total abandonment of all institutional protection. When for instance a thief takes your bag, he/she acquires at the spot a legal title on it. Because the diminishing of institutional protection will increase incentives for illegal dispossession, owners will respond to this by an increase of private monitoring and non-institutional protection (more locks, more guns, more alarm systems, more private detectives, more civil guards, etc.). The relationship between institutional protection and non-institutional protection will move to a new equilibrium. Although this new equilibrium will be optimal in the shadow of the new prescription period, this does not mean that overall efficiency is reached for it is possible that a longer prescription period might have led to a more efficient, cheaper mix of institutional and non-institutional protection of property rights. The higher costs of a less efficient mix of institutional and non-institutional protection of property rights constitute in fact the costs of shortening the prescription period.

Finally, the lengthening of prescription periods is negatively related to the search costs of the dispossessed owner, or inversely, the shortening of it increases the search costs of the dispossessed owner. The longer the prescription period, the longer the time to search for the dispossessed item, which allows the dispossessed owner to spread his/her search efforts in a more efficient way.

As illustrated in Figure 6.1, the optimal prescription period is the one at which the sum of uncertainty costs, investment costs, efficiency costs of protection and search costs is minimized (see also Depoorter 2010: 187). From an economic point of view, legislators should take into account these cost variables in determining the prescription periods. The efficiency point can however differ according to different categories of goods. This would theoretically require a wide variety of prescription periods. However, as the complexity of the legal system involves a cost at its own, it could be efficient to reduce substantially the number of different prescription period, even when this would imply that for one category the prescription period is inefficiently too long and for another one inefficiently too short.

In many legal systems, prescription periods may vary according to the good or bad faith of the possessor. The burden of proof is here again on the non-possessor. He/she has to prove the bad faith of the possessor. When failing in this, good faith on behalf of the possessor is presumed. By applying a longer

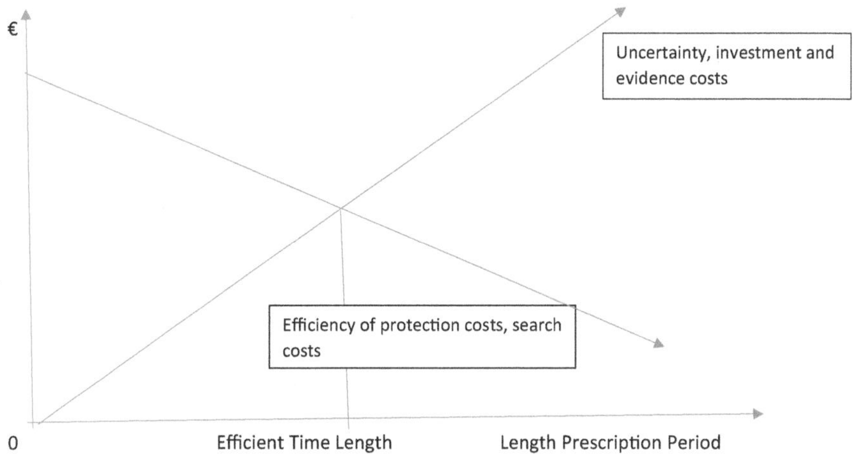


*Figure 6.1* Efficient time length of prescription period

prescription period against the possessor in bad faith, the legal system aims at giving a disincentive to agents who are intentionally dispossessing owners or are buying and selling knowingly dispossessed goods. Longer prescription periods provide them with less certainty. One can question however the efficiency of this distinction (Depoorter 2010: 186). On one side, it makes the system more complex, involving more costs of administration of justice. On the other side one can question whether a longer prescription period makes a lot of impression on bad faith possessors like thieves and resellers. Very probably effective criminal sanctions and high apprehension rates provide much stronger disincentives.

4 **Registration systems: history.** While verification by possession occurs through a direct visual check by the interested party and does not require further administration, verification by registration relies completely on written documents, systematically ordered by an administering body and open for consultation by the public. As one can expect, registration systems will develop when the literacy of the population and the importance of written evidence increases. In Europe, these tendencies became prominent from the seventeenth- to eighteenth centuries. Outside Europe however, examples of much older, well-elaborated registration systems can be found. In Hellenistic Egypt for instance each district had its registration book (*diastromata*), from which certificates on the legal status of land and slaves (*katagraphé*) were enacted by a public officer (*agronomos*) (Garro 2004: 14). The Edict of Colbert was the first attempt in France to set up a general registration system in the whole of France. Fierce opposition by the nobility and the notaries forced Colbert to repeal the edict in 1674. The nobility did not appreciate the

disclosure of the highly burdened status of their estates. Moreover, the notaries feared the loss of their monopoly on the drafting of deeds on land transfers (Garro 2004: 19). After the French revolution a *Code Hypothécaire* was enacted in 1795, providing for registration of mortgages. This was abolished with the introduction of the Code Civil in 1804. The drafters of the Code considered transfers of rights, affecting the legal status of estates, as an affair merely concerning the involved parties in which the public had no business. The absence of any verification system on the legal status of estates affected the finance and credit sector. In 1855, France enacted a law on the drafting of all transfers of estates and the vesting of mortgages and the registration of them. In Germany a general registration system giving public notice to land transfers and the vesting of mortgages, was pioneered by the Prussian king Frederick the Great with the General Ordinance on Mortgages and Bankruptcy in 1783. This ordinance was the forerunner of the later *Grundbuch*, regulated by the BGB of 1900, art. 873–902 (Garro 2004: 24).

In England a first attempt to establish a registration system concerned the conversion of equitable 'uses', recognized by the lord Chancellor, into legal estates. For this registration of the deed of conveyance in a court of record of Westminster was required. This system failed however. During the nineteenth century, initiatives for a registration system were taken by the parliament with the Land Registry Act of 1862. Also this failed because the registration was made dependent on the will of the purchaser. Finally the Land Registration Act was enacted in 1925. It is estimated that about 85 percent of the land in England and Wales is registered. Non-registered land concerns mainly land belonging to wealthy families, the Church and the Crown. Because these lands were not transferred in recent times, they are also not registered.

In the United States, the situation varies from state to state. Attempts to establish more uniformity, such as with the Uniform Simplification of Land Transfer Act (USOLTA) in 1976, failed (Garro 2004: 34). Due to the archaic and incomplete character of some registration systems in some counties and states, the private sector has developed, already since 1853, title insurance. Purchasers, suffering value losses due to a lack of title or defects in the title, are compensated by their insurance company. To cope with the deficiencies of outdated registration systems, many states adopted a stricter system, the Torrens system. This system was developed in Australia by the politician and lawyer Torrens. It was adopted by Australia, some Canadian provinces and many Asian and African countries. More than twenty US states passed enabling act for introducing a Torrens system. A report, made at the demand of the New York Law Society, pointed out however that the Torrens system was more expensive than the traditional registration systems. As a result, the further spread of the Torrens system stagnated and even some states repealed the statute, allowing the Torrens system (Garro 2004: 47). The existence side by side of quite different registration systems in the US is of course conducive for discussions about the comparative effectiveness and efficiency of both systems.

5 **Registration systems: legal consequences.** Setting aside many and more detailed legal differences, two main types of registration systems can be distinguished: (1) mere recording systems, or, in classical legal terminology declaratory systems and (2) purging systems, or, in classical legal terminology constitutive systems.

The mere recording systems have a passive function. They record the vesting and transfer of rights, mostly about real estate, submitted to registration. The recording of the conveyances, often in deeds drafted by professionals (lawyers, notaries), does not strengthen by itself the legal validity of the recorded title. The main function of this type of registration system concerns the systematic pooling of legal information about rights in order to allow third parties to check the legal status of an asset. Suppose for instance that A is the beneficiary of a will about the inheritance of an estate. A sells the estate to B and the sale is duly recorded. Afterwards it turns out that the deceased has made a later will bequeathing the estate to C, by which the former will in favour of A is revoked. The recording of the deed on the sale does not protect B against a claim from C. If C were able to be reinvested with the estate, B would eventually be entitled to damages vis-à-vis A, but loses anyway his right on the estate.

The mere recording systems are the rule in civil law-countries, with a French Civil Code ancestry. Such are the countries in the South of Europe (France, Belgium, Italy, Spain and Portugal) and countries in Latin America.

The purging systems have an active function. In these systems an officer of the system (the registrar, a 'Landrichter') has the power to investigate the validity of the titles, which are the subject of the registered documents. If the title is considered invalid by the registrar, the transfer will not be registered, by which the sale or the vesting of other rights cannot be effectuated. If the title is considered valid by the registrar, then the transaction can be registered and the sale effectuated. An eventual mistake by the registrar about the legal validity of the title cannot affect anymore the position of the acquirer in the transaction. Suppose that in the mentioned case, A and B registered in a purging system. B will be able to keep the purchased estate. Sometimes the law provides the possibility to the victim of a registrars' mistake to claim damages from the registration office.

In terms of legal economics, the mere recording systems operate with a liability rule: the transferee of the right in the transaction is only protected through a possible payment of damages from the transferor because he breached the contract by not delivering a good title. The purging systems on the other hand operate with a property rule: the transferred right is in any case guaranteed to the transferee. Damages to the party which lost its title have to be paid eventually by the registration office.

The question arises which of the two types of registration system is the most efficient. As already mentioned, the United States is in particular a theatre of fierce discussions on this topic, for the two systems operate state by state, sometimes even county by county.

Miceli and Sirmans (1995) distinguish in this respect ex ante and ex post efficiency. The first refers to the optimality in the behavior of parties on the market before the transaction. The second to the optimality of the behavior of parties after the transaction.

The mere recording system has the best score regarding ex ante efficiency. Knowing that the mere recording system provides information with only weak reliability, parties will take optimal information ex ante. This creates a demand to the private insurance market to gather information about the reliability of titles. Competition between title insurance companies guarantees in this respect optimal and cost-efficient levels of information.

The purging system on the other hand has the best score regarding ex post-efficiency. Because would-be transferees (buyers, tenants, usufructors, mortgagees, etc.) know that they are strongly protected by the system and are guaranteed the transferred right, the ex post allocation of the transferred right will be efficient, for the highest bidder will acquire the right.

As both systems score well on one or another criterion, it seems difficult to decide firmly in favour of one or another system. There are however also other considerations, which might tilt the balance.

First, it has to be remarked that the mere recording systems involve duplicate efforts. The official registration institutions as well the private sector (i.e. title insurers) spend information costs to secure the same bulk of transactions. This may tilt the balance to purging systems (Arruñada 2003).

Second, until now a ceteris paribus was assumed about the integrity and efficiency of public officers, working in the registration institutions. Dropping this assumption might lead to different conclusions. The purging system bestows a lot more power to registrars than the mere recording systems. In a country with a weak culture of public administration, vulnerable for bribe and corruption, it might be better to opt for a mere recording system. In these systems, public officers have less power, so there is less to bribe and the private market will supplement additional and more accurate information. Not only corruption may impair the efficiency of a purging system. When the registration offices are run by a fixed salary bureaucracy, this will lead to slowness of search and additional uncertainty and again necessitate title insurance (Arruñada 2003).

6 **Registration: a critical factor in economic development.** Most literature on registration systems, classical legal as well as legal economic one, focuses nearly exclusively on its verification function. Registration is analyzed as an effective institutional tool to lower information costs and increase certainty in market transaction. De Soto (2000) perceived a much wider impact of registration of property rights in the economy. Registration converts a mere physical asset into capital. Mere physical possession of an asset establishes only a link between the asset and the possessor. As a result, the economic potentialities of the asset are limited to the knowledge and the ambitions of the possessor. By bringing in this asset into a registration system, the economic potentialities of the asset are opened to the wider universe of the global

economic system. This insight is, according to de Soto, crucial for development economics. Poor countries are not poor by lack of assets or by lack of entrepreneurial spirit. At the contrary, third world businesspersons are often extremely inventive in order to survive in the jungle of a corrupt black market economy, in which property rights are not well protected. The poverty is often related to a lack of formalization of property rights, by which businesspersons become dependent on local power brokers and by which they are condemned to use their assets and talents in the small circle of the local economy. Millions of talented entrepreneurs in LDCs are by this cut off from the wealth enhancing machinery of the global economy. De Soto perceives six so called property effects of registration: (1) by registration the asset becomes represented in the conceptual universe of capital; the physical characteristics of the asset are 'translated' in the universal terms of the global market economy; (2) by registration locally limited and dispersed information on the potentialities of capital, is integrated into one system; (3) by registration, agents are made accountable. Agents do not have to rely anymore on local arrangements to protect their property; (4) registration makes assets fungible. Assets can be fashioned to suit any transaction (e.g. by submitting them to multiple ownership and abstract and sellable share; by using them as a security on the credit market); (5) registration allows for the networking of people. By registration agents become formally linked to the asset by which they can be integrated into wider networks such as water supply, electricity provision, radio, TV, telephone and Internet cabling; (6) registration allows verification of transaction. De Soto was able to put his theory in practice, first in his native country Peru, where hundred thousands of squatting families received a formal title on their house and land (Calderon 2003). Research confirms that the formalization of titles has had a positive impact on the investment in real estate (Field 2003b). Although the impact on access to the credit market through mortgaging trailed during the first years after formalization (ILD 2006) it increased considerably during later years (Morris 2004; Jansen and Roquas 1998; Field and Torero 2003; Karas, Pyle, and Schoors 2015; De Vijlder and Schoors 2019). Finally titling led also to higher labour participation as people have to spend less time to protect their property (Field 2003a: 34, 2003b: 19).

## 6.2 Case analyses

### *1. B. v. Staatliche Kunstsammlungen Dresden (represented by Freistaat Sachsen, represented on his turn by the Ministry of Sciences and Culture); Cour de Cassation (Belgian), 19 Juin 2009; Pasicrisie Belge, 2009, 1598–1604*

### A. Facts and legal sources

The case is about the property on a painting by Jan Brueghel the Elder, 'Plain with Windmills'. It was painted by Brueghel in Antwerp at the end of the sixteenth century and acquired in 1708 by the prince of Saxony, Augustus II the Strong. It remained in display in the Dresden Museum, Old Masters' Gallery until 1945, the end of World War II. Then it got lost. In 2001 B. (the claimant in Cassation, the Belgian Supreme Court) tried to sell the painting in Antwerp through the mediation of the jewellery shop Tako Ganochi and a car wash manager in the same street. B. pretended that the painting was given in 1945 to the Red Army as a reward for the restauration of other paintings, damaged by water. He had inherited the painting from his father, who had bought it from a Ukrainian professor. B. engaged an art expert from Brussels, who confirmed that the painting was an authentic work of Brueghel the Elder. He offered the painting for a price of $500,000. In some way the police was alerted by these sale attempts, seized the painting and informed the *Staatliche Kunstsammlungen Dresden* about the found. The Antwerp Court of First Instance decided that B. had to return the painting to the *Kunstsammlungen*, and the Court of Appeal in Antwerp confirmed this sentence. B. filed a Cassation Appeal against this decision in order to annul the decision of the Court of Appeal and bring this case again for another Court of Appeal.[2]

As legal sources, the articles 2279, 2229 and 2262 of the Code Civil are concerned.

Art. 2279 states that for mobile goods, possession is considered as title, but for the good faith possessor of lost or stolen goods a prescription period of three years is required.

Art. 2229 states that in order to acquire goods through prescription, the possession has to be continuous, non-interrupted, undisturbed, public and not ambiguous.

Art. 2262 fixes the prescription period for all claims in repossession at thirty years. This is also the case for claims against bad faith adverse possessors.

## B. Claims and defences

Since he acquired the painting through possession, according to art. 2279 Code Civil, B. claims he is the rightful owner of the painting. His possession meets all conditions of art. 2229 Code Civil. Also the condition of publicity, because he offered the painting openly to the jeweller and carwash manager in Antwerp. The defendant in Cassation, the *Kunstsammlungen*, asks to be reinvested with the property of the painting because the possession of it was kept secret for him and consequently does not meet the requirement of art. 2229 Code Civil.

## C. Sentence and considerations

The Court of Cassation rejects the appeal of B. and confirms the decision of the Court of Appeal. The main consideration concerns the requirement of publicity of

2 In Belgium, as in France, the *Hof van Cassatie/Cour de Cassation* (Court of Cassation) checks decisions of lower courts merely on the basis of their legality. If it decides that a judicial decision lacks a legal base it annuls the decision and sends the case to another court of the same rank.

possession. Several circumstances of the attempts of the sale of the painting indicate that B. wanted to keep the sale out of publicity. He did not offer the painting to an Art Gallery or another specialized art house, but tried to get rid of it to non-professionals such as a jeweller or carwash manager. It appears that B. assessed the value of the painting at €1,250,000 which is much higher than the price he was asking at the attempt of sale. These circumstances indicate that B. wanted to keep his possession secret at least for some actors such as the *Kunstsammlungen*. Because a label, tagged on the back of the painting, marked the *Kunstsammlungen* as the former owner, B. must have known that the *Kunstsammlungen* could eventually claim the property of the painting. The Court also states that the fact the possession is made public to some (the jeweller and carwash manager) does not imply automatically that the requirement of publicity, as stated in art. 2229 Civil Code is fulfilled. When the possession is deliberately kept secret for some actors, who might have an interest in the case, the requirement of publicity is not fulfilled. Because one of the requirements for possession is not fulfilled, the claimant cannot claim that he has become owner through possession. This implies that even the longest prescription period of thirty years, which applies also to bad faith possessors (art. 2262 Code Civil), will not apply to the position of the claimant.

## D. Economic analysis

A major advantage of possession as verification rule relates to its clarity. For interested parties (e.g. would-be buyers) a visual check of possession suffices for verification. In addition, also the length of the possession has to be checked in order to see whether prescription has occurred.[3]

The requirements for possession in civil law, which are inherited from the Roman law tradition, are related to this characteristic of clarity. When possession is discontinuous and shifts back and forth from A to B, it is confusing for the interested party to determine in favour of whom the prescription through possession is running. The same applies for other requirements such as non-interrupted and non-disturbed.

The economic rationale for the requirement of public possession is however more complicated. As we mentioned, the reliance on possession as verification rule comes with some costs. Verification through possession, and consequently acquisition through possession, increases the incentives for fraudulent dispossession (see before this chapter, 3. The optimal length of prescription period) and may push owners to additional protection costs. By imposing the requirement of publicity, the law alleviates these costs. By imposing to the adverse

3 When legal disputes arise about possession courts rely primarily on the criterion of clarity. In the case *Pierson v. Post* for instance the court awarded to Pierson the possession on the shot fox and not to Post, who made the most effort to chase the fox. At first sight such a decision may be inefficient for it could stimulate free ridership and make fox hunting less efficient. The act of Pierson – shooting the fox – is however much better to observe, while 'chasing and hot pursuit' –the acts of Post – are more diffuse notions (Bouckaert 2010: 118).

possessor to display his possession, the search costs of the dispossessed owner are diminished. If possession could be hidden, it suffices for the possessor to conceal the possessed good during the prescription period (three, five, ten, twenty, thirty etc. years) and come out when this period has expired. Dispossessed owners would have to rely on costly search methods, such as private detectives, in order to trace down their lost assets. The requirement of publicity has however only a limited reach. Many goods, especially many mobile goods, are made to be used in the private sphere of a household. It would hurt all common sense to require for instance that an eventually adversely possessed vacuum cleaner should be put at display behind the front window in order to meet the publicity condition.

Consequently, publicity as a requirement for adverse possession making to run the prescription has to be given different practical contents, according to the category of goods to which it is applied. A type of use (or non-use) which deviates obviously from 'normal' uses of this category of goods and which signals an intention of hiding, collides with the publicity requirement and does not make the prescription run.

The 'normal' use of a painting is either to display it in his/her private house, so that family members, friends and any visitor can enjoy its beauty, or to bring the painting into the art market by offering it to professional art traders such as an art gallery. In the latter case, the art gallery would have signalled the appearance of this lost painting to the Art Loss Register (see before this chapter, 2. Possession and registration). This would have allowed the *Kunstsammlungen* to claim the painting. As the different courts dealing with this case stated that all other requirements of possession were fulfilled and that the prescription period had expired, an eventual claim by the *Kunstsammlungen* would not have been successful. Consequently, if B. had offered the painting to an art gallery, the claim by the *Kunstsammlungen* would have failed and he would have received a price, higher than the one he offered to the jeweller and the car wash manager.

## E. Economic evaluation

From an economic cost-minimizing approach, the decisions by the Belgian courts deciding in this case can be sustained. An opposite decision would have rewarded hiding behavior by adverse possessors. This would push dispossessed owners to higher search costs and owners in general to higher protection costs. These decisions contribute to a more efficient complementarity between private protection costs of paintings (locks, alarm systems, private search companies, etc.) and institutional protection (police, courts). The case also indicates that for paintings with a high historical value, a registration system would be a more efficient verification method. All paintings, which are, for instance, registered and described in the different '*catalogues raisonnés*', could be put under a registration regime. In order to get a title on these paintings, transfers of them would have to be registered. This would allow buyers to check easily the reliability of the title on the purchased piece of art. Such a switch of the verification relates of course to '*de lege ferenda*' and falls beyond the classical competence of the judiciary.

## 2. *Prestige Properties Ltd v. Scottish Provident Institution and another; Chancery Division, 13 March 2002; [2002] EWHC 330 (CH); WLR 1011*

### A. Facts and legal sources

In 1997 Prestige Properties Ltd, the claimant purchased an office block, known as 25 St Mary at Hill in London City, from Legal and General Assurance Society (LG). The latter provided to the purchaser (the claimant) five files of documents containing seven registered titles, which included also parcel 116. This parcel was mentioned as unregistered land and consisted of three narrow strips. The titles related to six freeholds and one leasehold with a lease of twenty-one years. The property was sold for a price of £9,900,000.

In June 1999, Prestige started negotiations with Scottish Provident Institution (SPI- the defendant) for the sale of the office block. They agreed on a price of £12.65 million. The parties also negotiated a retention of £450,000, in case the purchaser did not acquire title absolute to parcel 116. In October 1999 the Harrow District Land Property, informed Freshfields, the solicitor of SPI, that no part of parcel 116 was unregistered land, that parcel 116 contained three components, each of which formed part of a distinct title ('green', 'blue' and 'orange land'), that the lease only included part of parcel 116 (the 'green land') but that this part had been removed by error by the Land Registry from the title and that the 'green land' could be added back to the title, but that the 'blue land' and the 'orange land' were part of other titles, owned by third parties. Consequently, SPI was registered as proprietor with title absolute on the 'green land', but it had no claim to be registered as proprietor of the 'orange' and 'blue land'. SPI refused to release the retention of £450,000 unless it was registered with title absolute to the whole of parcel 116. Subsequent negotiations between Prestige and SPI led to a compromise under which SPI agreed to pay £50,000 of the retention and £50,000 in respect of Prestige's costs. By this, the claim of Prestige still only concerns the second defendant, the Land Registry.

Despite requests, the registrar refused to agree that he would indemnify Prestige for any loss caused by the errors by the Land Registry.

The provisions of the Property Act of 1925, concerning the liability of the Land Registry, are the main legal sources for this case.

Section 82 (1) of the Act provides that in case of omission or error a rectification can be asked.

Section 83 (1) of the Act provides that someone who incurred a loss by the rectification will be indemnified. Section 83 (2, 5, 6, 8) provides that anyone who suffered a loss from an error or omission in the registry will be indemnified, that the indemnity will not exceed the value of the estate. Section 83 (10) provides that, when an indemnity is paid, the registrar can recover the amount paid from any person who contributed to the loss by his fraud.

### B. Claims and defences

The claimant, Prestige Properties Ltd, claims an indemnity of £500,000 from the Land Registry. This is the amount of the retention Scottish Provident Institution refuses to pay to Prestige Properties Ltd because it did not acquire absolute title to the whole of the sold property. The claimant argues that it has been induced in 1997 to the purchase of the whole property by the error in the files of the Land Registry and by the additional errors in the subsequent search certificate. According to the claimant, he is entitled to this indemnity because the Property Act of 1925 provides in Section 83 the possibility to recover a statutory indemnity when a loss is due to an error or omission in the registry.

The second (and only) defendant, the Land Registry claims that the loss, Prestige Properties Ltd suffered was wholly the result of the lack of care by Prestige, by not checking duly whether the plans in the file and search certificate were correct. On the base of Section 83 of the Property Act of 1925 the Land Registry is not liable for paying the indemnity.

## C. Sentence and considerations

The court decides that both parties, the Land Registry and Prestige Properties Ltd, are liable but puts 90 percent of the liability on the side of the former and 10 percent on the side of the latter. Consequently Prestige recovers 90 percent of £450,000 from the Land Registry but has to reimburse £50,000 to Scottish Providence Institution.

As a rule in liability law, the error has to be the effective cause of the ensuing damage. Based on the hearings of concerned witnesses (the solicitors involved in the sales), the judge concludes that the error was decisive for the damage to Prestige. If Prestige had known that two strips of parcel 116 were not included in the property, but were owned by outsiders, it would never have concluded a retention clause involving such a high amount of £450,000.

The next question, however, is which party made the error? Is the error only at the side of the Land Registry or did Prestige's lack of care also contribute to the damage?

According to Section 83 (3) of the Property Act of 1925 the victims of errors are entitled to indemnification, but Section 83 (6) and (10) of the same Act holds the person, whose lack of care contributed to the damage, partially or wholly liable.

Consequently, the judge analyzes the allegations by the Land Registry about the lack of care by Prestige.

The judge states that the party, asking documents from the registry (files, plans, certificates) may reasonably assume that these documents provide correct information and has no duty to double check the correctness of it.

It is the professional duty of the seller's solicitor to investigate the documents received from the Land Registry and to watch that this information is translated correctly in the drafting of the deed. It is the professional duty of the purchaser's solicitor to check whether the description of the sold property in the contract, accords with the description in the documents of the Land Registry. According to Section 83 (3) of the Property Act solicitors who obtained the due search certificates from the Land Registry are exonerated from liability for damages originating from incorrect information.

The judge acknowledges that Prestige Properties and its agents did not spend due care by not asking for registration of parcel 116 before the sale. In this case, they would have known that the property did not include the orange and blue strips of parcel 116.

The errors in the plans and the certificates of the Land Registry contributed however to a far greater extent to the damage. Consequently, most of the liability lies at the side of the Land Registry.

### D. Economic analysis

The court assigned 90 percent of the liability to the Land Registry. This assignment is economically sustainable for many reasons.

As explained earlier (see earlier this chapter, 3. The optimal length of prescription period) the main function of a registration system concerns the reduction of uncertainty in the vesting and transferring of property rights in society. This is especially the case for 'purging' registration systems, as is the case with the English Land registry. Potential parties in conveyances of property rights on land rely on this institution in order to be provided with correct information on the legal and geographical situation on the land, which is the subject of the conveyance. As mentioned before (see earlier this chapter, 4. Registration systems: history), the function of purging systems is not limited to the mere collecting of conveyances of real estate, as is the case in mere recording systems. The potential parties may also expect from a 'purging' system correct information of the legal status of the conveyed estate. When incorrect information is provided by the Land Registry in one case, doubts about the reliability of the Land Registry may spread into the market, which would induce future market participants to duplicating efforts through private search. As was already remarked (see earlier this chapter, 4. Registration systems: history) the weak reliability of mere recording systems triggers supplementation through private initiatives such as title insurance, which may lead to wasteful duplication. By assigning the liability most to the Land Registry and by condemning them to most of the indemnity, the court provides to the Land Registry an incentive to take more precaution in the future in order to avoid such mistakes. One may expect that such an incentive will lead to better precaution, more correct information and as a result, more certainty in the market for real estate. In this sense, the assignment of the liability to the land Registry is efficient.

A second reason concerns the asymmetry of information between the concerned parties, i.e. the provider of information (the Land Registry) and the demander of information (the selling parties: first Legal and General Assurance Company, second Prestige Properties Ltd). Although Land Registry enjoys a monopoly on its function and demanding search certificates from the Land Registry is a legally imposed duty for conveyancing parties, the relationship between the two parties is still of a contractual nature. The demanders of information pay the due fees and the Land Registry performs through the provision of information. When a mistake happens within the context of a contractual relationship, this mistake is often of a bilateral kind. Both parties could have made an effort to avoid the mistake.

This is also the case here. In theory, if both selling parties would have made more efforts and double- and triple-check the correctness of the information of the Land Registry, the mistake could have been avoided. From an efficiency viewpoint, it is however not indifferent to which party the mistake should be blamed. It is efficient to blame it to the party which is able to obtain the relevant information in the cheapest way, the so-called better information gatherer, which is, more generally, the cheapest cost-avoider. In this case it is clear that the Land Registry is the better information gatherer. It receives considerable means from public funds to build up encompassing information on the legal and geographic situation of land parcels. By shifting the obligation to provide correct information to the cheapest information gatherer, the court makes an efficient decision.

Finally, the Land Registry enjoys a monopoly position in issuing certificates, having strong legal value as pieces of evidence. Users of the Land Registry have no alternative to get such certificates. As there is no corrective drive of possible inefficiencies through competition courts have to provide additional incentives through severe sanctions in case of mistakes as in this case.

A last question concerns the type of incentives to be provided to the Land Registry in order to stimulate good performance. Besides damages to the victim, incentives can be given also through criminal and administrative sanctions such as fines, imprisonment, setbacks in career, dismissal, etc. Such sanctions involve probable less costs of administration of justice than litigation about negligence and assessment of damage. By excluding tort or contract liability for the Land Registry, the risk of mistakes is shifted to potential victims. In this case, they have to bear the costs of the mistakes by the Land Registry. In order to abate this risk private parties may proceed to double checking, leading to an inefficient duplication of efforts. The possibility of recovering an indemnity relieves parties largely from this risk.

In addition, a non-compensation rule would lead to so called 'demoralization costs'. According to Michelman, who introduced this cost category into the academic debate, demoralization costs involve

> the total of dollar value necessary to offset disutilities which accrue to losers and their sympathizers specifically from the realization that no compensation is offered, and the present capitalized dollar value of last future production (reflecting either impaired incentives or social unrest) caused by the demoralization of uncompensated losers, their sympathizers, and other observers disturbed by the thought that they themselves may be subjected to similar treatment on some other occasion.
>
> (Michelman 1967: 1185)

To put it briefly, non-compensation would hurt a general sense of justice throughout society, resulting in feelings of disutilities and a loss of trust in the legal system and public authorities.

A last question concerns the liability of the two parties, Land registry and Prestige Properties. As Prestige Properties Ltd is partially liable because of some lack of care, the other party could have invoked a defence of contributory negligence. This would have meant that, due to the fact that the damage to the victim was partially to blame to the victim, the injurer is exonerated from any liability. The judge in this case rejected clearly contributory negligence and applied comparative negligence by which the liability was apportioned to each party according to their contribution in the causation of the damage. Also, this approach can be sustained from an economic viewpoint (see Cooter and Ulen 1996: 303–306). In tort case the involved parties face the problem of evidentiary uncertainty. They face the risk that the court will reject the evidence and rule against them even when they were acting in a legally correct way. To avoid this risk parties will apply over precaution in order to strengthen their position. Under contributory negligence, both parties face the risk to pay the full amount of the damages. Under comparative negligence, the parties face only the risk to pay a part of the damages. Inefficient over precaution will be less likely under this rule. In this case, contributory negligent could have induced the sellers to take over precaution by double-checking the information, provided by the Land Registry, leading to inefficient duplication.

### F. Economic evaluation

The assignment of most liability to the Land Registry and the lesser part to Prestige Properties Ltd is sustainable for several economic reasons. As is the case with many judicial decisions, the outcome of which is economically sustainable, the considerations on which the outcome is based are too vague and not enough convincing. Sharper economic considerations would strengthen such decisions and provide as a precedent a stronger intellectual signal to future decisions and to conduct in society.

## 3. *Bligh v. Martin, 16 February 1968; Chancery Division; 1 All E.R. [1969], 1157–1162*

### A. Facts and legal sources

In 1945 several parcels, located in Horsham West Sussex, were conveyed to Martin, the defendant. The latter however was not aware, until 1965, that this conveyance included also a field of 3,817 acres of farmland. The same field was included in a conveyance of 1948 by the same grantor to Bligh, the plaintiff. In fact, the conveyance granted a field to Bligh, which was already conveyed to Martin. According to the conveyances, Martin was the rightful owner of the field, without however knowing it, until 1965, when he found it out. Bligh, being in the opinion he was the rightful owner behaved as an owner, while Martin, not aware he was the rightful owner, behaved as a non-owner, more precisely as a tenant and user of the concerned fields. From 1954 until Lady Day 1960 (March 25) Martin used the field by ploughing, sowing, harvesting and putting cattle on it. This was done at the base of a contract with Bligh. Between Lady Day 1960 and 29 September 1960 Martin had a seasonal grazing tenancy or licence from Bligh on the whole estate (Greenfields farm) which included the concerned field. From February 1961 until now (the time of this trial), the defendant used the field in the same way as during the first period.

Based on the use he made of the field during the mentioned periods, Bligh claims a possessory title from Martin.

This latter claim is based on several sections of the Limitation Act of 1939.

Section 4 (3) provides that

> No action shall be brought by any other person to recover land after the expiration of twelve years from the date on which the right of action accrued to him or, if it first accrues to some other person through whom he claims, to that person.

Section 10 (2) of the same act provides that when adverse possession is interrupted the period of interruption does not count for the expiration of the twelve-year period of Section (3), but when the adverse possession is taken up again, the adverse possession period from before the interruption will count.

Section 10 (3) of the same act provides that

> For purpose of this action. . . (b) receipt of rent under a lease by a person wrongfully claiming, in accordance with subsection (3) of the last foregoing section, the land in reversion shall be deemed to be adverse possession of the land.

## B. Claims and defences

The plaintiff Bligh asks for (1) a declaration, entitling him a fee simple on the concerned field, (2) a declaration that the defendant has no right to a title, (3) an injunction to restrain defendant and his servants from entering, (4) an injunction ordering the removal of poles on the field and finally (5) damages. The plaintiff argues that he has been more than twelve years in possession (1949–1968). Although he was not physically using the land, but contracted out the use to a third person, which happened to be the rightful owner, he was acting like an owner by managing the land, concluding contracts and receiving the rent.

The defendant, Martin, argues that when the rightful owner sets foot on his own but adversely possessed land, in this case in the quality of a tenant, he automatically becomes himself the possessor and interrupts the possession by the adverse possessor. Moreover, section 10 (3) of the Limitation Act does not apply to the situation where the adverse possessor occupies the estate and later rents it to a tenant. It applies only to the inverse situation, where the tenancy was already running when the estate was taken in adverse possession.

Finally, the defendant claims that a tenancy contract with an adverse possessor is void because it is based on mutual mistake. Both parties act in the shadow of false assumptions, namely, that the adverse possessor is the rightful owner and that the tenant is not the owner.

### C. Sentence and considerations

The judge awards the declaration of good possessory title on the field to the plaintiff. A first consideration concerns the nature of adverse possession. Sometimes, due to circumstances, adverse possession cannot be exercised through real physical control and use of the good. This is for instance the case in wintertime or when the estate is rented out to a third party. As no concurrent possession is possible, the fact that a tenant uses the land does not dispossess the adverse possessor. Consequently, the argument of the defendant that the adverse possession is stopped from the moment the rightful owner sets foot on his land, does not hold. The rightful owner acts here as a tenant and does not, in this quality, dispossess the adverse possessor. A second consideration concerns the summer period of 1960. In that period the adverse possessor rented the land to the tenant. The question is whether Section 10 (3) applies also to this situation. The defendant argues the contrary. According to the judge, nothing in the wording of Section 10 (3) of the Limitation Act indicates that this exceptional situation, in which the adverse possessor, thinking he was the owner, rented the land to the rightful owner but was thinking he was just a tenant, would be excluded from the application of that section. Finally, the judge rejects that the tenancy contract would be void on the base of mutual mistake. That would be the case if the tenancy contract related exclusively to the concerned parcels. The contract however related to the whole Greenfields Estate and the concerned field only constitutes one tenth of the whole estate. As no dissection of the concerned field out of the whole of contract is possible, this argument has to be rejected.

### D. Economic analysis

When one analyzes possession for verification purposes, the question arises as to who should be considered as the possessor in this case: Martin, the tenant, who uses the land physically and whose control on the land is quite visible, or Bligh, who acts as the owner and receives the rents from the tenant, a position which is less visible than the one of the tenant. At first sight, the tenant should be considered as the possessor, which would result here in the quite bizarre situation that the rightful owner gets his title through an adverse possession of twelve years.

Verification is however not the only function of possession, it has also an acquisitive one. After twelve years of adverse possession, the rightful owner may lose his title in favour of the adverse possessor. Counting the physical control of the estate by a tenant as adverse possession would however impair seriously the market of real estate.[4] Renting out a house or land to a tenant for more than

4 According to the civil law doctrine, prescription by adverse possession does not run in favour of agents, using the asset on the base of a 'detention'(Van Hoecke and Bouckaert 2018: 239) This latter is a right to 'hold' the asset, which is derived from a contract with the owner. By this, detention is distinguished from possession, in so far that the possessor has the intention to act as an owner, while the *detentor* has no such intention because he knows that his/her title derives from a contract. This

twelve year could result in the loss of the rented property. The tenant could then claim that he or she was in possession during twelve years. For owners the only way to protect themselves against such an unintended alienation of their property is to avoid a tenancy of more than twelve years to a single tenant. This would obviously impair the efficiency of the market in real estate. All tenancies in which the landlord would have preferred to keep his tenant for more than twelve years would disappear and be replaced by second best options. The difference between the first option (more than twelve years with the same tenant) and the second best option represents the loss in efficiency to society.

Not counting the use of an estate based on a contract such as a tenancy, an adverse possession involves however also a cost. The holder of a use right is, as already mentioned, more visible than the owner who retains other property rights (in the economic sense, see Chapter 1) such as the right to manage and the right of alienation. It requires more scrutiny to check the activities, through which these rights are practiced, than in the case of use rights. It seems however obvious that these costs are by far outweighed by the costs of impairing the real estate market by counting tenancy as adverse possession. For these reasons the decision by the judge of not counting the use of the parcels by the tenant as adverse possession, while counting the acts of the seeming owner as such, can be sustained from an economic viewpoint.

In the same line, also the decision by the judge to reject the idea of 'concurrent' possession can be sustained. Of course, rejecting that the person, who later turned out to be the rightful owner, has possession when he effectively uses 'his' land, sounds counterintuitive. By his acts he did not, however, actually dispossess the seeming owner for he continued his acts of management such as receiving the rents. Accepting a situation of concurrent possession would however jeopardize entirely the verification function of possession. A concurrent possession would raise the question of the mutual shares in the possession of the land. Such shares require however an abstract title which can only be defined in a written document and be verified by thirds through a public registration system (see earlier this chapter, 2. Possession and registration). Accepting concurrent possession would in fact eliminate possession, as a verification method for it is impossible to check visibly mutual shares of the concurrent possessors.

A last question concerns the legal validity of the tenancy contract between a person (Bligh) who thought he was the owner but was not and another person (Martin) who thought he was a mere tenant while he was, according to the grant, the rightful owner. It is clear that the contract was based on mutual mistake. Both

---

intention by the possessor is called the '*animus possidendi*', distinguished from the mere physical possession. The notion of '*animus possidendi*' was developed by the scholars of Roman law. During wintertime, possessors of meadows in the mountains could not practice their possession in a physical way. In order to avoid that wintertime would interrupt the acquisition of property through '*usucapio*' (acquisition through mere use), they developed the notion of '*animus possidendi*'. During wintertime the possessor remained in 'the spirit' of being a possessor (see Van Oven : 136).

parties were mistaken on the legal capacity of the other party. Mistakes in contracts cause inefficiencies when the contract would not have been concluded without the mistake and when the cost of avoiding the mistake was not higher than the mutual benefit of the parties in the contract (De Geest 1994: 167–181). In order to avoid such inefficiencies it is important that the party which can avoid the mistake at the cheapest cost ('the better information gatherer') is incentivized to acquire and display the necessary information. Incentives can be provided by voiding the contract when this is at the disadvantage of the better information gatherer such as the more professional party. In this case, it is however very difficult to decide which party is the better information gatherer. Both parties were conveyed the parcels in different grants and did not know from each other that they were granted the same parcels. The voiding of the contract would be at the detriment of Bligh because by this the necessary years of adverse possession do not accrue to him. Because he is not the better information gatherer, 'punishing' him by voiding the contract would not have enhanced efficiency in society. The only effect is of a distributive kind. The only party which should be incentivized is the grantor himself. He is in the position of the better information gatherer because, as the former owner, he granted the same parcels to two different persons. Because he is not a party in this case, his position cannot be further discussed.

Finally, it has to be remarked that the reason why the judge did not void the contract cannot be sustained from an economic point of view. According to the judge, the contract cannot be voided with regard to the parcels only. There is however no substantial reason why this should not be possible legally or should not be made legally possible, in case there is some legal obstacle.

## E. Economic evaluation

As with many other cases, the decisions of the judge are economically sustainable and probably reflect an underlying economic common sense intuition. At the same time, however, the considerations for the decisions could be made more convincing by advancing some more explicit economic arguments. Take for example the reason why the use of the land by the tenant cannot be considered as adverse possession. According to the judge the tenant does not 'dispossess' the seeming owner. It is clear that the judge has a legal notion of possession, and not a mere physical one, in mind when he argues in this way. By this however, his argument becomes rather circular: legally the possession of the seeming owner has legal consequences, because his acts of possession should be consider as legal possession. Pointing to the more consequentialist economic argument, namely, that equalling tenancy and adverse possession leads to unintended distributive consequences, avoids this circularity and strengthens the argument substantially.

Finally, the reasons advanced for not voiding the tenancy contract are also not convincing because a partial voiding should be possible. Again, an economic reason related to the economics of information would be more substantial.

## Cases

*B. v. Staatliche Kunstsammlungen Dresden; Cour de Cassation (Belgian), 19 juin 2009; Pasicrisie Belge, 2009, 1598–1604*

*Bligh v. Martin, 16 February 1968; Chancery Division; 1 All E.R. [1969], 1157–1162*

*Pierson v. Post, 3 Cai. R. 175, 2 Am. Dec. 264*

*Prestige Properties Ltd v. Scottish Provident Institution and another; Chancery Division, 13 March 2002; [2002] EWHC 330 (CH); WLR 1011*

## Bibliography


Arruñada, Benito (2003) 'Property Enforcement as Organized Consent', *Journal of Law, Economics and Organization*, Vol. 19, 401

Baird, Douglas G. and Thomas H. Jackson (1984) 'Information, Uncertainty, and the Transfer of Property', *Journal of Legal Studies*, Vol. 13, 53–67

Bouckaert, Boudewijn and Gerrit De Geest (1998) 'The Economic Function of Possession and Limitation Statutes', in Claus Ott and Georg von Wangenheim, eds. *Essays in Law and Economics IV*, MAKLU, Antwerp and Apeldoorn

Calderon, J. (2003) 'The Formalization of Property in Peru 2001–2002: The Case of Lima', *Habitat International*, Vol. 28, 289–300

Cooter, Robert and Thomas Ulen (1996) *Law and Economics*, Addison-Wesley, Reading, MA

De Geest, Gerrit (1994) *Economische Analyse van het contracten- en quasi-contractenrecht. Een onderzoek naar de wetenschappelijke waarde van de rechtseconomie*, MAKLU, Antwerp

de Soto, Hernando (2000) *The Mystery of Capital: Why Capitalism Triumphs in the West and Fails Everywhere Else*, Basic Books, New York

De Vijlder, Nicolas and Koen Schoors (2019) 'Land Rights, Local Financial Development and Industrial Activity: Evidence from Flanders (19th-early 20th Century)', Working Paper, Department of Economics University Ghent

Depoorter, Ben (2010) 'Adverse Possession in Property Law and Economics', in Boudewijn Bouckaert, ed. *Encyclopedia of Law and Economics Volume 5*, Edward Elgar, Cheltenham

Ellickson, Robert (1986) 'Adverse Possession and Perpetuities Law: Two Dents in the Libertarian Model of Property Rights', *Washington University Law Quarterly*, Vol. 64, 723–737

Epstein, Richard A. (1979) 'Possession as a Root of Title', *Georgia Law Review*, Vol. 13, 1221

Field, E. (2003a) 'Entitled to Work: Urban Property Rights and Labor Supply in Peru', *Research Program in Development Studies*, Working Paper no. 220, Princeton University

Field, E. (2003b) 'Property Rights and Household Allocation in Urban Squatter Communities: Evidence from Peru', Working Paper, Harvard University

Field, E. and M. Torero (2003) 'Do Property Titles Increase Access to Credit? Evidence from Peru', Working Paper, Harvard University

Garro, A.M. (2004) 'Recordation of Interests in Land', in *International Encyclopedia of Comparative Law*, Volume VI: Property and Trust, Chapter 8, Tübingen, Mohr Siebeck

Hansmann, H. and R. Kraakman (2002) 'Property, Contract and Verification: The Numerus Clausus Problem and the Divisibility of Rights', *Journal of Legal Studies*, Vol. 31, 373–420

ILD (2006) 'Dead Capital in 12 Latin American Countries', www.ild.org.pe

Jansen, K. and E. Roquas (1998) 'Modernizing Insecurity: The Land Titling Project in Honduras', *Development and Exchange*, Vol. 29, 81–106

Karas, Alexei, William Pyle and Koen Schoors (May 2015) 'A "de Soto"-effect in Industry? Evidence from the Russian Federation', *Journal of Law and Economics*, Vol. 58, 451–480

Miceli Thomas J. and C.F. Sirmans (1995) The economics of land transfer and title insurance, *The Journal of Real Estate Finance and Economics*, Vol. 10, 81–88

Miceli, Thomas and G.K. Turnbull (1997) 'Land Title System and Incentives for Development', 14th Annual Conference of the European Association of Law and Economics, Barcelona

Michelman, Frank I. (April 1967) 'Property, Utility, and Fairness: Comments on the Ethical Foundations of "Just Compensation" Law', *Harvard Law Review*, Vol. 80, no. 6, 1165–1258

Morris, Guerinoni (2004) La Formalizaçion de Propriedad en el Peru: develando el misteria', in *Commission para la Formalizaçion de la Propriedad Informal* (COFOPRI)

Van Hoecke, Mark and Boudewijn Bouckaert (2018) *Inleiding tot het Recht*, ACCO, Leuven

Van Oven, J.C. (1948) *Leerboek van Romeinsch Privaatrecht*, E.J. Brill, Leiden

Von Savigny, Friedrich (1865) *Das Recht des Besitzes*, Eine Civilistische Abhandlung, Gerold, Wien

# Index